THE TALL VOYAGERS

THE TALL
VOYAGERS

THE STORY OF BARNEY BURNETT

BY CLAIRE RANKIN

THE WARD RITCHIE PRESS   LOS ANGELES

TO MY SON
MICHAEL BEARD WOOD

INTRODUCTION

SOME PEOPLE ARE MOVED BY THE SEA AND SHIPS, AND OTHERS ARE NOT. Those who are moved reach that condition—a vastly varying condition—in a number of different ways. For some the contemplation of cracking a volume by sea-poetess C. Fox Smith by a window at twilight is a kind of voyage. Another's poetry is to stumble along the deck plates at the command to let go aft, dry-throated, half still in the night before, half in the grey, vaporous, early morning of dockland.

There are those who read and those who collect and those who *do*. Do—go to sea, work in the shore end of shipping, build ship models, paint pictures of ships, sail a nineteen-footer musingly, half in this century, half in the one before.

Ships make a temple in the mind where one can retreat. There are other such temples, but ships are especially satisfactory for the purpose. A coffee salesman of my acquaintance was by the other day to say that he had taken up ship model building again. He had been away from it—he had followed soldiering for awhile, lead soldiers from the Napoleonic and other wars. But we find ourselves in troubled times—in the coffee markets too, for all I know—and he was glad that his interest had swung back to building miniature vessels.

"It gives you something to think about," he said. What I took that to mean was that at intervals in his day he could lose surroundings less congenial and dwell on the pleasure of pegging down a few tiny deck planks. That evening when he got home he could reach up on the shelf, take down his copy of *Ship Model Builder's Assistant*, and

[vii]

amongst tobacco smoke, get some help on the problem of rigging jeers for the mainyard.

If most men lead "lives of quiet desperation" then all the more reason that a quiet corner of the thoughtful process should be set aside for the sorting over of one's own slowly collected charms, images, and memories.

Some of us who respond to this subject have in our mental baggage a sight of some rusting old-time vessel, the look and position of which —across sedge or rooftops—hastened our start along the sea trail. My aunt had a two-story house in Alameda and while from the street there was nothing much for a boy to see, from the parlor window on the second floor there were suddenly and dazzlingly two blocks away the yellow spars of the *Star of Alaska, Star of France, Star of Holland, Star of Finland, Star of England, Star of Lapland, Star of Shetland,* and *Star of Zealand.* That was in 1932. Twenty-two years before this the *Star of Zealand* had been dismasted off Cape Horn when she was called *Astal.* That is described in "The Tall Voyagers."

A next step for me was to start to collect, thumbing through old magazines for pictures of sailing ships to cut out. One of the evocative ones was a small tinted photograph of a busy wharf printed in *Popular Mechanics.* It was mislabelled, but the picture had unmistakable style. A four-masted bark was tied up, the foreground was filled with a procession of horses and carts. I wrote to the magazine but the original was no longer in the files; years later a glass negative of this scene—by this time with a corner broken off—came on the market and I purchased it for our museum. It is the *Astral.* She has just completed the voyage that Barney Burnett describes. New topgallant masts are being sent aloft.

Finally, after some years of collecting, I went to sea in one of the square riggers that I had seen from my aunt's window. The second World War called even sailing ships back into service. This bark had been built by the Sewalls in Bath, Maine and with one of my first paydays I bought a book I came to admire greatly called "Sewall Ships of Steel" by Mark Hennessy. It is a weaving together of letters written home to the owners by the captains of the Sewall square riggers. Barney Burnett describes some of these very same captains and voyages but from the other end of the ship.

So I was prejudiced in favor of this manuscript from the time Claire

Rankin first brought it by—it is a narrative that adds flesh and blood to my own collection of charms and memories.

But its real virtue is that it tells the story of a kind of sea lover who never stood by a window with a volume of poetry and who has probably never built a ship model or painted a seascape. Barney Burnett's motive doesn't seem to be a career especially—a seascape is spread before him and he has a desire to step into the canvas and to be a sailor there. The times served—most of his story takes place in the unusual decade punctuated by the first World War when square riggers could still be found to sail on, and schooners abounded.

A case could be made that Burnett is the truest of sea lovers because the brush with which he paints is fashioned out of himself. He uses it with broad strokes, sometimes with great detail, color, high spirits, and an illogic here and there that is prototypic. I have been shipmates with this kind of poet and their tragedy (or rather ours) is that their pigments are evanescent. Barney Burnett's are given a chance to last by the remarkable skill of Claire Rankin in transferring a sailor's spoken tale into the pages of this book.

KARL KORTUM
San Francisco Maritime Museum

CONTENTS

ILLUSTRATIONS

Taking leave of the departing towboat, officers and passengers of the four-mast bark EDWARD SEWALL *pause at the taffrail.*

Boarding seas fill the main deck, as the four-mast bark HAWAIIAN ISLES *takes a dusting in boisterous weather.*

The watch on deck stretch the enormous wings of the sea albatross, freshly caught for the Second Mate's camera.

Heeling to the freshening wind, the four-mast bark MUSKOKA *romps along the sea-road to Cape Horn.*

Seamen all . . . standing their watch on the pitching, wet decks of the Cape Horn sailing ship SONGVAL.

The four-mast bark WM. P. FRYE *sailing through the Golden Gate into her arrival port, San Francisco.*

Clewing up and furling her sails, the four-mast bark GRANADA *awaits the towboat, ranging up on her quarter to tow her into Seattle.*

Legendary San Francisco . . . port of ports for the windjammer sailor . . . sailing vessels discharging at the Howard Street wharves.

The four-mast bark ASTRAL *lying at the Howard Street wharf, September 18, 1910, shortly after her arrival, 154 days from Point Breeze, Pennsylvania. Her topgallant masts, lost over the side on the Cape Horn passage await replacement.*

Dropping her tug . . . topsails full and straining . . . the ship CAMBUSKENNETH *makes a picture of unforgettable sea beauty.*

Standing in tall and handsome . . . the four-mast bark JOHN ENA *leaves Honolulu . . . bound on the port tack for "Frisco."*

Discharged and waiting for cargo, ranks of sailing ships wait their turn at the coal tipples in Newcastle, New South Wales, Australia.

The Steward . . . chief of all domestic chores . . . except cooking, stands on the broad, sea-whitened main deck of the four-mast bark ARTHUR SEWALL.

Lifting to the broad sea-swell, the four-mast bark WM. T. LEWIS *sets out from San Francisco, across the Pacific to Australia.*

With towboats standing by, the sailors of the four-mast bark WM. T. LEWIS *unshackle her mooring chains at the Nobbies in Newcastle Roads . . . to free her for the sea-run back to San Francisco.*

The East Coast four-topmast schooner HORATIO G. FOSS *at the dock in Boston, Massachusetts.*

THE TALL VOYAGERS

ONLY TWO PEOPLE WERE PRESENT AT THE SMALL, PRIVATE CEREMONY in which I was launched into this world. My mother, and, according to custom, the family doctor. Outside, under lowering skies, it was a raw February day in the year of our Lord 1893. Inside, things were livened up directly by the lusty squall which ensued when the doctor vigorously smacked me athwart the stern in lieu of breaking a bottle of champagne against my noggin.

For all that I was a small unseaworthy craft the doctor, with the venerable wisdom of one who had launched many such as me, promptly equipped me with a spanker fashioned out of flannel, folded like a flying jib. The makeshift sail, crude though it was and held fast only by safety pins, served to keep me from foundering before I'd a fair chance to open my eyes and sight my native land. The city was New York, and the East River lay very close to my home port, though that I was not to discover until I got my land legs and was able to venture away from home without a pilot. By then, of course, I had abandoned the spanker in favor of the more conventional and suitable knee breeches worn by small lads of my time.

The long arm of coincidence, or perhaps the indicative forefinger of Fate, arranged my arrival so that my birthday fell on the twenty-fourth day of February under the Zodiacal symbol of Pisces, sign of the Fish, governed by Jupiter and Neptune. The Old Man with the trident was beckoning me to come to sea before I'd time or opportunity to know of aught else.

Save that I was a boy, there was nothing that first day to distinguish me from the rest of the babies Dr. Wilcox had delivered to our house. Three times before the gruff old physician had been at my mother's bedside, each time delivering a girl to parents who had little else than their love to offer the small newcomers who arrived with such appalling regularity.

A shabby three room flat, gas lit, with a cockroach infested kitchen, and eighteen dollars a week income from my father's wearisome and unremunerative activities as a rent collector comprised the slight security of the Burnett family. Such woefully slender assets were more than offset by the five mouths there were to feed before I inopportunely added mine, and my appetite for food was as lusty then as it was to become for adventure later on.

My father had not always lived in such straitened circumstances. He was the son of Captain Henry Burnett, a well educated, soft spoken, hard bitten skipper, one of the original founders of the Sandy Hook Pilot's Association in 1870. My grandfather was shrewd in his calculations, navigating either a ship or his business affairs to the best advantage possible. He cannily invested his captain's pay in real estate, first and second mortgages and the like, and he was more than comfortably well off by the time my father's attentions and heart were irrevocably captured by my mother—a handsome, blue eyed, black haired Irish lass who had nothing but her comeliness and Gaelic wit to bring her husband as a dowry.

As a result of his worldly views my grandfather withheld his consent to the marriage, and, even worse, the sanction of his well lined pocketbook. While neither act abated the ardor of the young lovers, who married despite his disapproval, it taught them early that the odds were against two trying to live as cheaply as one when a diabolical stork insisted on hovering over their modest roof as though curious to see just how many "blessed" bundles could be squeezed into their tiny menage.

The irascible old skipper must have been aware of the fact the young Burnetts were being reared in an atmosphere far from opulent splendor, yet he cagily remained at a safe distance, possibly feeling he might relent if faced with our actual plight. I say this because his tendency to weaken was manifested periodically by large orders of groceries which he had delivered to our doorstep, thereby proving his crusty old heart was not immune to a certain amount of sympathy, try as he might to conceal it.

Two years after I made my debut Dr. Wilcox again made the hasty trip down our cobblestone street to assist the stork in squeezing still another baby, a girl, into our flat. Oh, but we were a crowded lot of individuals! Sweltering in summer, freezing in winter, yet managing somehow to maintain our precarious existence.

Three years, then, and once more the doctor's horse and buggy clattered down our street. This time to contend with the grim reaper for my mother's life. But she was so exhausted by the bearing of children, the endless struggle to keep them clothed and fed, that the gruff old doctor was defeated. He forebore to tell us children, looking about under beetling brows with a bitter sort of compassion, and so it was that we were left alone with her until my father came home from his weary day of collecting rents to find us huddled together, solemn, round-eyed and quite forlorn.

That day remains in my memory, a bit blurred at the edges like an old tintype, but with the central figures emerging clearly so that I can even now see myself in retrospect, a small boy of five, sidling into the room where my mother lay.

I had come in to waken her so I might sing a little song for her. I had just learned it, and was very proud. When all my tuggings at her still hand went unheeded, I cleared my throat urgently and began singing in a piping treble.

> "Oh, Mrs. Hen lays an egg every day
> She seems so glad because she can lay
> And she sings 'Caw, caw, caw-dockle.'"

My song finished, I stood expectantly at her side, never once guessing she was enveloped in the great sleep from which no mortal wakens. I began to sing again, a bit uncertainly, when my three year old sister came into the room and tried to pull me away.

"Leave me be!" I said, pulling away, "I'm singing my new song to mama, to cheer her up a bit."

[5]

"Barney, I think our mama's dead," whispered the youngest of us all, and, though I wondered how she knew, I suffered her to lead me from the room, and we joined the others to wait for our father's return. There the tintype blurs, and I remember no more of that day.

My father, now a widower with five children, settled the problem of our care as best he could. He hired an immigrant Irish girl to take charge of his motherless brood. She proved to be strong and cheerful, and as time went by we adjusted ourselves to the loss of our mother.

It was inevitable, being the only boy in a family of girls, that I should eventually tire of the games that delighted my sisters and begin to conjecture about the world outside the crowded confines of our flat. The Irish girl, with so many children continually underfoot, was no doubt relieved at times to have one less to deal with, and so it was that after cramming down a never varying breakfast which consisted of oatmeal, baker's buns and coffee, I would saunter down the splintering wooden steps and out into the cobbled street which led me past livery stables smelling richly of manure, and finally to the grassy banks of the East River along which cows grazed placidly, switching their tails at the flies and gazing with calm bovine eyes at the fascinating river scene before them.

I, like the cows, gazed at the river hours on end, but there the similarity stopped, since they seemed incurious, almost bored, while I was wide eyed with wonder and excitement.

With a blade of grass between my teeth, which at times was a dirk, or a cutlass, according to my fancy, I lay hot cheeked, my imagination running riot as I watched the sailing barges carrying cargo from dock to dock, steered by a big tiller, wonderful to the eye of a boy whose blood answered subconsciously to the muted call of the sea. The mere sight of a jib boom on a sailing ship made my heart beat extra fast, and I would look until the sun on the water made my eyes ache, and go on looking until my stomach reminded me it was time to wend my way home.

I would rise from my prone position in the grass and stand, a small, unprepossessing figure, absorbing the sights and sounds of the riverfront hungrily to make sure they would remain with me until I could return the next day.

On the rare evenings when my father was not too tired I would ask him to tell me about my grandfather and the tales of the sea he had heard from him in his youth. Then I would hear about the pilot boats which were sailing vessels in those days, and the "Mary A. Williams" of New York, a schooner rig which was my grandfather's pride and joy.

I'd listen as long as my father would talk, then go to the crowded room in which I slept, surrounded by narrow beds in which my pig-tailed sisters slumbered, and close my eyes to think of a world of blue sea and sky and white sail until I drifted off to sleep, into a dreamland of a boy who stood at the wheel of a ship that vanished with sadden-ing elusiveness when I opened my eyes. I was six years old, a trifle young to go to sea no matter how you looked at it. It was very discouraging.

I was duly entered in school at the proper time, and the days be-came extraordinarily long. Amazingly so, when I considered how fleeting they had been in the halcyon days when I had spent them lying on my stomach, propped up on my elbows, surveying the pag-eantry of the East River.

At home, affairs were neither better nor worse, our regular diet of oatmeal, baker's buns and coffee supplemented at times by the gro-ceries my grandfather sent us. The best Java coffee sold for fourteen cents a pound, while milk was four cents a quart and deemed too ex-pensive to pour down the gullets of five growing children.

My grandfather died when I was seven years old, and when his will was read it was obvious that his displeasure did not last beyond the grave for he had willed all his holdings and the four story brownstone family home in Brooklyn to my father.

We took up residence promptly, and the dignified old house re-sounded for the first time in many years to the yells, muffled thuds, poundings and thumpings that go hand in hand with bannister slid-ing, blind man's buff, and the pranks so dear to the hearts of children. From three rooms to four stories was a delightful and bewildering experience, though scarcely more wondrous than our change of diet from the dispiriting round of baker's buns and coffee to meals that sent us from the table groaning with ecstasy.

My favorite room in the house was the study in which my grand-father had his ship models. There they still stood, gracefully adorning the mantel, the desk, the book case. Beauty in miniature, perfect replicas of the best in sailing ships. It was a bad room for me to do my homework in, and so, of course, I always went there.

My father was now managing my grandfather's holdings, and as the income from them was considerable we were all more comfortable than we had ever been. It was natural that his thoughts should turn toward marriage again. Nor were any of us surprised when he told us he was marrying the Irish girl who had worked so diligently to take care of us all. The marriage scarcely made a ripple in the household, so accustomed were we to regarding her as part of the family.

As for me, I was only waiting until I was old enough to go to sea, and my marks in school bore mute testimony to the fact. How could you learn to be a seaman sitting at a desk? The answer was plain as the nose on your face. You couldn't.

The "Santiago" was built in Glasgow, Scotland. She was a big old freighter with sixteen cargo booms and her charter was general cargo to all Cuban ports. No sleek greyhound of the sea was she, but old and shabby. A tramp steamer.

It was mid-winter, and I went aboard packing my first sailor bag. Big, full, round, loaded with warm clothes, mess gear of plate, pannikin, knife, fork and spoon, and—tobacco. Nearing the age of seventeen was I, and the tobacco was a declaration of approaching manhood.

The discordant braying of the steamer whistle sounded harshly, and we were under way. It was a chill January day, foggy and dispiriting, but there was no time to stand and mope for there was much to be done. Hatches to batten down, lowering booms in place, securing all cargo falls, and lastly, wasjomg her down.

Once out into Red Hook Channel, the "S. S. Santiago" headed down for the narrows between Bay Ridge and Staten Island, then on to Sandy Hook where we dropped our pilot.

It took us about five days to reach Santiago, our first port of call. Tossing through the windward passage between Haiti and Cuba we arrived there and anchored in the stream for loading and unloading. Down anchor, then the noise began!

Cargo booms, steam winches, sectional wood hatches, stacked up on the steel decks, and around us bumboats, cargo barges, floats, lighters, all loaded with stevedores from shore. It sounded like bedlam, everyone jabbering Spanish six to the dozen as we got booms and running cargo gear ready for discharging.

To reach the foc'sle it was necessary to walk for'ard along the deck, stepping gingerly over cargo skids, wire hawsers, hatch covers and tarpaulins, and the door that read "Seamen—Certified to Accommodate 12 Seamen" looked pretty good until you stepped inside.

The door was a big iron affair that hadn't been oiled for years, the threshold no less than a foot high. The smell of strong plug tobacco, on entering, hit you in the face like a tangible object. Bunks strung along the bulkhead in tiers three high on the wooden deck, while clotheslines, two or three of them, were always strung across the foc'sle. Dungarees, socks, work shirts, redolent of sweat, draped the lines. Along the midship bulkhead hung oilskins and sou'westers, and in the middle of the foc'sle stood the mess table and two long benches.

On the deck, by way of adornment, stood a few soup and bully tins for the boys to spray from time to time, and an occasional full gob of tobacco was dropped from the top bunk that didn't reach the mulligan can, better known as the home-made spittoon.

The bow port holes were covered with heavy smoke grease, and were never opened until flying fish weather was reached. The steam heat which came along the decks in pipes and ran into the foc'sle overhead always leaked, dripped, or found a way to let off some of its vapor, causing a sweaty bulkhead or a trickling of water along the foc'sle deck. An iron bucket provided our only washing facilities, and outside the foc'sle door on the port and starboard side was the "head" and combination washroom, equipped with a spout and pump handle for drawing ice cold water. Attached to the bulkhead was a live steam line for boiling clothes. All the comforts of home. Or so we were told.

As deck boy, I brought grub from the galley in black pans from amidships. It was also my job to sweep the foc'sle after each meal. The foc'sle was dimly lighted with perhaps two twenty-five watt bulbs, and that was considered a luxury as many ships were still using oil lamps. Outward bound conditions in the foc'sle were terrible, and it took a full week for the new crew to clean up after the last gang paid off. Once at sea, seamen tried to live as cleanly as possible, but they never cared how they left things for the new crew.

I made friends right away with an Irishman named Paddy Doyle. There was almost always an Irishman in every crew, and Paddy was one of the best. He took a great liking to me, and called me 'Laddie, me b'y' like a father. He taught me many things about the sea, among them the quickest way to say the lead line.

I can see him yet, tilting his head to one side, saying "Now lad, it's

Two-three and ten leather
Five and fifteen white
Thirteen blue
Seven and seventeen red
Twenty (2) knots
Twenty-five (1) knot, etc."

From him, I also learned the "Shoemaker's Compass," much talked of in our navy. He was companionable, merry, full of anecdotes, and I whiled away many an hour listening to his cheerful brogue.

Captain Cartier, a Frenchman who spoke French, Spanish, or English with equal ease, was master, and the crew was of all nations.

Our general cargo unloaded, we took on sugar in the raw and bales of leaf tobacco in the ports of Santiago, Manzanillo, Camaguey, and Cienfugos. As we went from port to port we would take on cargo and discharge from another hatch all day long, beginning at six in the morning and ending at nine at night. Then the bo'sun would stick his head in the foc'sle door and bellow, "All right, men, secure all booms and hatches! We're getting under way!" Work all day in the Caribbean sun, then get under way when we should have been in our bunks! A dubious pleasure at eleven dollars a month!

There were no unions in those days, nor overtime either. There was always lots of grumbling in the foc'sle, but it didn't prevent our carrying out orders promptly. It soothed our rebellious souls to grumble in front of our shipmates, and we always felt better when we'd gotten our grievances off our minds.

With hatches finally battened down, and all cargo gear secured, we upped anchor and were under way at last for New York, loaded with brown sugar and bale tobacco. About the latitudes of Cape Hatteras we bid farewell to the gulf stream, and followed the coast to the welcoming Highland light.

It was four in the morning when our pilot came aboard, and by seven we were passing up the narrrows.

A grey dawn, a red sky. What did I care? We were homeward bound. . . .

I PULLED THE BELL JOYOUSLY, AND IT WAS MY DAD WHO CAME TO THE gate to let me in.

"Hello, pop! I just got in." I wanted to hug him, but compromised instead with a handshake that made him wince.

"I'm glad you didn't stay away any longer," he said dryly, "I might have lost a hand." His eyes rested on me fondly, belying the sarcasm.

We entered the house together, and I put my sailor bag down and looked around silently, appreciating anew the parquet floors, the hand painted ceilings, the pictures of grandfather's pilot boats in rich gold leaf frames. Four globes of ship design covered the four burner gas chandelier. After the foc'sle of the "S. S. Santiago" it was like stepping into fairyland.

We went into the study, and Dad settled himself comfortably in his rocking chair while I took the captain's chair at his old roll top desk.

"Well, pop, what's new?"

"Well," he said, "there's a postcard for you from Captain Smith of the Standard Oil Company."

That was news! For seven long months I'd had my application in with Standard Oil to sail on one of their thirteen sailing ships which carried general cargo, and I grabbed the card like a kid reaching for his Christmas stocking.

"How long has it been here?" I asked anxiously.

"Three, maybe four days," Dad answered.

"Oh boy! This is what I've waited for! A chance to ship on a big square rigger! Now I'll have some real excitement." I jumped out of my chair, afraid I might miss the opportunity of a lifetime. "No time to lose, Dad. See you at supper."

I hoofed it to the foot of Broadway, Brooklyn, where I took the now obsolete Roosevelt Street ferry to New York. For three cents I took the horse car to the Battery, getting off at State Street to walk to 26 Broadway, the main offices of the Standard Oil Company.

Captain Smith, a former British sea captain, had, by virtue of his dignity as port captain, both inner and outer offices, and I restlessly prowled the floor of the latter while waiting to see him. Now and again I stopped to admire the framed paintings which adorned the panelled walls. To this day I can remember them.

There was the four masted bark "Daylight." The "Astral," the "Atlas," the "Radiant," and the "Arrow." All beautiful square-rigged ships, some British, some American, but all belonging to the glorious world of sails and spars.

"You may go in now," announced a prim-faced clerk. I lost interest in the paintings. Reality was waiting.

Captain Smith sat at ease behind his massive desk. I walked up to the desk, cap in hand, and stood uncomfortably while he looked me over.

"I understand you want to see me, young man," he boomed genially. His gaze was shrewd and appraising.

"Yes, sir!" I produced the magic card I'd received. "Captain Smith, I'm Barney Burnett—er, Theodore. Your card came four days ago, but I just arrived this morning on the "S. S. Santiago." You didn't get some one else, did you?"

"No, son, I didn't." The captain ended my worried suspense with merciful dispatch. "You're not too late. Knowing your grandfather as I did, I felt pretty sure you'd be a chip off the old block, so I waited a bit. I have orders for you to join the American bark "Astral," now discharging cargo at Point Breeze, Philadelphia. Are you ready to join this ship?"

"Yes, sir!" I was a bit crestfallen that being the grandson of Captain Henry Burnett had saved the day, but tried to conceal it.

"You're to ship as boy. Wages to be five dollars a month."

"Oh, thank you sir!" I said in tones of heartfelt gratitude. He glanced at me sharply, then smiled when he saw I was sincere. He bid me goodbye, wishing me luck, and I trod on air as I started back home again.

I left the next morning, assuring the family I'd see them again for a final farewell when the "Astral" docked in New York.

I arrived at Point Breeze the next day, and went straightway to where the "Astral" lay at the foot of Franklin Street wharf.

Never in my life had I seen anything that looked as big to me as did that four masted bark with her massive structure of spars and rope. Two thousand, nine hundred and eighty tons! She was a huge bark, a monster ship, to my way of thinking. I fell in love with her then, with her graceful lines, and I promised her silently I'd do all I could to make her voyage a pleasant one.

The first person I saw when I stepped aboard was the chief mate, Mr. Douglas, or, as I later learned they called him, "Old Squint Eye." Spitting tobacco, hard-boiled as they came, and looking for all the world like a wrinkled Sioux Indian with his bronzed leathery cheeks, he surveyed me from the poop as though I were a worm.

"Are you the chief mate, sir?" I asked reverently, looking up at him in awe.

"I think I am," he growled testily. "Who are you?"

"Sir, I was sent down here to join this ship by Captain Smith. My name is Theodore Burnett."

"Oh, yes! You're one of our deck boys, aren't you? Well, you'll bunk in the midship house. Now get your work clothes on and sweep the decks down." He turned and walked away. Decks were never swept down better.

We loaded most of our cargo at Philadelphia, and there I met Captain Dunham, the skipper, a down-Easter from the state of Maine, Mr. Moran, second mate, bo'sun Frank Martin, "Chips" the carpenter, one George Neilson from Norway, and "Sails" the sailmaker, a George Strong of Bristol. There, too, I met my apprentice shipmate, deck boy in the port watch, Halsey Davis of New York.

[13]

The riggers came aboard and got to work bending sail. The "Astral," one of the famous ships built by Arthur Sewall and Company at Bath, Maine, began to look ready for the sea. Ropes, halyards, buntlines, braces—oh! there were ropes fore and aft all over the deck.

The wintry nor'easters were in season over the North Atlantic, and, as we loaded the ship's provisions of salt beef, salt pork, canned goods, lime juice, and a couple of tons of potatoes, the commonplace items took on new meaning as gusts swept down over the Delaware River, humming their gale tune in the riggings of the "Astral," whose royal yards stood one hundred and seventy feet from the deck. It began to be borne in upon me that here was a ship being provisioned to sail around the Horn.

At last came sailing day, and the skipper shipped a full dozen riggers to handle the lines on the tow between Philadelphia and New York, where we were to pick up the rest of the cargo. This balance of cargo consisted of two thousand kegs of black powder. Not the safest shipment to be found!

The towboat arrived, a powerful seagoing tug belonging to the Moran Towing and Transportation Co. of New York, and after making fast to us the gang stood by fore and aft, waiting for the skipper. He finally arrived, brief case in one hand, a box of cigars in the other.

"Mr. Douglas, take in the gangway," he said matter-of-factly, as though going around the Horn were an every day affair, "and single up the lines."

The captain of the tug shouted through his megaphone lustily. "I'm ready when you are, captain!"

"All right, sir!" barked Captain Dunham. "Mr. Douglas, you can let her all go fore'n aft." Intoxicating words. They meant we were on our way.

While the skipper held down the whistle cord, the powerful tugboat backed the big sailing ship, now drawing twenty-one feet aft, out into the Delaware River.

My excitement over sailing was a bit premature, for when we reached the point where the river widened on its way to the sea we were slowed down by a pea soup fog, and finally had to anchor while the opaque mist blew in for two straight days and nights.

The monotonous drip-drop of the fog's heavy moisture settled in the rigging, and I was assigned to anchor watch by Frank Martin, the bo'sun.

We lay as a ghost ship, caressed by the swirling grey fingers of fog, ringing our ship's bell for a twenty-second interval every two minutes. Now and then I gazed aft at the midship house, dimly lighted by oil lamps, and thence to our tug, securely tied up alongside her charge. For all the fog and my lone watch, I felt indescribably content. My roving spirit had come home.

A brisk nor'wester followed the lifting of the fog on the third day. It was a twenty-four hour tow to New York from the Delaware breakwater, the night was clear and cold, and the lights off the Jersey shore winked like yellow diamonds.

The tug shortened her hawser before entering Ambrose Channel, and proceeded to tow us to anchorage off Bay Ridge. The riggers went ashore in the tug, and we were left anchored, waiting for our cargo of black powder and farming tools for California.

The next morning the lighters were brought alongside, and up went the powder flag. The stevedores went to work, the powder was taken aboard, and placed in a specially built magazine under the main hatch. On the starboard side, derricks and lighters were busy putting general cargo into the fore and mizzen hatch.

The Commissioner came aboard that same day to sign what crew had joined the "Astral" in Philadelphia. In the meanwhile, Captain Smith had placed an order for the balance of our crew with the different shipping masters, who in turn got in touch with the boarding houses on Cherry Street, Front Street, and Water Street.

Seamen then always made the rounds of the New York shipping masters, as they were called, to look for a good ship. On the blackboard the order would go. "Wanted: Twenty A.B's for the American bark 'Astral.' Voyage—San Francisco. Wages, $18.00 a month. One month's advance only." This advance, which could be drawn prior to setting sail, was known as a "dead horse." In the meantime, ship's articles were being drawn up by the U. S. Shipping Commissioner.

I heard some of the crew who had come aboard at Philadelphia requesting shore leave, and, not to be outdone, I put in my request too. As boy, I was lowest in rank, but my hopes of getting home to say goodbye were as high as anyone else's.

Captain Dunham called me in the after cabin just before cabin table.

"Young man," he said, smiling at me in kindly fashion, "we sail tomorrow in the p.m., and when I was your age I stayed aboard my ship. I have heard you say you waited a long time for this berth. You have it. The next step is to stay aboard and learn all you can. That is all."

The bland refusal to leave disappointed me badly, but I forbid myself even the dubious comfort of discussing the matter with Halsey Davis. I was, as the skipper had pointed out, aboard a square rigger, and I intended to be as hard as the next one.

Boylike, I'd counted on that visit to tell the family of the wonders of the "Astral." No matter. The only favor I wanted on that ship I had already won. To be a member of the crew.

The next day a small tug came up under our quarter, testing his whistle for a stand-by to take a line. On board he had our foc'sle gang.

The Jacob's ladder was dropped over the port side, just forward of the break of the poop, and Mr. Douglas and Mr. Moran stood side by side on deck, ready to "greet" the arrivals. The bo'sun stood by ready to lend a hand if necessary.

The men stood on the t'gallant rail with heaving lines, lowering away while sea chests, sailor bags, mattresses, and broken bundles of "ship's tailors" stores such as oilskins, blankets, mess gear, and the like, for which these poor devils had given their eighteen dollar advance, were brought aboard.

Over the side they swarmed, drunk as lords, with every nationality including Indian amongst them. All had been rounded up on South Street, and on and on they came over the starboard quarter, stumbling, swearing, hiccoughing and singing. Advancing to meet their hard-boiled hosts, the mates, who stood frisking their "guests" for whiskey bottles and firearms.

It seemed impossible that such a motley crew could ever take a ship such as the "Astral" to sea. I looked at Captain Dunham, who stood on the poop deck, expecting to see I knew not what. He stood there calmly, his stern down-Easter countenance never changing expression, evidently so accustomed to this pre-sailing sight that it had become commonplace. His unruffled attitude was vastly reassuring, and in turn I was able to resume my own scrutiny of my shipmates.

For'ard the drunks went to the foc'sle to pick out their bunks. What a hubbub they made! Laughing, singing, cursing, complaining, shoving. The drunk tank of a jail could have housed no worse.

The bo'sun, patience exhausted, strode to the foc'sle door and shouted over the clamorous commotion:

"All you men! We're getting under way! Two men in the chain locker, the rest of you on the foc'sle head and heave anchor! And I mean now, not next week!"

The towboat was waiting, the Stars and Stripes flew gallantly in the breeze at the end of the monkey gaff, while the Standard Oil Company's house flag flew from the main truck. Up on the foc'sle head, the crew shipped the ten foot long capstan bars while Chips attended to the unlocking and locking of the windlass. Then, out they sang . . .

> "I heard the Old Man say
> We're bound to California
> To me, hooda, to me, hooda
> I heard the Old Man say
> We're bound to California
> To me, hooda, hoo-da-da

Chorus:
> "Blow the winds, hi-ho
> We're bound to California
> Oh, there's plenty of gold, so I've been told
> On the banks of the Sacramento,

> Sheet home the lower tops'l
> And we're on our way
> To me, hoo-da, to me, hoo-da
> Then we'll set the upper tops'l and
> we'll stretch 'em tight
> To me, hoo-da, hoo-da, da

> Blow ye wind, hi-ho
> We're bound for California
> Oh, there's plenty of gold
> So I've been told, on the banks of
> the Sacramento."

"Vast heaving!" shouted the mate, "Fish hook!"

The gang worked surprisingly well considering their tipsy condition. There were stumbles here and there, a slip of the hand from time to time, but all in all they were doing a good job. My doubts concerning their seamanship vanished, and never again did I attempt to gauge a man's nautical ability by his appearance when he boarded.

The anchor was catheaded, the tug took a strain on the hawser, and we were under way. Chow was called soon after. A hungry lad, the terms that meant filling your stomach at sea were already known to me. Chow, slops, "Get the grub, Peggy," it all meant but one thing. Eat.

We were now on our way out the narrows, and as I came to the galley door on our starboard side the German cook we had was dishing up the pans for the foc'sle crew. I was waiting patiently for the midship house grub when Thompson, the cabin boy, came along with his metal-lined basket for the skipper's mess. He was still drunk.

He took one surly look at the cook and snarled, "Why you lousy, horn blowing s.b.—where's my grub?"

The cook was an intelligent, clean cut fellow, well built, and with the map of Prussia all over his face. He had been trained on the "P" liners out of Hamburg, Germany, and was as respectful as they came. I stood at the galley door, wondering how he'd react to such abuse.

Thompson was about twenty-seven, old enough to know better, yet he stood there sneering, obviously expecting to bully the cook into a servile attitude by the sheer weight of his belligerence.

The cook slowly put down his utensils, then, with no change of expression, led with a right to Thompson's jaw that sent him over the eighteen-inch threshold and out into the starboard scupper, blood spraying in every direction. He then quietly resumed dishing up, while Thompson got to his feet slowly, looking far more sober than before.

I went away round-eyed with the midship house grub, for the silent eloquence of the cook had spoken volumes. It had been a fine thing to witness.

The tug was now nearing Scotland lightship. After chow the bo'sun came to the foc'sle shouting, "All right, you fellows! All hands on deck! Get aloft a few hands and loosen your tops'ls, t'gallants, and you kids (meaning Halsey and me) get aloft and loose the royals!"

This was the moment I'd been waiting for! Up, up, up I went, agile as a monkey, Halsey close after me.

Gaskets off one after the other. The cry came from aloft, "Sheet home tops'l! Sheet home upper t'gallant!" Then, in shriller tones, Halsey and myself, "Sheet home royals! Ah, it was a grand moment.

Fore, main, mizzen, all were set. Then, "Spanker!" "Tug is now blowing to stand by!" "Let go hawser!" The deep throated cries were music to my ears.

Three shrill whistles from the tug and the "Astral" was on her way —a greyhound released for her run.

"Haul down colors! All hands muster aft!" barked Mr. Douglas.

We filed aft, and the mates picked out their port and starboard watches. The mate takes her out, the skipper brings her home.

All sails set, thirty-two on the "Astral," and then the routine of the sea began. We steered ESE from Scotland lightship, and the wind freshened about midnight. In came the royals, along with the flying jib. We were deep laden, drawing twenty-one feet aft. At eight bells, midnight, the wind hauled to the eastward, and that meant "Lee fore brace," and so on to cro'jack, but at the lee main brace we were then shipping seas.

Mr. Douglas warned Halsey and myself to hold on tightly to whatever was near if the "Astral" rolled under, and we solemnly nodded that we would. I was on the lee main brace with Halsey when she rolled, and although we obeyed Mr. Douglas we were washed the full length of the deck. Three of the crew fared likewise, and all five of us wound up aft in the scuppers, blubbering and gargling sea water. I didn't have the sense to be frightened. Yet I'd come a long way since I'd abandoned textbooks in favor of the sea.

The following day found the drunks going about their duties as though they'd never heard of hard liquor, and the way they worked proved they were good seamen with not a "stiff" among them. Before we were through we were to be thankful for this happy state of affairs.

It wasn't long before stores were whacked out. The fresh provisions were finished, and we were in for salt horse. The watches had drawn for their "trick at the wheel" and lookout. Then the Peggies were drawn, a week at a time.

"Peggy" was a term that had to be explained to Halsey, and I, with three voyages behind me, was only too glad to be able to teach something to someone.

"At the beginning of the voyage," I explained, "each watch draws for Peggy days. Peggy each day gets the grub from the galley and takes the empty pans back, sweeps the foc'sle, washes the foc'sle table, trims and fills the foc'sle lamp, and carries the daily allowance of water from the carpenter shop to the cooks and fills the foc'sle drinking tanks. He is done at the end of the week and doesn't have Peggy again until his next turn."

"Sort of a chambermaid," snorted Halsey when I had finished. "No wonder they call it 'Peggy.'"

"It isn't as bad as it sounds," I said, nor to my mind was it. It was all in how you looked at it.

The next event, if such it could be called, took place in the second dog watch on Saturday.

From the break of the poop came the stentorian cry, "Slopchest is opened!"

The men flocked aft, as women to a bargain basement. The call meant that shoes, coats, dungarees, jumpers, underwear, hats, caps, stockings, oilskins, boots, playing cards, pipes, cigarettes, tobacco, soap, towels, bandanas, and even concertinas were for sale by the skipper—who owned and controlled the contents of the slopchest. They were sold for profit, not to exceed ten per cent, but all was bought on credit until the men were paid off before the U.S. Shipping Commissioner at the end of the voyage.

I looked at the men as they bought, but refrained from doing any buying myself. At five dollars a month I couldn't afford extravagances and I'd come aboard at Philadelphia with a well-filled sailor bag. The men's selections reflected, to a certain degree, their natures. Some bought only necessities, others selected anything that caught their eye with a prodigal disregard of settlement day.

True windjammer life followed in the succeeding days. Sail changing in the tropics, and, finally off the River Plate, sail changing to double heavy. And always the "Astral" sped along, a thing of infinite grace, dancing to the ever-changing rhythm of the waves without a single falter.

Halsey and I talked now and then of our families, and how we came to be at sea. Halsey, it seemed, had been sent on the voyage by his father, who hoped it would improve his health. He eyed me with disbelief as I spoke of my love for the great canvas-winged birds of the sea, and with his lack lustre eye upon me I became silent. He was not fond of the sea, nor did he feel himself a part of the "Astral." In my heart I pitied him because his father had made him try to be a sailor when he was not fitted for it.

We were now sixty days out, and were off Buenos Aires. Although it was the middle of June the air thirty degrees south of the line had a distinct chill.

Through the flying fish weather I had sat many times about the hatches, listening to the hardened seamen of the crew spin yarns about the pamperos of the River Plate. The wind, I believe, gets its name from the Pampas plains of the Argentine, and it blows with almost cyclonic force.

The "Astral" was not slighted by the pamperos. For the first time I saw her under three lower tops'ls and fore topmost stays'l, and then she began to show her mettle. Into the teeth of the storm she rode, the gale tune in her rigging sounding as though Neptune were using it for a giant lyre, her decks awash, leaping toward each new sea.

Ships nearly always had their Cape Horn sails bent by the time they hit the latitudes we had now reached. From there on it was rotten dismal weather, with blow after blow until the greater tempests of the Horn itself were reached.

We sighted the Falkland Islands, then Tierra Del Fuego—meaning the land of fire—a fine, romantic, misleading name for the most desolate spot I'd seen.

We were getting way down under now, with all running gear up off deck. The watch kept handy making sennet under the foc'sle head, and each day Chips rationed out water to the crew. Our decks were awash with seawater most of the time, and daylight was only six hours long. We reached our Cape Horn latitudes about the twentieth of June, and then, under tops'ls, lower t'gallants and fore topmost stays'l, the battle with the Westerlies was on.

The only company we had were the Cape pigeons and the albatross, circling the "Astral" gracefully, regarding us with bright incurious eyes. The snowy wings of the albatross and the sullenness of our surroundings gave a feeling of unreality to the days, creating the grey indistinctness of a half-remembered dream.

The wind was unpredictable as a woman, now blowing three out of four days at gale force, now vanishing, leaving us becalmed. We were on the starboard tack, making southerly all the time, often having to take in our lower t'gallants and even our upper tops'ls. For some reason surpassing all understanding, this almost always happened in the middle of the night, and up we'd go, climbing the rigging in pitch blackness, the ship rolling thirty degrees, her decks filling on each roll, the wind howling derision at the desperate fumblings of our benumbed fingers.

The westerlies are accompanied by terrific squalls of snow and sleet which blind a man even as they chill him to the bone. One such night, on the eight to twelve watch, it became necessary to take in the main upper tops'l, and then the dreamlike quality of Cape Horn latitudes assumed the dread aspect of a nightmare.

"All hands on deck!" bawled Mr. Douglas from the poop deck.

The job at hand required eighteen men, all of them bundled bulkily into warm clothes, their oilskins tightly strapped to their bodies, each one working as fast as he could. The port watch filed out of the foc'sle in obedience to Mr. Douglas' order, into the ink black night of unleashed fury. The mountainous seas, forty feet from trough to crest, tossed the "Astral" as though she were a toy.

The men gathered around the main fife rail, fumbling in the Stygian blackness for the upper tops'l gear. The bo'sun stood by the halyards, a burly, indistinct figure.

"All ready on your down hauls?" he shouted into the storm.

"All ready!" came the faint reply, the words carried away by the force of the wind.

Now it blew gale force. The bo'sun lowered away the upper tops'l yard, the men shouting as they pulled. They bunted it up tightly, the while they struggled to keep their feet on the lively deck across which seas surged on every roll. It was every man for himself, and "One hand for the ship, one for yourself" was a saying that was true that night.

"All right, men! Belay everything! Up, and tie her up snug!"

Into the weather main rigging, into the maw of the gale, went both watches. As they climbed, their bodies were pinned against the rigging with wind pressure.

The more experienced men were up there first, moving slowly out on the lee and weather yard arm, and my admiration for their skill knew no bounds. Many's the man who's been thrown into the whitely hissing cauldron of the sea, and nothing to do about it but for some of the men to cross themselves and murmur, "One less."

I was up on that yard along with them, working as hard and fast as I could, and for half an hour we remained aloft while squall after squall struck the ship. We worked with our bare hands for greater speed, and it was beginning to freeze. The gang now started moving down on deck, but I stayed up with the last man though my finger tips were beginning to feel numb. By the time I made my way down to the deck, my fingers were frozen.

An old German sailor, wise in the ways of the sea, pulled me over to the lee scuppers that were always full of sea water and made me put my hands into the ice cold brine. The pain was excruciating, but he knew what he was doing, for it helped take the numbness away.

Now the mate was shouting, "Take in the fores'l!"

"Lad," said the old German sailor, "it's a-blowing when they take that in!" I nodded at him numbly, speechless from the pain in my hands.

There wasn't much chance of being washed away from the fore fife rail, unless a breaking sea should catch the bow on a downward plunge. Should that happen, it meant grab anything, and hold tight while a hundred tons of icy green sea poured down upon you. This was the tempest.

Up she went, belay all, one man to clear up the gear, the rest of them to furl'er. Nothing now was left of the "Astral's" full panoply of thirty-two sails but her fore topmast stays'l and three lower tops'ls. Stripped for action, fighting her way through the tempest, she no longer seemed the monster ship I had first thought her, but a Lilliputian vessel dwarfed by the wilderness of waves which threatened to engulf her.

The nights were now long and miserable. Followed by short hours of daylight with naught to gaze at but a billowy waste of leaden sea that merged into sky with scarce any change in coloring.

The foc'sle was fast becoming an unfit place to live. The bogie, or stove, burned well enough, but with the sea water running through the scuppers, coming in one side and spilling out the other, and the "Astral's" bell ringing on every roll she took, there was little enough of warmth or cheer for the men at the end of their watches.

The wind dropped considerably in force the next day or so, the seas rolling high, with no crest breaking. The skipper, oddly enough, didn't seem encouraged by the seeming improvement.

"I don't like that barometer reading," he said to Mr. Douglas in my hearing. I lingered a bit, unashamedly eavesdropping.

Mr. Douglas puffed on his paper cone capped pipe reflectively, "It looks like all hell is going to break loose from its moorings," he answered slowly.

[23]

I went on my way, pondering his reply. In my innocence, or igno-rance, I thought we'd already been through the worst of it.

The Cape pigeons and the albatross still followed our ship faith-fully. The cause of our popularity was the refuse thrown to them by the cook, though we were now living on stews of salt beef and pota-toes, with cracker hash for supper. This unusual delicacy was made of salt beef, potatoes, and ground-up sea biscuits.

Halsey and I, boylike, were completely undisturbed by the state of the barometer. We decided to relieve the monotony of the days by catching sea birds. Before long our enthusiasm infected the bo'sun, and he joined us in the harmless sport.

We cut up salt pork in small pieces, putting it on pin hooks which we cast out from amidships on the port side, for all the world as though we were fishing. It wasn't long before we had about fourteen Cape pigeons and two albatross on deck. Then Mr. Douglas spoke his piece.

"When you fellows get through having your fun, pick up every one of those birds and put them back into the sea. I don't want you to injure one of them—and there'll be no *albatross quills!*"

The superstition of the sea rode with us, and while Halsey and I were inclined to scoff, we obeyed orders. Later on I was glad we had, else I might have made the mistake of attributing what happened directly to our folly.

All hands watched the antics of the lovely sea birds as they wob-bled up and down the deck. They amused us for quite awhile, then we put them back to their mother sea, for they were helpless without it and could not soar into flight as long as the deck was beneath them.

Where their rookeries are located, only a shipwrecked seaman could tell. That is, if they are off the Horn itself—and if they are, then you would have to knock at the portals of Davy Jones' locker to inquire.

The wind freshened to gale force again on July ninth, and with it came such squalls that the "Astral" lay over from wind pressure, ris-ing shudderingly to a heavy sea before making her plunge into the trough.

The main deck submerged on every roll, the mad sea racing clean across us. Yet our bulwarks were six feet high.

"All hands on deck!" came the cry from the poop deck, and it was Mr. Douglas, looking tough and grim.

[24]

"Bo'sun," he ordered, "take in the mizzen lower tops'l."

To take in the mizzen lower tops'l was about the worst job we could have been given, for in the waist of the ship, or abaft it on the main deck, was the most dangerous part of the ship for a man to try to keep his footing.

Somehow, we made it. We worked together with the closest of teamwork, the sort borne of the common urgency of self-preservation. Then, the mizzen lower tops'l made fast and gear triced up, we moved for'ard to take in the fore lower tops'l.

All seamen felt better clewing up a sail on the foremast, for they had the shelter of the break of the foc'sle head. The "Astral" was now under the main lower tops'l and fore topmast stays'l, "By the wind."

At four a.m. again the cry, "All hands on deck!"

"Wear ship!" shouted Mr. Douglas, and the words struck fear into the hearts of the crew. The fear was not cowardice, but the knowledge that of all orders, this was the equivalent of suicide if the Almighty God did not protect you and guide you. No vessel can tack ship in any heavy gale or storm. She must "wear ship."

To "wear ship" meant two reliable men at the wheel while the skipper and the mate stood on the poop deck. Now as never before, the pooping of one mountainous sea could sweep them and every man Jack of the crew to his death. The waves were now running fifty feet high and combing.

"Put your wheel up," came the order.

The gang at the weather cro'j'k braces waited, second mate Moran at the lead. Their faces were tense, watching.

The "Astral" started to pay off, the roll heavy as the sea came on the beam, then on the quarter. The men on the braces squared in, mizzen, main and fore. Now she ran before it.

We of the crew could look up at the stern of the ship, now lifted high by a sea which swept over both rails, stopping at nothing. Now the bow was down and lifting to the sea, and it swept on and we waited for the next.

She was combing again, but we rose to it, for the yards were braced for the port tack. No mishaps, strange to say, and the gang cleared up the deck, the ends of our ropes washed aft, tangled and snarled, but the worst was over.

Mr. Douglas stood behind a weather dodger we had rigged up out-

[25]

side the starboard stays of the jigger, smoking his t.d. with one of the paper cones I had made him to keep his pipe going in any sort of weather.

"How do you like this, young fellow?" he asked.

"It's—well, it's just what the old timers said it was," I said blissfully, "I wouldn't trade it for anything!"

Mr. Douglas favored me with an approving glance, then turned to the bo'sun. "Have all hands stand watch on the poop deck from now on," he said. Officers were never inclined to be chatty with the crew, and Mr. Douglas was no exception.

At midnight that night, the watch, wheel, and lookout were relieved. I watched my chance, then clambered down from the flying bridge to the midship house.

I was wet, cold, and hungry. I got in quickly, shutting the iron half-doors behind me. The old stove, stayed to the deck, felt wonderful. Clothes were strung over rope lines all around it, the oil lamp globe was smoky, and sea water rushed back and forth over the midship house deck. I turned in, oilskins and all, and slept from sheer exhaustion.

There was no communication then, outside of International code flags to report the names of our ships. No radio, no wireless, and, in our case, not even a ready life boat. Not that it would have lasted long in those latitudes!

With the roar of the gale in my ears I slept, hearing even in my sleep the "Astral" groaning as though she were in anguish. Some think a ship has no soul, but they are wrong. Every old time sailor has had the thought at some time that his ship couldn't take much more.

At three forty-five a.m. I awoke, half frightened out of my wits, for a terrific crash had just occurred on deck. Loud shouting and orders could be heard, and hoarse frenzied cries of "All hands on deck!" came to the midship house. Such a crash it had been!

I think every one of us moved faster than we ever had before. We answered the call, each with the unspoken thought in our hearts that this might be the finale for the "Astral."

We moved through complete darkness, each man feeling his way aft. All hands mustered aft, the mate waited.

The main t'gallant mast had gone by the board, taking main royal and main upper t'gallant yard, but leaving the main lower t'gallant yard hanging on a stub. This yard was all steel, and weighed two tons. There it swung, and below it was our cargo of black powder.

The sea was a mass of flying spume, the vengeful gale howling at hurricane force. And such wreckage and utter chaos with the main t'gallant mast, main royal yard, main upper t'gallant dangling half in the boiling sea, the other half with rigging, back stays, braces, halyards, draped across the main yard and main tops'l yard!

"All hands stand by on the poop deck!" shouted the mate.

We edged our way aft warily, trying to watch in the inky dark, for any minute the other masts would go.

"Watch aloft for falling blocks, bolts, chains! Anything can fall now!" warned Mr. Douglas. The valiant "Astral" was fighting for her life.

Every roll of the ship was forty degrees. The "Astral" shuddered, strained and groaned as she took the merciless pounding of the wind and waves with heart-rending gallantry that brought a lump to my throat.

Back on the poop deck the crew waited. Waited for the inevitable crash of fore and mizzen t'gallant masts.

Again the mate ordered one man on lee wheel.

"Burnett!" shouted the bos'un, "Burnett! Lee wheel!"

Now the six foot wheel took two men to handle it, and Oscar, my German wheel mate, and I stood in one spot for the next sixteen hours watching the near destruction of a fine ship due to stress of weather.

Over she'd go to port, then with a lift from the sea and a heavy roll to windward, then back to port with a snap like a gunshot. Came the cry, "There she goes!"

The fore t'gallant—with royal, upper and lower t'gallant yards! Tons of rigging plunging headlong into the sea, crashing down upon and smashing the foc'sle head, the ship's rail and the port life boat like shells.

"Bos'un!" shouted the mate.

"Yes, sir!"

"Take a couple of men with you and hacksaw the starboard mizzen turnbuckles, or use a heavy topmaul on them." Mr. Douglas spoke as though this were daily ship routine.

The bo'sun didn't blench. He was away, working fast because of the danger. One man was enough, for the next port roll there was crack! crash! and away went the mizzen t'gallant mast.

I stood at the lee wheel, trying to disbelieve what I was witnessing. I stared through the wreckage of the wild scene somberly. No man could live in such a sea, and our ship was fast going to pieces it seemed to me.

In the darkness I could just manage to focus my eyes on the old Seth Thomas screwed to the bulkhead back of the wheel. It read five twenty-five a.m., and it might as well have been midnight. We were enclosed in utter darkness, the wreckage pounding against the ship's side as though demanding admittance to our hull, banging and smashing against the port side. Nearly all the lifts had been carried away, leaving our fore, main, and cro'j'k yards swinging just on goose necks.

At six, a seaman relieved me at the lee wheel while I went for coffee. As I crossed the bridge to the midship house it seemed as though nothing but green sea was below me. The deck was not visible, only the crashing waters about the fife rails and hatch combings.

I watched for my first chance, then dashed for the midship house door. Gaining the musty dampness of inside was better than anyone could imagine, for the bogie was fired up, the lamp in the gimbals was smoky, and although wet clothes hung everywhere I saw Sails and Halsey Davis comfortably dunking their pilot bread in their coffee.

We all sat wondering if we'd ever see our loved ones again. I reached for the treacle jar, and put my pilot bread on top of the bogie to toast. It burned, so I spread treacle on my hot burned sea biscuit. I was so ravenous that I ate about six, burned or not, along with two big pannikins of coffee to wash them down. I had some Prince Albert left, and I rolled a cigarette and smoked it. The bench I sat on was soaking wet, for every skylight of the "Astral" was now a strainer, but I very nearly fell asleep. No time for sleep, though. One last puff, then back to the lee wheel.

Daylight revealed a terrible picture to us all, a scene of unbelievable wreckage. A ship in distress was the "Astral," an all but vanquished ship, waiting for the death blow. This was Cape Horn. Bleak, desolate, a burying ground for ships.

The one thought uppermost in the mind of every ship's captain was to keep clear of the God-forsaken shore, with its mountainous snow covered peaks and jagged rocks, and the apparently bottomless waters around the island known as Diego Ramirez. Captain Dunham must have had cruel forebodings on this score, yet he moved amongst us men with outward assurance, speaking only to issue an order, and then in a voice of unshaken authority that admitted of no despair.

From my position at the lee wheel I could see the crew, equipped with hack saws, pinch bars, top-mauls, axes, marlin spikes. Mr. Douglas snapped orders, and they went in groups, watching for even a moderate lull. They cut, chopped, and sawed, and every now and then some large piece of rigging passed astern. With each one I breathed more easily, for it gave me new hope for the "Astral."

Then I noticed a few men trying to get a gantline made fast to the lee tip of the cro'j'k yard, now cock-billed at a forty-five degree angle, swinging up and down threateningly with every roll of the ship.

The bos'un went into action, and forever after I thought of him as a man of high courage. Followed by two men, he worked slowly out on the lee side of the yard until he was on the tip of the yard arm —and that yard was plunging into the sea with every roll to port.

He had lashed himself with a gasket, and each time, while I held my breath, he came up with the yard on the windward roll. Almost frozen, soaked to the skin, he secured the ninety foot cro'j'k yard by dint of heroic effort, working back slowly when he was done, his homely features etched with relief that he was finished.

Now the mate's attention was riveted on the main lower t'gallant yard that hung on a stump of mast not more than six inches above her goose-neck. No lifts, her braces completely carried away, she swung as a clock's pendulum, her sail crackling and snapping to ribbons.

"Bos'un!" shouted Mr. Douglas. "Get all hands aft, and damned fast! That main t'gallant yard is going!"

The men rushed aft, looking aloft apprehensively as they went. No sooner had they made it than a forty-five degree roll sent the yard crashing into the sea. It cleared the t'gallant rail and main deck by mere inches, its two tons of steel careening past and plunging into the sea with a thunderous splash.

I was temporarily beyond speech, the rest of the crew evidently sharing my plight. If that two tons of steel had struck the main deck it would have gone on through, striking the black powder in the hold, and, indirectly, the bell of Lloyd's of London, which would have tolled brazen tongued announcement of the loss of the "Astral."

When we recovered from our fright I believe we all felt a fresh surge of hope and courage, and I think more than one hardened sailor in that rugged crew gave thanks to God without his shipmates' knowledge.

In the days that followed there was no noticeable change in the weather. We were now far south of the Horn, about fifty-seven degrees south, and the crew worked without rest to clear the wreckage, meanwhile keeping a sharp watch for icebergs as we were now in their latitudes.

The battered "Astral" ploughed through the angry green seas, a mere speck on their apparently limitless infinity. Young as I was, it brought home to me the realization of the immensity of the universe when contrasted by the comparative insignificance of man.

The stars and moon, when visible at all, were pale, wraithlike, scarcely discernible in the cold pewter sky. The chill air silvered into fine ice-like particles which glistened eerily on the ship's deck, the rigging, our clothing, aye—even our beards and brows. We slid through that watery desert as a phantom vessel, a sombre picture in grey.

Yet, despite the fear gnawing at our hearts, we kept faith with the "Astral," marvelling hour on hour that she never leaked a drop despite the incredible pounding she was taking. The master craftsmanship of the Sewalls who had built her was now apparent, for underneath her beauty lay staunchness as well.

A new moon, pale and slender, made its debut, and with it came new hope as we were again ordered to "wear ship." At last we were making good our "westing."

On July twenty-first the heavy black clouds which had replaced the gunmetal skies were pierced by a brave streak of sunlight, and there, off to the starboard side, was land!

It was not the kind of land for good landing, for it was the forbidding coast of Chile. A rock-bound, mountainous coast, its jutting peaks shrouded in snow, yet it brought a grin to our faces and a light to our tired eyes. We were around the Horn, with all hands safe.

We beat north, the strength of the sun increasing with each mile we gained, and the days grew longer so that we were no longer almost constantly hedged in by darkness.

Chips made a new main t'gallant mast, and with our other extra spar he cut a t'gallant yard. We rigged "raffees" on the fore and mizzen, a triangular sail rigged from the top of the lower mast and sheeted home on the top of the upper tops'l yard.

Came the south-east trades, Pitcairn Island, Juan Fernandez, sunshine and fair wind. The crew sang, and played accordions during the dog watch. We were as carefree as we had been fear laden before.

Holystoning of the decks began. Painting, scraping, every activity was bent toward getting the "Astral" shipshape. She looked strange with just a main t'gallant mast, bereft of her splendid wings. A crippled bird.

The doldrums came next. Heavy rains, light airs, the seas now calm and glassy. Underneath our bare feet the decks felt hot, and sails hung in a bight with the courses clewed up. We washed clothes, took bucket baths on deck, and revelled in the double privilege of not only being clean, but wearing dry clothes as well.

Ship talk began to focus on the number of days it would be before we got paid, and what we'd do when we got ashore. We discussed the Johnson-Jeffries fight, to be fought while we were at sea, and argued amongst ourselves as to who might have won. I bet on Jeffries, then could hardly wait to reach San Francisco to find out if he'd won.

The doldrums held us for two weeks before we picked up the light airs of the north-east trade, our home-stretch wind. We passed the time playing cribbage and poker. There was no money to change hands, but the slopchest was available and I think the boys bought nearly everything the skipper had.

We scrubbed out the foc'sle, with its sieve-like skylights opened night and day. The water barrels were all full. This was sailing ship life at its best. Our worries had disappeared with the last of the black clouds, everything was serene, and the "Astral" glided effortlessly through a field of blue dotted by nodding, white-capped daisies.

It was just one hundred and fifty-nine days out of New York when the Farallone Islands loomed up before us. A solid, reassuring sign that soon we would pick up the pilot boat.

How we hailed that pilot! The first new faces we had seen since leaving New York. The first moment we could get information about world happenings in the five months we had been at sea!

[33]

"Who won the fight?" we yelled.

"Jack Johnson!" came the reply, and that wiped the grin off my face for a minute!

We could see a big towboat making for our ship. With binoculars we could make out her name, the "Sea Rover," and a powerful and seaworthy tug was she.

"Stand by to take the towing hawser!" Mr. Douglas shouted, and the crew really jumped to his command.

That afternoon we dropped anchor in San Francisco Bay. The mate called all hands aft.

"The captain has gone ashore for the money and the Commissioner," he said. "I want you men to paint the hull of this ship around. Do that, and you are through. Pack your bags and stand by to pay off, and the towboat will take you ashore."

We went to work painting the hull. She looked beautiful in her new coat of French grey, the Stars and Stripes floating proudly from the monkey gaff, the Standard Oil flag on the main truck. But for all her paint she showed what she'd been through. Aloft, she showed her battering.

Passengers on ferry boats gathered at the rails to point at us. They read about it next day, for the "Astral" was as fully written up as any visiting celebrity.

Thanks to my bet on the fight, I paid off before the Commissioner with just $2.56 to show for doing man's work in extreme peril while rounding the Horn. I pocketed the money feeling a bit foolish.

My seamanship might be improving, but my commonsense seemed sadly lacking.

THE NEXT MORNING WE WERE TOWED TO THE HOWARD STREET WHARF, an open dock. The "Cissie" of Liverpool, another four master, was brought up astern of us and made fast. On the other side of the dock lay the German four-masted bark "Palau" of Hamburg, while astern of her was a three-masted bark of Yarmouth, Nova Scotia.

In the bay anchorage there were some fifty-odd sailing ships, while each day more ships loaded with cases of salmon came in. These were the Alaska packers' fleet, their foc'sle heads covered with cannery hands, fishermen, all cheering and shouting. They had been up there ever since early spring, and they, like the crew of the "Astral" could hardly wait to set foot ashore in a town that was known the world over for its hospitality to seafaring men.

East Street was a bustling thoroughfare, and rubbing elbows on its narrow sidewalks were sailors, fishermen, boarding house runners, crimps, pimps, and masters of the "shanghai gang" whose business it was to furnish a ship a crew. Any ship, to any port in the world.

The bos'un warned Halsey and myself about the shanghai artists, explaining the routine they followed.

The bars were always packed with seamen and men from every walk of life, and in every bar were "runners" from the shipping offices. They knew how to talk ship's language, and they'd walk up to a bar, throw five silver dollars on it, and cry, "It's my shout, boys!" an English expression from the public houses, meaning "It's on me."

While they urged the boys to drink, the crimps eyed their prospective victims calculatingly. Sometimes the bartender worked in cahoots with them, and ofttimes a good wad of money was paid for a single member of a crew.

The ship would be loaded, laying in the stream with sails bent and anchor hove short. A truck, horse drawn, stood by awaiting the crimp's beckoning hand, and after all the boys in the bar had several jolts of whiskey under their belts some of them could be talked into signing ship's articles, with many a scrawled "X" for signature.

Then came the signal for "outward bound," and the Mickey Finn. A well-planned fight, the victims loaded into the truck, and down they went to the waiting tug which carried them to the ship that was ready to sail.

That was one method of "shanghai," though there were others, and we listened as the bos'un explained. Ever after I was alert for such tricks, for I had no desire to be shanghaied.

It was wonderful to put our feet on dry land after all those months at sea. Halsey and I walked the length of Market Street and back, taking everything in, wishing we were with some older members of the crew. We didn't quite have courage enough to invade Barbary Coast, though neither one would admit it. Instead, we both agreed that we were "tired" and returned to the "Astral" early, thereby creating the impression we tended to be dullards.

The second day at the dock a fine team of well-groomed horses and an elaborate carriage drew up in front of the gangway and stopped. An official looking gentleman stepped out.

"Good morning, Captain Dunham!" he called up to the captain.

"Good morning," replied the skipper. He turned to Mr. Douglas, who stood beside him. "Mr. Douglas, muster what men we have left in the crew, and we'll drive to the offices of Standard Oil Company on Market Street."

I was one of those taken along, thanks to my early return the night before, and when we arrived at Standard Oil we were one by one asked to give testimony as to the loss of our ship's rigging off Cape

Horn. To me, it seemed a rank injustice in view of what we had gone through, but I had the sense to curb my tongue, and was soon glad, as I discovered it as simply routine questioning.

After much discussion the adjusters made their decision. "Loss of ship's rigging due to an act of God. Due to stress of weather. Case closed."

That night, Neilson the carpenter decided he wanted to tour Barbary Coast, and, to my great surprise, asked if I'd like to go along. He only had to ask once!

Our evening clothes consisted of faded blue denims, blue cotton shirts, and peak caps. My pockets held a couple of packs of Sweet Caporals. Chips had money.

We started with the Hippodrome, where three hundred hostesses were on tap to dance with anybody and everybody. Movies went on continually, and the orchestra played "The Turkey In The Straw," "Casey Would Waltz With A Strawberry Blonde," "Take Me Back To New York Town," and Eva Tanguay's "Won't You Come and Splash Me in the Ocean Blue?"

At the sides of the hall were regular church pews, with a six inch shelf the full length of the pew, where singing waiters lay down six beers at a time and slid them with unerring aim in front of the customers who had ordered.

Chips drank, and I danced. He was feeling flush, and loaned me money enough to cut a few capers. I soon found the trick was to select your partner before some homely hostess clutched you. As soon as you got your partner she led you to the one hundred foot bar where she ordered and you paid the bill. The bartender then handed her a commission check on her sale, and up went her skirt while she slid the ticket in the top of her stocking. The stockings I danced with were all bulging. With tickets, and a bit more.

I wasn't too good a dancer, and the girls weren't my idea of anything at all. They were either blowsy and fat, or thin and hard as nails. I made my way over to Chips.

"Is this all there is to Barbary Coast?" I asked.

Chips looked up from his grog and grinned.

"Hell no!'" he said emphatically. He clapped me on the shoulder. "Come on, kid, I'll show you around. You ain't seen nothing yet!"

We left the Hippodrome. Chips seemed to know where we were headed. I strode along beside him trying to look rough and ready, a sailor home from the sea. I'd been initiated into the ranks of those who had rounded the Horn, and it was plain I was now ready for sin and sex. In my mind, they were synonymous.

San Francisco's Barbary Coast was a plucked bird in comparison with what it had been before the earthquake. That was what Chips said, and numerous deserted buildings bore mute testimony to his veracity. But, if it was plucked, it was still one hundred per cent chicken and you could buy it any way you liked it.

Chips shopped around. Partly because he enjoyed it, and partly because he was getting a tremendous kick out of showing me the sights. For an hour or so we wandered in and out of places buying drinks and eyeing the girls. Some were scantily clad, some revealingly clad, and, in one place, they wore nothing but slippers and stockings. My face flushed often, and the telltale blush each time provoked remarks more startling than the sight which induced it.

"We-ell," drawled one slumbrous, sloe-eyed brunette after a deliberately prolonged scrutiny, "You may be a seaman, kid, but you ain't hardened—yet."

"Let the kid alone," advised another languidly, "Maybe he's saving it for his old age."

"Stow it!" thundered Chips, pausing in his dalliance with a buxom blonde, "This is his first time out, and you chippies ain't going to spoil it."

"Migawd!" the brunette said, batting heavy lidded eyes, "A virgin? Maybe I better run and slip something on—." The suggestions which followed were graphic and quite apt.

"Chips," I said, when we'd regained the street. "Er—are you having a good time?"

"Don't let those two-bit whores get under your skin, Barney," he said, laughing, "Come on! Now we'll really get squared away!"

"I'm sort of hungry," I said lamely, avoiding his eye. "I thought maybe we could get something to eat."

"Eat!" He stared at me in amazement. "Listen, fellow—you can always eat!"

There was nothing much to say. Not unless I wanted to confess that I saw nothing exciting in going to bed with someone who would bounce with anyone for a price. No storming a citadel here, no purple passage of romance. No goddess to invade your dreams.

We wound up in a bagnio that Chips assured me was the ne plus ultra in brothels. It was a three-story house, uncompromisingly plain outside, but decorated with much ornate furniture, gilded mirrors and heavy carpeting inside.

The Madame must have weighed two hundred pounds. She was well corsetted, impeccably dressed, and had an eye like a dead haddock. She rustled up to us after the negro maid had ushered us into the parlor. She asked what sort of girls we'd like. There wasn't a one in sight.

"How do we know unless we look 'em over?" Chips asked. He favored me with a knowing wink as she padded away to summon her girls. "No use in buying a pig in a poke," he observed cheerfully. I nodded dumb acquiescence.

The harlots strolled in. Every man to his taste, and God help a seventeen-year-old on a night like this . . . Chips had been right, though, in making his final destination. The girls were cleaner, less vulgar, and they made no raucous remarks. The madame's eye was on them, and business was business.

Chips was in his element. He ogled and quipped, pinched and caressed, and finally disappeared in the direction of the stairs with a Junoesque blonde. I was left alone. Or, rather, alone with eleven girls and the madame.

The girls smiled teasingly, and asked if it were the first time I'd been in such a place.

"No!" I blurted rashly, thinking to forestall any quips anent my innocence.

"Then what are we waiting for?" At my elbow stood a lissome topaz-eyed girl who looked no older than I. She slipped her arm through mine and drew me in the general direction where Chips had vanished. The madame nodded indulgently.

Then I had the inspiration!

"Look," I said hesitantly, my foot on the first red-carpeted step of the supposed stairway to Paradise, "I just came along with my friend. I better go. You see, I haven't any money."

The girl laughed, and her mirth was not pretty to hear. "So that's what's eating you!" She misunderstood me completely. "Listen, sailor, to be with a clean kid like you after some of the dirty old bastards I see—well, it's an honest-to-God pleasure. Come on up, honey. This one's on me!"

I went on up.

Afterwards, Chips and I made our way back to the ship. Chips was unwilling to leave, and I pulled him half the way. He was three-fourths drunk, full of argument, and unhappy about leaving the blonde.

"How come a big strong kid like you has to go running back to the ship just when the going's good?" he asked resentfully, "If you didn't like the girl you could have gotten another."

"I didn't have any money," I said shortly. I was not in the mood to discuss the events of the evening. It wasn't the girl, particularly.

"Then how did you get upstairs?" Chips asked, obviously disbelieving.

"I was invited," I snapped, goaded into truth.

Chip's jaw dropped a good quarter inch. "For free?" he asked incredulously. I nodded grimly.

"My Gawd!" he ejaculated, "In all the times I've been in those places I've never gotten so much as a free beer!" We trudged the rest of the way back to the ship without speech, save when he'd look at me from time to time and shake his head in wonder and murmur, "My Gawd!"

Back in my bunk, I did a lot of thinking. I reviewed my first bout with sin and sex, and in my mind they were no longer synonymous. I wasn't revolted, yet neither was I looking forward to a similar episode. Nor was I proud of being a "courtesy" customer.

The word "customer" jolted me back to normalcy. The conquest of a chippy in a parlor house was no more to be compared with the real thing than a stagnant pond with the clean, tempestuous ocean. There was as much difference in women, I was beginning to suspect, as in bodies of water.

It wasn't many days after that I quit the "Astral." I was approaching my eighteenth birthday, and I wanted to go to sea again. First, though, I wanted to see the family. The hitch was, I had no money.

I went to Murray and Ready's Employment Agency in San Francisco to get a job. They shipped me out to Portola, California, where a powder monkey job awaited me on the Western Pacific, $2.50 a day plus three square meals.

Came the day when I had money enough to get to New York. I got out of there as soon as I could, and headed for the nearest railroad station. It only took seven days and four different railroads to reach New York, but my impatience made the trip seem longer than the entire voyage around the Horn.

What a welcome I got when I walked through the old iron gate! They all fell on me at once, and we kissed and embraced all around until everyone, including myself, was sure I was home.

Over and over they asked me about the trip around the Horn, and I answered every question as best I could, and even a few that I couldn't.

It was only when my sisters asked me about Barbary Coast that I hedged a bit.

"How were the women?" asked one daringly, "Were they as wild as everyone says?"

"How wild does everyone say they are?" I parried, laughing easily enough.

"You girls let up on questioning Barney, and go to bed," ordered my Dad, "Let us men talk for awhile." Away they went reluctantly, giggling and whispering, after kissing me goodnight.

My Dad waited until they had trooped out of the room, then looked at me and grinned.

"Well, Barney," he said, chuckling, "You can tell me—how wild were they?"

THE FIRST OF NOVEMBER FOUND ME HEADING FOR MY OLD HAUNT,
South Street. Winter had returned full force, and while I bought
some deepwater flannel shirts, woolens, and a generous supply of
tobacco, a ship bound for flying fish weather, away from the biting
gales of the North Atlantic, was what I was hoping for.

Into every shipping office I went, but things were deadly dull. I
finally bethought me of Moore and Eggete, the shipping office, and
strolled in there. I'd no sooner hit the front door than they asked me
if I were a sailing ship man.

"Yes, sir!"

"I've a good chance for you, then."

"What ship?" I asked curiously.

"The 'Laura M. Lunt' of New York."

"Where bound?"

"Halifax, Nova Scotia."

Good night! And I had hoped for flying fish weather! I thought it
over carefully. With shipping so dull there didn't seem to be much

alternative. I didn't want to be on the beach for the winter, and I never could turn my back on the North Atlantic at that time of year.

"All right," I sighed resignedly. "You can count on me."

"Can you get your clothes right away?" A shipping master never felt sure of himself until he had a crew ready in his office *with* their clothes.

"Yes, sir."

I got my sailor bag from the Seaman's Institute, then came back to the shipping office and sat around most of the afternoon until three more men came in from a boarding house. We were told that the "Laura M. Lunt" was eight hundred net tons, the largest hand-pulling schooner on the Atlantic seaboard. A three-master, her skipper, a Captain Martin of Rockland, Maine.

The crew included Hans Tuft of Mandell, Norway; Harry Bergstrom of Horton, Norway; Yens Nelsen of Denmark; the cook was a Liverpool Limey from Nova Scotia, and the mate was Mr. Meyer of Danzig, Poland. Once again I was the only American in the crew.

Our wages as A. B.'s were thirty dollars a month, the second mate got forty, and the mate received fifty. The cargo was coal. Coal for Halifax, than which there is nothing colder.

We heard the heavy tread of feet on the rickety old wooden stairs, then into the offices strode the skipper.

"Captain, I have all your men here with their clothes and they're ready to go aboard," piped up the shipping master promptly. Captain Martin looked pleased.

We all signed articles. They read something like this: "And the crew will work the cargo with the necessary stevedores and load lumber at Ingramport, Nova Scotia, for a final port of discharge at Philadelphia, Pennsylvania." None but the hardiest and most experienced would have covered the trip at all.

We upped our heavy sailor bags, and off we started. We made quite a sight going down South Street in that day of sailing ships, our sailor bags on our shoulders, our clothes mostly European cut, peak caps at a forty-five degree angle. Red or blue bandanas, Blucher shoes, and, protruding from the lee corner of our mouths, the famous clay pipe. 'Twas that, or a cheekful of Copenhagen snuff.

The tug "Shamrock" awaited us, and we climbed aboard. The ship lay anchor off Red Hook flats, Brooklyn. With the crew sitting on the hawser rack, huddled into their woolens against the wind that blew cold from N.E. down the water front, the tug steamed down the East River and Buttermilk Channel.

Once alongside the "Laura M. Lunt," the tug blew several short blasts to stand by. The cook came out and took a bow line, and we piled aboard.

Next came getting the stores aboard while the tug hung on. And, at last, the order, "Heave anchor!"

All hands had dropped their bags in the foc'sle and we shipped our windlass pump handles while the cook grabbed his chain hook and took care of the lapping turns on the old wooden drum. It was his job to make sure the chain did not ride over its own part of the drum.

In came the anchor chain, one link at a time. We hove in sixty fathoms and catheaded the anchor. The tug gave us his hawser and we towed up the East River, out through Hellsgate. A man to the wheel, the rest to supper.

When we arrived at City Island anchorage in Long Island Sound we were wind-bound, and there was nothing to do but anchor. The "Laura M. Lunt" lay in snug harbor for three full days and nights while the storm blew itself out. Not a single one of us had the slightest idea of what hell we would go through before we would eventually be paid off ninety-five days later at the foot of Shackamaxon Street, Philadelphia.

The morning of the third day at City Island, the cook told the skipper he would be needing some more stores. Pots and pans, and the usual requisites for a long trip. Captain Martin said he would be going ashore and would see that the stores were sent aboard by the men who rowed him in.

Hans, Harry, Yens and I responded. We ducked into the foc'sle to get our pipes and tobacco, glad to get a little action if it only meant rowing the old man ashore.

It was a cold, dull day, with the wind beginning to haul toward its winter quarter in the nor'west, and the cloud formations were breaking. We got busy clearing away the strong backs which gave support to the keel of our life boat, and, with everything clear, Hans and I climbed in.

"Lower away!" ordered the second mate.

Steady lowering, and she kissed the waters. I unhooked the stern-tackle while a strain was held on the fore until Harry and Yens slid down the bow fall. Once down, we unhooked and cast off, grabbing our sweeps and stroking together to the Jacob's ladder at the starboard gangway. There we sat and shivered, waiting for the skipper and Von Meyer.

"I scal tank I vil ask the skipper for five dollar," Hans said to Harry while we held on.

"Yah, by golly, I scal do the same," said Harry.

"Sounds like a fine idea," I chimed in.

Yens, wearing the Icelandic sweater his mother had knitted for him before he left Copenhagen, grinned contentedly, "Yah! Ve can have penga!" The old man sure had a surprise in store.

Von Meyer came down and took a seat in the stern sheets to steer, while Captain Martin sat on the port side of the boat steerer. "Cast off, and give way together!" said Von Meyer curtly.

We headed into the dock, where a ladder nailed to the pier was the only means of getting ashore. The skipper had just placed one foot on the ladder when Hans Tuft nailed him.

"Oh, captain!" he sang out, "Do you tank ve could get a few dollars to buy some tobacco and varm mittens?"

Captain Martin flinched slightly, knowing what to expect from the rest of us.

"I suppose that goes for the rest of you," he said sarcastically. He dug into his pockets and fished out his wallet. He gave each of us five dollars, the equivalent of five days pay. "You men can sign for that money on board," he said, ascending the ladder, "Mr. Meyer, I'm sending some stores down. Wait for me, and we'll go aboard together."

We tied the boat up to the lee side of the pier, leaving Von Meyer to wait for the skipper. He paced up and down, military fashion, but we snickered amongst ourselves for the hat he wore was one he had bought somewhere around the San Pauli Dance Pavilion in Hamburg's water front.

We headed for Monahan's "Sea Breeze Cafe," our five dollars burning a hole in our pockets. We walked in, to be greeted by as salty a crowd of coasters and deep watermen as ever sheeted home a sail. There sat Papa Dick, Russian Finn John, Red Pete, Hulga Thorgsen, and Lobscouse Harry. What a gathering!

Monty Monahan set up the drinks on the house at once, shouting boisterously, "It's on the house, boys!"

Lunch was on the counter, all you could eat. A piano stood in the corner, and the pretzel bowls did a rushing business, while someone played "Take Me Back To New York Town." A pint of good liquor could be had for fifty cents.

The party was still going full tilt at seven-thirty. We thoughtfully sent Yens down to the dock to see if the skipper had showed up.

He found the second mate still plodding his boat. The skipper hadn't shown up, but the stores were all there.

"I vunder vot is der matter vit dot skipper?" Von Meyer said unhappily.

"Ve should worry," replied Yens, glad the skipper hadn't asked him to wait at the dock. "Ve are having vonderful time. If you vant us, ve are at Monahan's." He left Meyer to his lonely promenade, and came back to the fun.

At ten o'clock we headed for the pier, twice as warm as if we'd spent our money on mittens. A snappy wind blew from the nor'west, and when we hit the cold night air things began to happen. One by one, as we waited for the skipper, we passed out. I was just coming to at about two in the morning when he showed up.

He cocked an observant eye at us, then said to the weary Meyer, "Shake 'em up! The wind is fair, let's be going aboard."

I heard him. I was nearly frozen, and my head felt as though it would slip its moorings, but I felt sorry for Meyer so I obligingly got to my feet and shook hell out of the rest of them.

"Vare are ve?" mumbled Yens sleepily.

"Vot ship is dis?" asked Hans, looking around foggily. I didn't answer. I was working on Harry, trying to waken him while the skipper stood by and watched. He spoke only once.

"I trust the mittens will be satisfactory," he said.

Once the men had come to and the stores had been passed down into the boat, we shoved off and gave way.

"Rockland, Maine, will be our first stop," Captain Martin said as we rowed out, not half so expertly as we'd rowed in, "There I'll be leaving the ship and you'll get a new skipper." We rowed on without comment. None was expected.

As we approached the vessel we could see the cook had taken care of putting up the riding lights. We came alongside, bent a heaving line onto the stores, and landed them on deck. The mates were on hand, for they had to do their share of all the work.

They hooked on the boat tackles, and we sat taut, waiting for the men to come up out of the boat. It was a fifteen foot shinny from boat to poop deck, and that was only a small part of the shinnying.

The mate, Mr. Wagner, fore-handed the boat tackles and the crew stretched out along the rope. One man sang out, and we pulled in rhythm of the chanty-man.

Up she came. First the stern, then the bow, and so on until it was "two blocks." But, in making fast the stern, someone hollered, "Come up behind!"

Well, we were stupid. We all let go of the rope like a bunch of stiffs, and down she went—the rope burning the mate's hands, only to hit the water with a heavy splash. The ship's stores dumped into Long Island Sound, and sank before we could rescue them!

The bow of the lifeboat was secure, and the stern hung in the water. We looked at each other like simpletons, each demanding who had yelled "Come up behind."

The German mate was holding his singed paw, jumping up and down and raving like a maniac. He cursed fluently in German and English, bringing the skipper to see what was going on.

He jumped at the stern boat fall, and shouted, "Men! This time you're going to walk it up. And you walk too, Mr. Mate," he added acidly.

Seven men grabbed that tackle fall, and away they went, stamping their feet on the deck in perfect step. The stern of the life boat came up to two blocks when the skipper, old coaster that he was, blew his whistle to "fast heaving." Then he put a stop on her and blew two shrill blasts. This meant "Come up behind."

The gang seemed to sober up, and all hands got busy putting strong backs and boat gripes to lash her in tight. This time the lifeboat was secure, and Captain Martin left orders for coffee at four a.m. and that we were getting under way.

These orders had the poor cook running around in circles. He was really doing double duty. Keeping us in food, clearing the wooden drums of riding turns as the anchor came in, and tailing on to a halyard when setting sail.

We hove short, and all hands went aft to "set 'schpanker'" as Mr. Wagner called it. It was pitch dark and cold as hell, if such a thing can be.

Three men on the peak, four on the throat, but with the ropes swollen and wet from the nor'easter, and the sail itself like a damn board that spilled a couple of gallons of ice water at every hoist.

Neither side had gotten that spanker up fifteen feet when the mate called, "Belay that peak, and all hands on throat halyards!"

Old Hans Tuft, tough as he was, exclaimed, "She's the heaviest son of a bitch I been in for a long time!" Brightening, he added, "We can do this with a chanty!" We obliged by breaking into "Blow the Man Down." It *did* help.

By jumping from one halyard to the other, it took us one hour to set that spanker! Then we had the mains'l, and the fores'l, all set to the tune of the chanty. Then back onto the foc'sle head to heave our guts out on a windlass that brought in one link to three ups and downs of the windlass pump handles.

It took all hands, no matter what we did, and sorry we were to be finding it out with anchor aweigh!

At least she paid off in fine shape, sheets eased, anchors catheaded, and a man to the wheel. Watches were set next, and I was on Von Meyer's starboard watch. From then on it was "Give a suck on the pumps," at one and seven bells. The "Laura M. Lunt" had to be pumped out every watch as long as we were on the damned hooker.

We listed to a smart nor'wester, and soon the skipper ordered the fore and main tops'ls set. We headed east, going like a winged horse for three days, and anchored in the harbor of Rockland in good time.

We took Captain Martin ashore and were given orders to wait at the landing for the new skipper. If we'd known what we were in for I think we would have all jumped ship there and then.

We waited, Meyer and I, arguing hotly over which country had the best navy. Finally an irritable looking man, cold eyed and cruel mouthed, approached the second mate. "Are you men from the schooner 'Laura M. Lunt'?"

"Yes, sir."

"I'm Captain Nelson, and I'm taking over. We'll go aboard now." He seated himself in the boat and gazed straight ahead, unsmiling.

To a new skipper, a seaman meant no more than ship's stores. There was never an introduction, nor do I recall a case where any familiarity existed between master and crew. And, for some reason, the formality worked both ways.

The day before Thanksgiving we arrived at Halifax. The tug put us alongside the dock. The harbor was a cold one, open to all nor'eastern gales. Seas rolled onto the piers that would toss a Newport yacht like a cork. And now we worked from six to six.

Coffee at five-thirty in the morning, and "turn to" a half hour later. It was the coldest place anyone could imagine. Our drinking water was in big casks, lashed to the ringbolts in the deck. Each time we wanted a drink we stuck the tin cup through the square cut in the bung and broke the ice over the surface.

The coal was worked with hoppers which held about a half ton in each lift, and it snowed and blew every day. Working that boom guy every day out of seven, our feet ice cold, our faces chapped from the freezing wind, was no idyllic existence.

The stevedores were the waterfront riff-raff of Halifax. They would have stolen the fillings from their grandmother's teeth. Those fellows would unbend the jibs at night and sell them to a junkie!

At six p.m. we'd knock off and go to the foc'sle where our supper was ready. There was no talk of washing up, for we never had enough hot water to shave, let alone get our filthy hands clean.

The fire was kept going by whoever came into the foc'sle, and we cleaned the lamp by spitting into the globe and wiping it with a page from an old magazine. After chow we'd take turns at the one bucket there was to wash in, and it took bravery to wash in the ice water it contained.

We all drew ten dollars and went ashore one Saturday afternoon. The water front of Halifax in 1911 was lined with quaint wooden buildings, one and two stories high, and every other store sold clothes for seamen.

After a few shots of Canadian whiskey to warm us up we began buying woolen socks and underwear. We'd all had a fair sample of the "Lunt" and we had no intention of freezing to death. In those days of schooners and square riggers we steered with a four foot wheel, out in the open regardless of weather, the weather cheek almost frozen when steering by the wind.

Once back on ship we didn't go ashore again. Our foc'sle was warm and comfortable with its four wooden bunks and little pot-bellied bogie.

By December twentieth the ship was unloaded, the hold cleaned, and the gear on deck made ready for the sea. Captain Nelson proved to be a jumpy, irritable Swede. He gave the impression of one driven by some grim demon who wouldn't let him rest.

We were taken out to anchor in the harbor, and the sky was thick with wintry clouds as we dropped port anchor. During the night the wind increased to a howl in the rigging, and I called the mate and we gave her twenty more fathom.

By four a.m. the skipper had the mate let go the starboard anchor, and by the time it was four next morning both anchors were out to full cable length of ninety fathoms each. The nor'east gale was blowing in force, our harbor sea one such as is known only to the folk in Halifax.

Christmas Eve found the wind hauling enough to make a fair wind for our ship, and Christmas morning the skipper told the two mates we were getting under way.

The two mates were in such terror of the skipper's temper that they generally stepped over the threshold of his cabin together, each making sure he would not be the last on deck. They jumped as though the Kaiser himself were speaking.

We were all watching from the door of the foc'sle, and no sooner had we said "Merry Christmas" to each other than the captain stuck his head in at us.

"All right, you fellows! Ve're getting under way!"

The idea of getting under way on Christmas really rankled, and none of us moved with any spirit. I think we might have dumped him by accident, but for one thing. It was Christmas whether he knew it or not.

There were the ninety fathom of chain outside the hawsepipe on each anchor, and we could just about stand our deck in the wind. It seemed that a superstition of the sea was being borne out by the captain's insistence on getting under way on Christmas. I have many times seen captains strive to get a ship unloaded by Saturday in order to get under way on Sunday, only to give back that day two for one, and lose rigging with it.

We shipped our windlass bars, and Captain Nelson passed round a bottle of whiskey as his Christmas gesture to warm up the men. Then, generous soul that he was, he said, "Boys, I will help you. I'll sing a chanty."

He let out to the tune of

"Oh, Sally Brown was a fine mulatto
Oh, oh, Sally Brown—
Her father was the keeper
Of a New Orleans tavern,
And I spent my money on Sally Brown."

He went on, chorus after chorus, until the crew had a fine sweat under their heavy woolens.

I had reached that point in seamanship where I knew the next step was to speak what was on my mind. I approached the singing skipper, and he stopped in mid-verse and stared at me.

"You'll live to regret this, sir," I said coldly, "It just takes the difference of one day to change the entire passage of a ship."

"Shut up!" he shouted, livid with rage, "Get the anchors up!"

Now he was mad. He acted tougher than hell, barking out orders left and right.

"Man to the wheel!" "Get those side lights up!" "Clear up the decks!" "Mr. Wagner, tell that cook to get some food aft!" "Mr. Meyer, slack those lee boom lifts! Every time we get under way you have to be told!"

Two days later we arrived at Ingramport, Nova Scotia. Here the skipper picked up a mizzen topmast of pine spar, and every day from six to six we loaded laths and lumber for our return trip to Philadelphia. On deck we had a load of laths twelve tiers high.

For ten days we toiled with Nova Scotian workmen and mill hands, loading the "Laura M. Lunt," wondering who she was to have had such a ship named after her.

The spar for the mizzen topmast was floated from the mill, brought on deck, and lashed. We never saw that spar again, for it lay below a deck load.

The cook got sick and left. The captain paid him and told him to send down another cook when he got to Halifax.

The following night the new cook arrived. Within twenty-four hours we discovered that he was blind. He would pick up foods, smell them, feel them.

"Good God, Hans!" I muttered, "We can't take this man to sea! He'd be washed overboard! What shall we do?"

"You report it to the skipper," said Hans glumly, "I don't vant to."

Yens came into the foc'sle. "Barney!" he said in his broken English, "Cook don't see!"

"You're right, Yens," I said regretfully, and went aft to brave the old man. He surprised me by agreeing the colored cook was blind, and said he would like me to see him safely aboard a train for Halifax.

After lunch the crew cleaned up the galley and I saw old Ben to the train. Now that his near blindness had been discovered he used a cane to feel the ground ahead of him, something he had not done aboard ship.

Our new cook Ansel, a Nova Scotian schooner cook, proved to be all right, and on January fifth the "Laura M. Lunt" was ready for the sea.

An open bay made getting under way easy. The fore and mans'ls went up, as usual, to the tune of a chanty.

> "Whiskey made me go to sea
> Whiskey, Johnny
> Whiskey bought and whiskey free
> Whiskey for my Johnny."

The wind was nor'east, and dirty. Captain Nelson, after seeing the fore and mains'l set, ordered a double reef in the spanker. The barometer was on a spree.

January seventh I was at the wheel at eight p.m. when eight bells struck aft, and the lookout promptly struck his eight on the foc'sle head bell. Captain Nelson, standing nearby, looked worried.

"Mr. Wagner," he said "take in the inner jib, and put a double reef on the mains'l." The sea was heavy, Sable Island light off the starboard bow. The skipper relieved me at the wheel, and though I gave him "full'n bye" he would not repeat the order. For'ard I went, to help the crew tie up the inner jib.

The "Lunt" was sticking her bows under to the foot ropes on the jib boom. Not so good, but I always felt better when the inner and outer jibs were tied up. Six of us hoisted that mains'l after tying in a double reef.

Back to the wheel I went, waiting for the order "Relieve the wheel and lookout." The skipper went to his cabin, and I looked at the compass. The wind had now hauled to the east, and I kept her "full'n bye."

The seas grew in span and size, now combing dangerously and running twenty feet high. The air grew warmer, rain clouds gathered, then the downpour and blow!

Captain Nelson appeared on deck in his oilskins. He strode over to the mate at the weather rail. "Mr. Wagner, the barometer is now down to 29.60. Secure everything forward and stand by. I think all hell is going to break loose!"

Again the wind hauled to the southeast, the blow was heavy, with an engulfing downpour of rain, and the "Laura M. Lunt" was making heavy weather of it. She rolled at twenty-five degrees, in such complete darkness it seemed a curtain had been drawn across the moon and stars.

The skipper remained at the weather rail, peering intently through the rivulets which ran off his hooded oilskins. He seemed to be waiting for something to appear.

"Mr. Meyer," he said, finally, "take a sounding of bilges fore and aft."

Second mate Meyer reported soon enough. "Two feet, six inches, sir."

"Have all hands man the pumps and stay with them throughout the watch," the captain replied, looking worried.

By midnight, the weird situation the captain had anticipated occurred. We had two winds of gale force blowing at us from directly opposite sides. We lay in the trough of the southeast gale, while off to the northwest the sky was breaking, the air growing clear as crystal.

The difference between the two forces was almost unbelievable, for while the southeaster carried a temperature of sixty-five degrees the northwester we could see coming from our position on the poop deck carried zero temperatures! Captain Nelson's compressed lips and furrowed brow showed plainly he was debating what to do.

When a nor'wester strikes, every sea sweeping the ship turns to ice. A hundred tons of ice is quickly added to a deckload. The ship becomes topheavy, and when she rolls over she does not come back. Her crew are either swept away, or freeze to death on a water-logged ship.

The galley and the foc'sle were now awash, and glad we were we didn't have old Ben, the near-blind cook, added to our troubles.

Then the nor'wester struck! All hands eased over the booms and shifted the tackles, for the ship was taken full a-back. Now we were on the starboard tack, the bitterly cold nor'west seas meeting the sou'east seas.

By four in the morning we were getting the full force of the furious gale. Ice was forming over the entire ship, the foc'sle head sheeted with glistening white, the deck load beginning to sheathe itself in the deadly weight that could spell our doom.

Captain Nelson ordered a double reef in the fore'sl and Yens and I began securing the reef plank that went from the deckload to the forward house.

The "Lunt" suddenly took a dreadful roll, as though she were trying to shed the excess weight of her smothering deckload. The reef plank went sliding, and—Yens! He had no chance to grab for anything. He just held onto the plank and both headed for kingdom come.

I saw his plight, and, between sliding and grabbing, I managed to reach the top back of the port t'gallant rail. There, with one hand on the fore topmast stay, I reached out with the other and grabbed Yens' oilskin coat, I clung to his coat for dear life while the port rail went under with the next roll, taking with it the reef plank he had been holding. The whole thing was over in a matter of seconds, and Yens, when it was over, clapped me silently on the back.

"Dot vas close!" he acknowledged shakily.

Two more hours of incredible labor, and we had the fores'l set. By that time the deckload was encased in solid ice. Each time we rolled, the ship hesitated longer before coming back, as though she were tired of struggling against insurmountable odds.

"Cut the deckload lashings!" shouted the captain.

A twelve foot deckload, with seas breaking completely over it! We tried to hurry, but turnbuckles and chains are not easy to let go. We fumbled when we tried to snap the buckles by striking them with a top-maul, and to unscrew them was the only way.

It took us hours. Hours of seemingly futile effort. Then the deckload began leaving the ship with every roll, away into the sea, lightening the burden of the ship, lifting the weight of fear from our hearts.

Then the ship took one directly on the bow! She dove, after rising to it, and in so doing she came close to disaster.

The forward well deck filled in, flooding the galley. The lashings of the foc'sle stove let go, setting the foc'sle afire. Fire and ice! Through the glacial coating of the foc'sle the rosy flames could be seen, and meanwhile the "Laura M. Lunt" was shaking herself free of her deckload with all the abandon of a loose woman.

[55]

Everyone stopped whatever they were doing to put out the fire. We passed sea water in buckets, and the skipper held the wheel and looked on.

When the fire and the excitement had died out we began to see the full extent of the damage.

"Have a drink of water, mate," said Harry to me. His voice sounded suddenly rusty.

A glance revealed that the crew's water barrel had gone by the board. Water, water, everywhere and not a drop to drink.

We were iced half-way up in our rigging now, the glimmering silver white transforming the "Laura M. Lunt" into a veritable snow maiden of a vessel. The charred embers of the foc'sle were already cloaked in wintry white, and as we staggered through the combing seas it was apparent she was in immediate danger. Her ice-laden bow nosed deeply under, while her sodden hull lurched with a disastrous lethargy.

We of the crew were soaked through, bone cold, tired beyond relief, yet we stumbled back to the pumps and the losing game went on.

"Don't stop at those pumps, boys!" said Captain Nelson. He looked ten years older, his shoulders sagging underneath his oilskin like those of an old man. "It might save us from freezing to death," he muttered, half under his breath, as he walked away.

The gale continued unabated, and snow squalls and furious sea merged into a smother of white.

"Take in the mains'l, fores'l, spanker, and bend the storm trys'l on the mizzen!" the skipper bellowed.

Somehow we managed. Our wrists broken out with saltwater winter-chap, our hands cracked open with sea cuts, while in our boots swished sea water warmed by the blood from our feet.

And now it snowed! The air was a smother of fine white particles, blotting out vision, powdering the ice-laden decks, making the turn at the wheel well nigh blinding. And all the while the "Laura M. Lunt" rolled and tossed, the seas going clean across her, taking each time the laths that were still left on deck.

Captain Nelson, walking among us, noting the gaunt cheekbones and tired glitter of our eyes, knew we were about played out. He did not look much better, for he walked with fear for his ship as a constant companion.

We rigged up a contrivance of sorts on the cabin stove, and the cook heated up canned "Willie," canned roast beef put out by Burnham and Morrill of Portland, Maine, and this, with pilots bread and coffee, we lived on for the next three weeks.

I was at the after pumps in front of the captain's door, when Captain Nelson came out of the cabin and stood by me, silently. No one was at the wheel, for we were hove to. Soundings showed six feet of water in the hold.

"Barney," he said, "I don't feel I'll ever see my wife and children again. And if we waterlog there won't be one of us left to tell the story."

"Oh no, captain!" I protested, reassuringly as I could, "We'll come through. I wouldn't think such thoughts! We'll just go on trying to get a suck on these pumps!" He put his hand on my shoulder for a moment, and after an unsuccessful attempt at a smile he went back into his cabin and closed the door.

"Men, stay at those pumps! It's our only chance!"

Our sidelights were useless because water had found its way into our kerosene. When night came we had to burn our slush lamp—poor consolation when we had been blown offshore into steamship lanes. One night when the lookout reported a steamer headed straight for us, we dragged out the slush lamp and lit a flare. The steamer saw it just in time to avoid going through us. She swept by, her lights gleaming, and how we longed to be aboard!

Now we lay hove to, with salt water ice glistening clear to the crosstrees. To get at any rope we had to break ice with belaying pins, and, as we pumped and continued to spell each other, silence gradually took over. We worked without word, almost without hope.

Twenty-one days of sail splitting, loose laths washing fore'n aft, the jib boom looking like a big candy stick. Now and then a sickly ray of sunlight penetrated the storm clouds momentarily, then withdrew, leaving us to our steady ration of misery.

At last came a day when we were able to put sail to the "Lunt." Fores'l, mains'l, spanker and jib, we got them all up, only to take them in again as new gales descended upon us!

Now our sails were getting many seam rips, for they filled away with a slap and bang on each roll. We lowered them, and sewed them out in the cold with our cut, raw hands that hadn't seen fresh water for fifteen days.

On the morning of January twenty-fourth we sighted Dutch Island,

R.I. We sailed into the harbor, but there we encountered such heavy ice we were forced to drop anchor. The captain ordered anchor watches, and still those cursed pumps had to be kept going.

At eight that night we got a "suck" on the blasted pumps, and that was news indeed! There was real joy on the faces of the men, and we rallied round the captain as he broke out a bottle to "Splice the main brace."

Each man held his pannikin, and the skipper gave a toast to "A harbor of rest." Amen! We drank to that toast!

The next day found us at the boiling point. We'd been told we couldn't go ashore. That for our "harbor of rest!"

Sick of the whole bloody mess, I went aft to the old man to tell him we would not turn to again if we couldn't go ashore for one night and draw ten dollars each.

The skipper nearly hit the skylight, and started to use language that he knew best, but it didn't bother me any. I'd already seen how tough he was . . .

I went for'ard to tell the crew, but before I'd a chance to say anything Captain Nelson charged up, mad as a Madrid bull. He swung open the foc'sle door.

"Now you men!" he shouted, "I want to tell you right now—if it's dancing you want, I'll play the music but you pay the musician! I'll start with you, Barney, by putting you to a test in seamanship! I just want to make sure you're an able-bodied seaman. You go and put a long splice in the main throat halyards. Yens! Come out here!"

I was scowling, and Yens looked uneasy because he couldn't put his thoughts into English, and Hans—Hans didn't wait to be called. They had all been to sea many years, and they were talking to a man who spoke their language. Then they started!

Never in my life, before or since, have I heard a skipper called the names those two fellows used. "Cue fitter," "stockfish eating bastard," ending with "Enter that in your log book, you son of a bitch!"

I was young, obedient, and knew where the Act of Congress started and ended. So, while they ranted at the skipper and the two mates paced the poop deck, I finished the splice I had been set to do.

"All finished, sir," I reported.

"Go to your foc'sle," he growled, "That's all!"

No one went ashore that night. The next day, however, the captain chose Yens and me to take him for fresh stores. The rest of the crew looked glumly on as we lowered the lifeboat.

"Two good men are enough to put me ashore," said the skipper sarcastically.

We cleared away from the ship, and the ice in the harbor was thick and heavy. It was a dirty job getting to the dock, but Yens and I made it, eager to be ashore. Then, at the dock, the skipper told us to wait there for him.

At nine that night he came back with the stores, a cigar in his mouth, bourbon on his breath. Yens and I had had no dinner, no supper, and danced our feet for seven hours to keep from freezing. That was our reward for proving we were able seamen!

The next day we got under way again, and there wasn't a member of the crew who had much strength left after the unusual labors of getting her off.

Fortunately we sailed down the Atlantic seaboard without incident, for we were in no condition to weather any sort of storm. On January 30th we finally hove in sight of the Delaware Capes, a tug came alongside, close enough to bargain with the skipper, and the tug captain stuck his megaphone out the port window of the pilot house.

"Hello, captain!"

"Hello," replied Captain Nelson laconically.

"Where are you from?"

"Ingramport, Nova Scotia."

"Looks like you had a rough passage."

"Not good," said the captain indifferently, brave as brass now the danger was past.

"Do you know your port of discharge, captain?"

"Yes, Shackamaxon Street wharf, Philadelphia."

"Well, captain," said the tugboat skipper, "I'll take you up for two hundred dollars."

"Too much!" snapped Captain Nelson, "We are not a millionaire's yacht!" But he did have to go to a dock ninety miles up a river covered with twelve inches of ice.

We of the crew stood by the fore rigging, listening with relish to the preliminaries of haggling over the price. The tugboat captain rang down a bell and a jingle, meaning full steam ahead. One way of forcing the captain's hand.

Captain Nelson flung up a detaining hand. "One minute!" he yelled, "I'll give you one seventy-five!"

The tugboat captain stopped his tug. "All fine, skipper!" he shouted, "I'll take you up! There's just one other matter, skipper. I can't take you up unless you sheathe your vessel from the stempost to abaft the chain plates of the fore rigging!"

Captain Nelson fairly stamped the deck in rage, for he had been neatly caught.

"Such sheathing is an ordinance of the Delaware River," explained the wily tugboat captain. "Do you have lumber for it?"

"No," said Captain Nelson, short and sour.

"H'mm. Well, captain, I can go to Lewiston and get it for you for just twenty-five dollars." The tugboat captain was smiling, innocent as could be.

Captain Nelson gnawed his lips, paced a bit, then said grudgingly, "All right. Get the lumber, and don't forget, nails too." He turned and shouted, "Mr. Wagner, we will shorten sail and drop anchor!" He was defeated, and he knew it.

The tug was back by ten-thirty a.m. with lumber and nails, and all hands got busy sheathing the schooner from the waterline up to keep the ice from cutting and crushing through the hull. Up anchor, and on our way to Philadelphia. That night we were safely moored to an open dock. To greet us there were a couple of waterfront tailors who passed around whiskey, cigarettes, and their cards.

The next morning the captain paid us off. We all had about ninety-five dollars coming, and it looked like a million. We took a last look at the "Lunt," and said in farewell to each other, "See you on South Street!"

From the ship I walked directly to the address on the card the ship's tailor had given me. Now there was a sailor for you! Instead of going to a good store and getting our money's worth, we fell for the "dog's wool and oakum" suits of the waterfront. No wonder they used to sing "Strike up the band, here comes a sailor!"

I did go for a Turkish bath, and there I met most of the crew, for they'd all had the same idea. What a time we had in that Turkish bath! Even the guy who rubbed us got half-crocked, and every remark called for another drink.

Clean again, and after some well-earned sleep, I bought a ticket on the Penn R. R. for Jersey City, and from there I headed for home.

"It's good to be home," I said to my Dad as soon as I saw him, "Especially when a fellow said I'd never see it again." He grinned at me, and I grinned back.

We understood each other, my Dad and I.

I STAYED AT HOME A FEW WEEKS, THEN HEADED FOR BEN HALL'S
shipping office at Quincy Slip. I was now a hardened deepwater man,
and ready to ship as an A. B., or able seaman.

I hadn't been in the shipping office long when a smart looking
skipper walked in. He and Ben shook hands, and as they did so the
captain, Captain Tinker of Deer Island, Maine, glanced through the
wire cage at the seamen with their sailor bags, waiting to hear the
number of A. B.'s wanted.

His ship was the three masted schooner "Robert A. Snyder" of
Deer Island, Maine. Tonnage net three hundred and twelve tons,
carrying four A. B.'s, a colored cook, a mate, himself and his wife.

"I've some good men for you, captain," said Ben.

The skipper wheeled, regarding us critically. Three of us were very
young, the fourth a grizzled Irishman about fifty years old who was
obviously a real schooner man.

We stepped up to the table one after the other, answering the skipper's careful questioning to the best of our ability. On a schooner, everyone on board must be able to do his work. If one man becomes ill, the work, heavy as it is, must be divided among his shipmates.

We answered his questions satisfactorily, for he had us put our names on the dotted line. Then he threw a couple of dollars on Ben Hall's desk.

"Here's a little beer money for the boys," he said cheerfully as he strode out. A good captain, and a smart one.

Ben took care of us in short order. He called a runner. "Take these men down to Perth Amboy," he ordered. We shouldered our sailor bags and were off.

We arrived at the dock about four-thirty p.m., piling aboard gladly, throwing our bags over the rail. We were greeted by Ned, the colored cook, his teeth showing white in a welcoming grin.

"I'll have a good supper for you in about half an hour," he assured us, and vanished into the galley.

At six o'clock the skipper climbed over the rail, and with him was his wife, Florence. She was really pretty.

The mate, who had one glass eye, stepped to the foc'sle door.

"All right, boys!" he sang out, "We're getting under way immediately. We're bound for Brunswick, Georgia. It's a fair wind, boys!"

Soon the sail stops came snapping off the booms, and the messengers ran to the drum heads of Captain Tinker's newly installed six horse power gas engine. This was the turn of the times from hand-pulling power.

Up went the fores'l, mains'l, and so on, until all sail was set. Our schooner was under way, a bone in her teeth.

Before long Ambrose Channel lightship was bearing abeam, and the order "Set the watches" came from the poop deck. Three days later we were racing past the Savannah bar. A tug hove in sight. It had an awful time trying to catch us, but on we flew for Brunswick lightship.

"All hands on deck!" shouted Mr. Montgomery, the mate. "Take in tops'ls, flying jib!"

The captain took the wheel while we worked. The tugboat skipper lifted his megaphone to his lips.

"Have your men stand by on the starboard side for our hawser!" he yelled.

We went forward, waiting for the towing line. With towing hawser all fast we lowered and tied up the lower sails, the mooring lines gotten up from lazarette and fore peak.

"Relieve the wheel!" shouted the skipper.

The towboat took us up the Satilla River. The shores were lined with thick jungle growth, and as we towed along at slow speed we could see many water snakes.

As we passed Brunswick we were told to proceed to Owen's Ferry, far into the state of Georgia where the cypress timber was heavy. We sighted a saw mill or two along the river bank, and, along the east side of the river, numerous small creeks over which branches of palmetto trees twined.

When we reached Owen's Ferry a large group of Georgia negroes stood on the dock, plus a few white officials from the mill. The scene was one of great natural beauty; tall cypress sticks lay waiting in the swamps, chained together, ready to be loaded. The air was fragrant with the woodsy cleanliness of freshly cut timber.

The first evening at the dock we went aft, asking the captain for five dollars with which to go ashore. It was a perfect night, the balmy climate making us forget the driving wintry blasts north of Cape Hatteras.

Over the rail we went, onto the rickety old dock. Smoke drifted lazily upward from the saw mill, and thick brush and dense woods surrounded us.

There was a lone road and we headed for it, walking at least two miles before we came upon a clearing with a small cluster of shacks, each showing the glow of an oil lamp inside. It didn't look promising, but a seaman goes ashore in every port whether it looks promising or not.

We soon discovered we were in a village of real Georgia negroes. There was one very small general store, very dilapidated, with advertisements of every kind plastered on its scabrous front.

In we went. The storekeeper was a kindly old negro who prompty told us to make ourselves at home. An old woolly-headed negro sat in one corner of the store, strumming tunes on a weather-beaten banjo, eyeing us in a way which made it evident it was unusual for whites to visit the village. He knew little of sailors for we thought lightly of color distinction, race, or creed.

We sat and chatted with the storekeeper for a bit, then he volunteered the information he had some hard cider put away. Three glasses apiece and we started dancing Swedish polkas on a floor measuring five by five. My head spun faster than my feet and I wound up outside on the ground, wondering why that spun too.

I came to on the shoulders of the Finn shipmate, who was trying to pack me back to the ship. However, he was carrying a double load, and after much struggling and swearing he finally put me down about twenty feet off the dirt road and left me to sleep it off.

At daybreak I awoke, lifting my head to stare around confusedly. I could see little but swamp and fog, and remembered but vaguely what had happened. I got to my feet, and after much stumbling around finally found the road back to the ship.

I got a warm greeting from the mate. In other words, he gave me holy hell. "Now get a bos'uns chair and scrape down the foremast!" he barked, when he had finished.

Scraping down the foremast in my condition wasn't exactly a picnic, but I got to it at once. It wasn't the time for me to sound off.

Two days later our deck load was ready, the towboat "Radiant" gave us a hawser, and with orders for South Boston we were homeward bound, back to the cold New England winter.

Once having cleared the coast we eased the sheets and headed nor'west. The wind was bound to haul to the south'ard, and all ships bound to Boston headed for the Gulf stream, that lovely blue water abounding in sharks.

Captain Tinker was standing by for a noon sight with his sextant one day when he noticed fins cutting water astern. The wind was light, almost a calm, and schooner men often considered the shark a "Jonah" of the sea, believing they had something to do with fair winds.

No skipper relished the banging of his booms and sails due to rolling in a calm sea, and the sight of a shark meant getting out the shark hook and a heaving line, then off to the cook for a fat piece of salt pork.

Captain Tinker ordered the wheel put in beckets.

"Now to get the man-eater!" he said briskly.

I was well pleased, for I had never seen a shark caught and was keen to witness the kill of a cannibal fish.

It took no skill at all. We just shoved the piece of salt pork on the twelve inch shark hook, bent the heaving line on, then just abaft the starboard mizzen rigging, I cast the hook into the sea.

The wily scavengers of the sea hear all, see all, and know all that goes overboard. It wasn't long before our Jonah came up to the bait cautiously, then went away and came back again. On the return trip he grabbed the hook, pork and all.

When he had it well fast in his jaws, I pulled, making sure I had him. Now came the fun! He was a full nine feet long, and I kept a nice strain on him while the gang made ready.

I passed my heaving line along to the boys, who waited with the double block. The shark was now thrashing his tail madly, churning the blue waters to a frothing foam.

The gang took a strain, shouting "Now for fair wind!"

"Come up with him!"

Already I had slipped a running bow'lin over his head, for his tail had to be lashed lest one swipe from it should knock a man galley west.

Now in he came, on to the deck load.

"Stand clear! This fellow is a tough customer!"

One of the hands came aft with an axe, watching his chance at the tail. Once stilled forever, we used our sheath knives, dissecting the ugly Jonah, casting him piece by piece into the blue waters of the Gulf stream.

Whether because of the shark killing or no, we did fetch a strong sou'easter that night and away flew the "Robert A. Snyder" with her fair wind.

A few days later we picked up Chatham light, the weather clearing and setting in for a nor'west gale. The clouds were breaking and a patch of clear sky was visible between fast-moving clouds. Far off to the southeast the dawn was breaking, and the air took on a crisp freshness that warned us of the approach of the nor'west gale.

As the first gusts of nor'west were felt, I was relieved by the look-out for coffee. I munched pilot biscuits as I drank the scalding brew, standing in the galley door talking with Ned. Over in the corner of his galley bench I noticed a model of a full rigged ship with wooden sails.

"Say, Ned!" I said appreciatively. "That's really fine work. Who are you making it for?"

"The skipper's wife," said Ned bashfully, ducking his head. He reached down, to cover his shyness, and dragged six well-browned loaves of bread from the only kind of oven we seamen ever saw aboard an American windbag. The "Shipmate" was the trade name, and many's the good meal they've turned out.

"Think she's pretty nice, eh, Ned?" I hadn't seen too much of her, but what few times I had encountered her she had been pleasant and the crew seemed to rate her ace high.

"Yassuh!" Ned was emphatic. "She comes from quality folk!"

We spoke no more on the subject of the skipper's wife, but I wondered what it would be like to be captain of a ship and have a pretty wife at my side as I sailed the seven seas. Not for me, I decided. A man couldn't love the sea as I did and have room in his heart for a woman.

We were taken in tow by the tug "Betsy Ross" and put into Neponset, Massachusetts. Sails made fast and covers on, the boys rushed into the foc'sle to pack up.

When we filed aft for our pay the skipper asked me to step aside. I was a bit surprised, but when the men were gone he put an end to my speculations.

"My mate is going down East," he said quietly, "I would like you to go mate with me."

I was highly elated, pleased almost speechless by his offer. My fifth trip to sea, and I had just turned nineteen.

"I'd like nothing better," I said earnestly, once I'd recovered my breath.

My wages, he told me, would be forty-five dollars per month. I was to bring my own bedding. I would have slept in the rigging if I'd had to.

Mate of a three hundred and twelve ton schooner! Who was a green youth now?

I BID MY SHIPMATES GOODBYE.

"Goodby, Mr. Mate," they said jovially, "Keep a sharp lookout!"

After their departure the foc'sle was dead, deserted. I started over the deck load with my sailor bag to enter the domain I had always held in great respect. I had often wondered when I would be entitled to be an occupant of quarters aft. Well, here I was. And, I was mate!

Mr. Montgomery turned over his room to me. It was on the port side, just off the officer's messroom. After he had left, I gazed around. Over the outside of the door was a sign, "Certified For Mate." That was me!

Inside, I saw the desk with the ship's log book on top, the sunken inkwell, with grooves for pens and pencils. The cover slanted and lifted up, for all the world like a school desk, and inside was a Bowditch, Azimuth tables. Over the desk was an oil lamp in a wall bracket and gimbals, beside it an old calendar from the Plymouth Cordage Company which bore a lithograph of the American full-rigged "A. J. Fuller."

As I glanced through the open door I could see Ned setting the table for Captain and Mrs. Tinker, and, the new mate. A tablecloth with napkins! I grinned delightedly, lit my pipe, and fell to putting my room in order.

When the mess bell sounded I put my jacket on and stepped over to the pot-bellied bogie, waiting for the captain and his wife. Once they were seated I took the chair that was to be mine as long as I was mate. Dinner was pleasant, and I answered the skipper's questions and made polite conversation with Mrs. Tinker, reflecting that it was almost like being at home. With a difference.

The next morning the skipper told me we would sign articles the next morning at the Commissioner's.

"I've ordered the crew, and I will also let you have a quadrant for this trip until you are able to buy a sextant," he said.

The next morning I headed for Boston on one of the ding-dong trolleys. Nor'east storms had descended, and it was in hip boots, blue flannel shirt and mackinaw, my deepwater pilot's cap over one eye that I dropped anchor in the office of the U. S. Shipping Commissioner.

I saw the skipper talking with one of the finest commissioners who ever signed on a crew. Mr. Grant, whom I got to know very well in later years.

One by one we signed our names. All my crew, it seemed were Scandinavians. The captain treated, and we drank boilermakers afterwards, known to seamen as "rotgut and suds." We all got chummy, and the topic was ships . . .

After two or three drinks I could feel the air getting thick, so I left, telling the men not to forget that we turned to for coffee at four-thirty in the morning and that the tow boat would be there at five.

I made my way back to the ship alone. The snow was deep, but on reaching the poop deck I stood studying the weather, then read the barometer. It was climbing.

The unaccustomed privacy and comfort of my room was wonderful. For awhile I just sat and luxuriated in my quarters, wondering if the shade of my arrogant old grandfather was lurking close enough to be impressed. A bit of this, and I turned to and slept like a log.

At four-thirty a.m. the cook called the crew, shoving his agate coffee pot, hot and steaming, and a pan of pilot bread along the slide. I took my coffee in the galley, while outside the towboat made fast.

"Let go all!" shouted the skipper, and out we backed into Neponset Bay, The "Mianus" was started up, and while warming we let go the tug while she moved ahead and threw us a heaving line with a hawser bent to it. The tug took the strain, and we were under way.

"Set the mains'l!" I shouted, giving my first order as mate.

"Everything drawing! Ease the sheets! Man to wheel! The rest of you clear up the decks!" So ran my orders, my thoughts running a little ahead, anticipating.

The tugboat was now blowing "Stand by to let go." Then a long and two shorts—"Let'er go and stand clear."

The "Robert A. Snyder," with sheets off, was away like a hare running from the hounds.

As the days passed I grew better acquainted with Mrs. Tinker. She was about twenty-five years old, and with no feminine companionship it no doubt grew somewhat dull for her at times. I, with five sisters at home, had some idea of what was considered fitting for well-bred female ears, so each time we met we had a bit of a chat.

Six days out of Neponset found us sailing into the gem-like Nova Scotian bay called Shulie, surrounded by thick forests of pine, fir and spruce. It was a snow clad landscape, with the saw mill at the head of the bay.

Both men and women stood on the dock to greet the American schooner. They presented a colorful picture in their warm woolens and felt boots. The men stood stolidly, staring, puffing on short clay pipes browned with age.

Lines were passed ashore for making fast the vessel. We unbent our throat halyard and bent the hook into the hawsers that were run off to a big tree on the bank and set up taut. This was done to keep our three-masted schooner from turning over, for the tide at the head of that bay runs completely out to dry rock bottom. We could load only once every twenty-four hours, and that for only six hours at a time.

The next tide found us doing some fast loading, and as we worked the skipper's wife promenaded around the deck, enjoying the beauty of the scenery.

It was my duty to move around the deck to see if the men were doing their work satisfactorily, and, as I went, "Tell me, laddie," asked a stevedore in a strong mixture of Scotch and Irish, "Who is the pretty lassie?"

"Oh," I said, comprehending immediately, "You must mean the skipper's wife."

"Now, that'll hold you lads for a bit!" said another. Mrs. Tinker had been duly noticed and admired.

Friday afternoon, the boss from the saw mill came over to request the presence of Captain and Mrs. Tinker at the village barn dance the following night. A raffle was to take place, and Mrs. Tinker was asked to bring something.

"Good!" she said, pleased with the idea of having something to do. "I'll make a blueberry pie."

"It ought to bring a great amount," said the foreman seriously. It was obvious that he, too, admired the captain's pretty wife.

Saturday morning found the deck load of the "Robert A. Snyder" really moving aboard. The news soon got around that Mrs. Tinker was to make a pie for the raffle.

"If it's anything like her, it'll be good."

"I'll bid five dollars for it," said another.

"I'll just raise that five," said another. And so the talk ran, and no one noticed Captain Tinker on the dock. The captain, as he told me later, got an earful.

The skipper met me in the cabin. He was warming up around the cabin bogie.

"Did you hear those blue noses?" he shot at me.

"I sure did, Captain," I said, smiling in spite of myself, "They mean to have that pie."

He stared at me, a fighting Yankee gleam in his eyes.

"Only if I go broke will they get that pie," he said firmly. His jaw set stubbornly, and not another word did he utter.

Nova Scotian nights are long, dark and cold, and the crew went in a body to the barn dance. The captain and his wife were taken in a horse-drawn sleigh.

The crew and I walked up the road, the snow packed and crunching underfoot, our breaths steaming in the chill night air. The boys had drawn five dollars each. I, as mate, had drawn ten. We were ready for the raffle.

We arrived at the general store, the big barn for the dance just one hundred feet behind it. We were visitors and "Yankees," and while the Boston tea party was a closed book as far as I was concerned, it was not always true of the ports we sailed into east of Eastport, Maine.

One sleigh after another drove up in front of the big barn, the occupants alighting hurriedly while the drivers blanketed their horses on the lee side of the barn where a half-shed was built to protect them from the biting winds.

We went into the barn, looking at the bracket oil lamps and reflectors hung here and there on the walls. Admission was free. Coats and shawls were draped over saddle-hooks. A piano and two fiddles furnished the music, and it was surprisingly good. The best food I had seen since leaving home was on tables at the end of the barn.

We danced with husky, rosy-cheeked girls. The tunes we danced to were "Annie Laurie," "A Beautiful Picture In a Beautiful Golden Frame," and, for our benefit, "Take Me Back To New York Town." We entered into the spirit of it with a zest that left the girls breathless.

The raffle was announced, then, and we all fell silent as the bidding began. We were biding our time until Mrs. Tinker's pie was put up.

The blueberry pie made its appearance, and Mrs. Tinker stood beside the auctioneer. She wore her Boston going-ashore clothes, and men and women alike stared at her. The women making fashion notes, the men just plain ogling.

"She must be a Yankee," whispered a jealous female disapprovingly.

"She's the daughter of the captain on the Yankee schooner," whispered someone else. Captain Tinker's ears turned a bright magenta.

"What am I offered for this blueberry pie?" called the auctioneer.

"I bid two dollars," shouted a Nova Scotian.

"I'll raise it to three!" called another.

"Five!"

"Seven!"

It went on, until it got up to eighteen dollars, and all the time Captain Tinker remained silent.

"Eighteen, I've been offered eighteen!" called the auctioneer. His voice crackled with excitement. Such bidding, and all for one blueberry pie! Then Captain Tinker spoke.

"Twenty dollars," he said firmly, thrusting his chin out as he looked around.

"Going, going—gone! Sold to the gentleman in the blue suit for twenty dollars!" The auctioneer mopped his brow and Mrs. Tinker smiled demurely at the captain.

The auction now over, tea and cake were being served in one corner of the big barn. I brought out my "Russian Finn Piano," better known as a harmonica, and with the prompting of a couple of deep swigs from a bottle of Scotch I stood by the piano and went to town on the "Oceana Roll."

> "Billy McCoy was a musical boy
> When he played that ol' piano
> On the cruiser Alabama
> Every morning, noon and night
> The crew all whistled and sang with delight
> Every morning on that ocean
> Everybody had a motion
> That was squirmy—"

That is all I remember of it now, but it was the real thing in those days and I felt quite the gay young blade as I played it.

At about eleven o'clock everyone started home. Outside, in the frost-laden air, good nights were said, men passed whiskey bottles around for one last warming gulp, and sleighs set off with their occupants calling merry farewells.

I joined the crew and we tramped down the river road, snowdrifts up to our knees, singing "O blow the man down!" We were very light hearted, and we still had our money. Captain Tinker had the pie.

By Monday afternoon the deckload was finished off, and that night we pulled away from the dock, all secure and tied down. With the wind off the land and the tide in our favor we set all sail and came down the Bay of Fundy like a frightened deer. Full'n by, nearly all the way to Boston light ship where we were obliged to take aboard a pilot coming from a Nova Scotian port.

Ice formed as each spray hit the ship. The nor'west wind freshened to a gale, and Captain Tinker never left the poop deck after we picked up the light ship at three a.m. The "Robert A. Snyder" was now under a strain, with everything but the flying jib set.

I went below at four a.m., and I'd been in my bunk perhaps five minutes when I heard a loud snap! crack! A commotion broke out on deck almost immediately.

"Clew up the mizzen tops'l!" shouted the captain. "Call the mate on deck!"

I jumped from my bunk, swearing violently. Who was the guy who had said, "Sell the old farm and go to sea?" That son of a bitch was crazy!

I was on deck in a jiffy, stopping only to gulp down a cup of black coffee that had been on the bogie all night.

The starboard topmast back-stay turnbuckle had carried away, and at once I had the men fetch two strops and a newly rove-off "Handy Billy." The tops'l came in none too soon. One more minute, and the mizzen topmast would have gone by the board.

Daylight was breaking, and the harbor lights were disappearing. We needed no tug until we were off Gallup Island where we hove to and waited for the doctor's quarantine boat to come alongside. All hands were mustered on top of the deck load aft. The doctor looked us over, then queried the captain.

"Any venereal?"

"No, sir!" answered the skipper promptly.

"All right, captain, I'll sign you a clean bill of health." The name of the quarantine boat was the "Vigilante," and her captain, "Old Tony," and the cook, had been in the boat and with the service it represented for twenty-five years.

The tugboat "Mamie Ross" was headed for us under high pressure. Chug, chug, she went. There's a little song the towboat men sing as they pass vessels.

> "Got a tug, got a tow
> Chug-chug
> Got a tow, making dough
> Chug-chug—"

They're telling God's truth.

Captain Tinker sang out to make fast the tugboat.

"Mr. Mate, take in all your sail and tie 'em up!"

All hands had a good breakfast, thanks to the faithful Ned, and we fed the pilot, too. Again we were slowed down for the U.S. Customs boat and Immigration.

"No contraband, every seaman's papers in order. Proceed!"

Now we were bound for Chelsea docks, just opposite Charlestown.

"Winter in Boston is a bugger," said one seaman, standing by the foc'sle head.

"Amen!" breathed another.

Mrs. Tinker made her appearance on deck as we passed the East Boston ferry. She was sparkling-eyed and animated, eager to go ashore. The skipper was lucky, I thought, then caught myself. Who wanted an anchor to tie him down? Not Barney!

We arrived in Chelsea at eleven-thirty a.m., and, with everything ship-shape, the gang awaited the skipper for their pay-off. Before long a man representing the U.S. Commissioner came aboard, Ned called us to dinner, and we sat down together for the last time.

At two p.m. the skipper arrived to pay us off.

We were paid off according to rank. First myself, as mate, seamen next, then Ned.

I folded my greenbacks, and they looked no greener than deep water to me. I knew, then and there, that I was a rover. I went to my cabin and packed my bag.

A knock at my door, and I opened it. It was Captain Tinker. I just stood there, looking at him. I liked him, and I liked his ship.

He, in turn, looked over my shoulder at my partially packed bag. "You're not leaving me, are you?"

"Yes, Captain Tinker, I am," I said honestly, "I've a hankering to go deepwater again."

"Too bad," he said regretfully, "I thought I had the makings of a real coasting mate in you."

"Thank you, sir," I said, wishing I could express what I felt. "I— I'm sorry."

I bid my goodbyes to Mrs. Tinker and Ned, extended my hand to the captain, and ashore I went with the crew.

I was home again.

It was spring, and there was little time to waste. Yet I sat with my Dad on the brownstone stoop and listened to the boat whistles on the East River, a scant two blocks away.

The hurdy-gurdies were out in force, as they were every spring. Kids were playing marbles, little girls jumping rope, boys rolling hoops or skating with the new skates they'd gotten for Christmas and hadn't been able to use because of snow and ice. Ice cream carts were plentiful, with newly-painted signs "Ice cream sandwich—2¢. Jumbo size—3¢." It was homelike, touching. I couldn't wait to leave for a foreign port.

At supper we pricked up our ears when my Dad spoke tentatively of installing electric lights in the house. Afterwards, I went out the kitchen door to the old swing that hung from the maple tree in our big back yard. Just over the fence was the back of the Epiphany Church where I had been confirmed, and I waved at Father Mc-Quirk who was walking back and forth, reading his prayer book in the church yard.

A flickering kerchief caught my eye. It was Mrs. O'Neill, waving from her stable apartment. Poor old soul, she had worked in the family for twenty-five years, yet no recompense had been mentioned for her in my grandfather's will. She now lived, by tacit agreement with my Dad, in the apartment over the stable with her cat, Maud. I waved back at her, feeling deep sympathy, for she was of the faithful Irish stock for which New York and Brooklyn were famous.

The Irish. They were our cops, firemen, conductors, trolleymen, motormen, and practically controlled the "Belt" line of horse cars that ran around New York. I loved them all.

I walked slowly back into the house. I looked at the tall china closet with its three hundred pieces of Limoges china. The top bore a bronze plate with the inscription "Presented to Captain Henry Burnett in 1901 by the United New York and Sandy Hook Pilot's Association for his services rendered as a pilot."

"No ship was ever too hard to board
No weather was ever too bad."

I went up to my room, and everything was in order behind the stained glass door that rolled shut. Every door in that house either rolled or slid. The curtains of my windows were twelve feet from floor to ceiling, and from the ceiling hung a cluster of six gas lamps with globes of marine design. Whales and ships. My dresser top was Italian marble, its mirror flanked by gas lamps. Bookcases lined the walls. It was a luxurious room, yet I felt stifled and longed for the clean salt tang of the sea.

Somehow I slept that night, but the next morning I packed my sailor bag and bid my Dad goodbye. I hated to leave, yet I knew I couldn't settle down ashore.

I headed for South Street. Springtime was boomtime, and there were chances to go to any port in the world. At Pier Four, East River, Andrew Carnegie's ship of wood, copper and brass was fitting out for a trip to the North Magnetic Pole. Shipping masters were running frenziedly the length of South Street to obtain crews.

I headed for the shores of South Brooklyn, and there I saw a four-masted bark loading at the Twenty-third Street long pier. I could read her name, the "Wm. P. Frye" of Bath, Maine.

The gang plank was out, and I went aboard. She was a big ship, three thousand tons, and a square rigger. A gentleman, well-dressed as skippers go, was walking the poop deck as I made my way aft.

Straight up to him I went, deepwater fashion. "May I see the captain?" I asked.

"You're looking right at him," he said, "Captain Nickerson. What can I do for you?"

"Well, sir," I said boldly, "This is an American ship, and I'd like a chance at the bos'uns job. I'm capable."

"Can you handle twenty-four A.B.'s?" he asked sharply.

"Yes, sir," I said. No hesitation here.

He looked me over appraisingly, then said, "Well, you have the job. Get your dunnage and come aboard. Your quarters are in the half deck."

I thanked him heartily, and you couldn't have seen my tail for smoke the way I went over that gangway. I headed for home to ask my Dad for a loan of thirty-five dollars to purchase some navigation books and four charts. North and South Atlantic, North and South Pacific. I needed a parallel rule, too, and a pair of dividers.

It was typical of my Dad that I was given the money at once. And, as I was going out the iron gate after saying my goodbyes, he stopped me.

"You'll need one of these," he said, putting something into my hand, "Take care of it, son." It was his watch.

That night I slept in the Seaman's Institute. For fifty cents I was given a clean bed and room, replete with agate pitcher, china bowl, and commode. I lay awake looking at the four bare walls unseeingly. I was thinking about my new job.

I made my purchases the next day at the Negus Navigation Store on Water Street, stopped back at the Institute for my two sailor bags, then had the devil's own time getting to the ship as she had meanwhile been shifted to Beard's Erie Basin. It was late evening when I climbed aboard and headed for the half deck where a few of the ordinary seamen were playing cards.

I looked around for what was "Certified for Bos'un."

"Are you the bos'un?" one asked curiously.

"I believe I am," I replied coolly. I found my quarters and turned in, leaving them to speculate on what brand of bos'un they'd been blessed with.

Before breakfast the next morning I went up on deck to meet one of the finest deep water mates I was ever to encounter. Mr. Kiehne, first mate of the "Wm. P. Frye." He was stern, gentlemanly withal, but his weather-beaten face was never acquired by sitting in Battery Park.

Our orders came fast. The next day we took up our tow for Sparrows Point, Baltimore, in the Chesapeake Bay. Our tug was the "Jupiter," and after thirty hours at sea we sighted Cape Henry lightship. A fog was coming in, too thick for the tug whose fog signals were blowing with persistent regularity. Some big steamers, bound out of Baltimore, gave us a close shave; the mate's whistle sounded, and I went aft.

Mr. Kiehne said, "We are loading coal at Sparrows Point for Bremerton Navy Yard, and when we get in here and tied up, get that hold cleaned up right away. Pile away all that dunnage for'ard, get the shifting boards up, and have all those ordinary seamen clean up the half deck."

"Yes, sir." It never paid to yap. Take an order, listen carefully, and use your head. Mates and skippers talked very little outside of ship's business.

The tug blew to stand by. I had expected that. The fog was too thick. No use worrying about water depths, for those tow boat men knew their business.

A long and two shorts. "Let go hawser." We couldn't see the tug, but we could hear her towing machine heaving in the hawser.

The "Wm. P. Frye," a truly majestic ship, came slowly to a stop. Captain Nickerson walked calmly to and fro.

To the man at the wheel he said, "Wheel amidships."

The seaman echoed, "Wheel amidship, sir."

"Let go your port anchor," came next.

Mr. Kiehne, watching, grunted finally, "That's got her. Make fast the compressor. Bos'un, set anchor watches."

The fog was now thick as pea soup. The rigging aloft dripped with it. We ate in companionable silence.

Thirty-six hours later the fog cleared and we proceeded to a temporary berth in Baltimore. There were no watches now. A ten-hour day, no unions, and seamen on that ship received eighteen dollars a month. As bo'sun, I got twenty-five. The chief mate got sixty. Such were port wages in New York in the year of 1914.

The "Wm. P. Frye" had a 'tween decks and trimming hatches, popular in the coal and grain trade. The hold was dark, as was the 'tween decks, except for the light which came from the fore, main, and mizzen hatches.

I climbed down about eleven in the morning to see how the men were doing. Everyone was working fine and no complaints, and I decided to pitch in and help them move the 'tween decks dunnage. Only half the hatches were off on deck.

Grabbing an armload of small dunnage, I started forward, never giving a thought to the trimming hatches. I groped my way through the darkness, and suddenly I plummeted through space, my arms holding the lumber . . . I landed on my right eye, twenty-five feet below, hit the keelson, and judged rightly after the first stunning impact that the warm fluid flowing over my hands and face was blood. I had landed directly on my face, and there I lay in a pool of blood for about twenty minutes.

The mate finally peered down the hatch from the main deck.

"Bos'un, are you hurt?" he called down.

I was but half-conscious, and though I tried to answer, it sounded like gibberish.

Down the iron ladder he came. He turned me over gently, and I heard his swift intake of breath. "Great Scott!" he muttered.

He upped the ladder full speed, bringing someone back to help sling me up on deck.

The gang worked fast, rigging up a purchase on the main stay, and a canvas cargo sling. The mate took charge, barking orders left and right.

As I began feeling less faint, I groped for the iron ladder. My right eyebrow hung down flaplike over a seemingly sightless socket, my face was bruised and cut, and the blood spurted hot and bright down my cheek. I didn't want to be helped out of that hatch like a sick child. Not while I could still move.

I climbed the thirty feet on my own, but had to be supported when I reached the deck or I would have fallen.

The ambulance rushed me to the hospital where I was sewed up like a rag doll losing its stuffing, and I was put in a bleak white room to rest and await further examination.

Three days later I was returned to the ship, rebellious at having been told I might lose the sight of my eye. I sat on my bunk, my head in my hands, involuntarily fingering the patch of bandage.

The mate came down to see how I was getting along.

"How are you feeling, bos'un?" he asked.

"Mr. Kiehne," I said slowly, "A ship is no place for a sick man. I guess you better pay me off. I'm not all together yet."

"I don't like to see you go," said Mr. Kiehne, sounding like he meant it, "But you know best how you feel."

My spirits were low when I went aft to pick up my money. It came to so little I sold my gun and cartridges for seven dollars.

I waved goodbye to the crew, and headed for home.

I STAYED AT HOME FOR QUITE AWHILE, UNTIL MY EYE HAD HEALED.
Then, in December, chafing at my enforced inactivity, decided it was
time to look for a ship. The vessel that took my fancy was a rakish
looking, four-masted bark, the "John Ena" of San Francisco.

Up her gangplank I went, watching for either a hardboiled mate or
the dog that might belong to the aft gang. I saw neither, so I stepped
over the gangway and down on the deck. A brawny six-footer walked
aft to greet me.

"Well, and what do you want?" was his nice opening. "I'm George
Heyward, the mate." A burly Nova Scotian, he stood at ease, sizing
me up.

"I'm looking for a chance to ship, sir," I said. I was as tall as he was,
and doing a bit of sizing up on my own.

"Have you ever been deepwater before?"

"Yes, sir."

"And what ships have you been in?"

"The American bark "Astral," and the "William P. Frye," sir."

"Are you an able seaman?"

[83]

"Yes, sir."

"Well," he said, apparently satisfied, "Get your clothes and be on board tomorrow morning. Turn to at seven."

By eight o'clock that night I was all packed and ready to go aboard. My farewells to the family were brief and affectionate. We had finally learned that prolonged goodbyes were harrowing experiences that need not be.

When I reached the long dock where the "John Ena" lay, I put my bag on the wharf and stood looking at her. Nothing is prettier than the proud bows of a square-rigged ship, her tall masts with yards symmetrically braced.

There she lay, gray hull, silent, her towering spars whispering of former voyages, of strange ports, and of happenings aboard. It was bitter cold, and her scupper holes had sprouted long white whiskers of icicles reaching almost to the water's edge. She listed ever so slightly, having very little ballast.

I went aboard, said goodnight to the ship keeper, and walked for'ard to the foc's'le. A good-sized rat jumped from the table as I opened the big iron half-doors, but he didn't bother me. I considered rats as part of ship's stores. I chose a bunk, and soon was fast asleep.

In the morning I discovered that breakfast consisted of burgue, or oatmeal, cooked to the consistency of billboard paste. Then there was slum, better known as stew. The smell and taste were fine, but I found later that the recipe was one the cook had found in Penang, and liked so well he made it four times a week so he wouldn't forget it.

The coffee was pretty hard to down the first morning, but after awhile we grew accustomed to its singular flavor. As the saying went, "It's all in the blend," but we decided the captain had forgotten to order any "blend" while at the ship chandler's. Brown sugar, and no milk, for this was long before the passage of the bill to benefit seamen.

I had been aboard a few days when I realized I had struck no home. There was a great deal of shouting and bullying, the old way of handling men, and, in 1914, the law was still in favor of the masters, mates, and ship owners. Seamen and their rights were seldom considered.

One night, as we lay in dock, with the gang in the foc's'le spinning

Loaded with barley and ready for the sea the steel four-mast bark
DIRIGO lies to her moornings in Elliott Bay, Seattle.

Braced up on the port tack the DIRIGO heads out past Cape Flattery for the lonely Cape Horn road.

Courtesy of the San Francisco Maritime Museum

Both watches have hauled out the stored sails for bending anew and they shoulder them aft, along the main deck to their proper locations.

Lying on the main deck, the men arrange the sails for easier heaving aloft to the waiting, naked yards.

Over the flying bridge on the main deck . . . hook in the gantline block, and sail bending goes on.

The "gang" runs aloft in the port fore shrouds
to secure the sails on their yards.

The starboard watch haul on the gantlines, "schooner fashion."

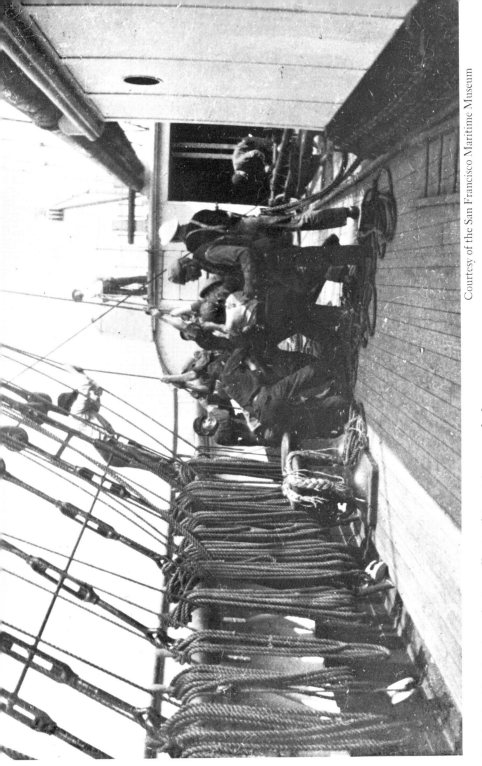

With a leading hand on the topgallant rail to get in some slack, the waiting watch on deck bends to the hauling with a will.

Courtesy of the San Francisco Maritime Museum

Strung out along the footropes of the ninety-foot main yard, both watches secure the main course to the yard with strong rope gaskets.

Courtesy of Carleton B. Allen

A wet deck . . . a heeling ship . . . a brisk wind . . . and a strong pull as she rolls.

*Rap full of a rising wind ... the "puller", the mighty foresail,
urges along the hurrying four-mast bark,* HAWAIIAN ISLES.

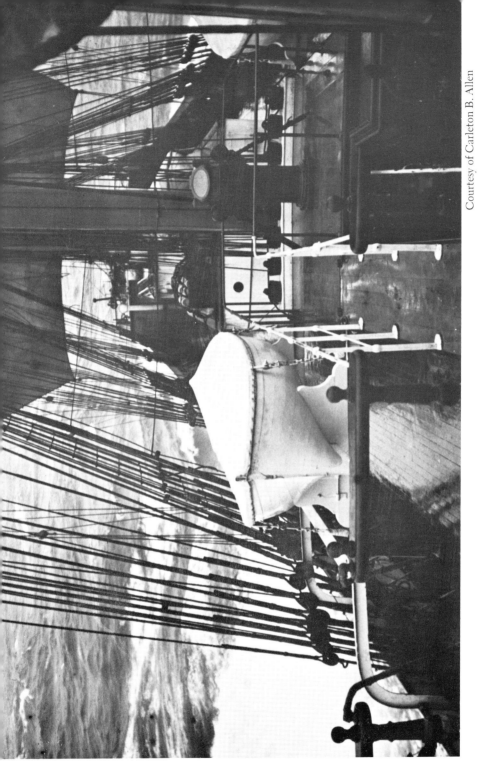

Courtesy of Carleton B. Allen

Dipping into the cold sea, the four-mast bark HAWAIIAN ISLES, *makes wet weather of it.*

Standing watch on the standard compass bridge, Captain Walter Mallet of the four-mast bark HAWAIIAN ISLES watches his reeling ship on her way around Cape Horn.

Taking "green water" on deck as she rolls makes the trip along the main deck more dangerous than it looks here.

Leaping onto the mizzen fife rail, a sailor keeps himself dry-footed as the hard-sailing vessel begins a wet roll to the leeward.

*Flooded decks and a confused sea . . . hatches double barricaded against
the hurtling, heavy seas . . . the Cape Horn road in full fury.*

yarns and playing cards, something went wrong on deck. What it was, I could not tell you to this day, save that it was something foul.

I was sitting on the edge of my bunk, and the bogey was red hot, making the foc'sle a cozy place to be. All at once loud voices snarled outside, the door opened, and the two mates and the skipper looked in, staring about as though bent on singling one man out from the rest.

Suddenly, "There he is, Mr. Heyward!" shouted Captain Olsen, pointing at a big, heavy set German known as Tampico.

"Go on in, mister!" sang out the great, brave second mate, standing well back, "Give the bastard what he's looking for!"

Mr. Heyward advanced on the German. He was a powerful man, the mate was, standing well over six feet and carrying his weight mostly above his waist. He grabbed Tampico abruptly and pounded him without mercy.

There we sat, we of the crew, and watched the bewildered German absorb the battering punishment of Mr. Heyward's fists. His face became a gory mask as a nasty cut opened up over one eye, and a tooth impaled itself in his upper lip. It was a sickening sight, and we ached to pitch in and come to his aid. Yet in those days you were taught to keep your mouth shut, no matter what happened, and woe to the man who didn't conform!

The poor German grabbed his "bindle," the few paltry things he possessed, and staggered out the door, with no one in the foc'sle yet the wiser as to what had caused the trouble. He was half-dead from pain and fear, and, never stopping to take steps for the gangway, he made straight for the starboard hawse pipe and slid down the anchor cable to the wharf. He disappeared in the bitter cold night, a half crouching, painfully lurching figure, still reeling from the effects of the harsh beating he had been meted out by the mate.

In the foc'sle it was now very quiet. The atmosphere of peace and contentment replaced by the brooding of silent, sullen men.

We lay at the dock at Erie Basin for two weeks before the order came to tow to Philadelphia in ballast, there to load case oil for Kobe, Japan, via the Panama Canal. This was doubly good news, for not only did it mean we would avoid passage around the Horn, but that we would still be in port for Christmas.

The next morning, I, with three other men, was scrubbing the deck navy style, when Mr. Heyward tapped me on the shoulder.

[85]

"Put your broom away, and go aft," he said coolly. "Your job will be cabin steward from now on." None of us had heard that our cabin steward had been discharged, and, though I was surprised I tried not to show it.

"All right, sir." Order were orders, and aft I went. Inwardly, I was fuming. Taken off the deck to be made into a flunky without a by-your-leave. Then a cheering thought struck me, and I grinned to myself. As cabin steward, I would not only eat well but I could dispense a bit of contraband in the direction of the crew from time to time! Oh, they had themselves a cabin steward, no doubt about it!

Everything went well until Christmas night. It was a typical Christmas aboard a square rigger in port. Every yard blanketed in snow, the ropes and rigging a spun-silver spider web of snow and ice, the wind blowing cold and clear outside, while within all breathed of warmth and cheer.

I had more than eaten my fill of the Christmas delicacies which were to be found aft, and my heart smote me when I thought of the poor devils in the foc'sle. True, my sympathy was caused more by imagination than fact, for the food aboard the "John Ena" was several cuts above that on most square riggers.

Imbued with the spirt of Christmas giving, I went down into the lazarette. There I rummaged around until I had an armload of canned lobster, chicken, pickles, jams, and plenty of fruit. I found my way out again, putting my loot under the wheelbox while I reconnoitered.

There was no one on deck, so I picked up my cargo and walked for'ard, quiet as a two-legged mouse. It was nearing eight p.m., and I knew the boys in the foc'sle would enjoy a mug-up, as they say in Gloucester.

I opened the door of the foc'sle carefully, so as not to drop my load, and stepped inside quickly.

"Well, boys!" I said, putting my ill-gotten gains on the center of the table, "Merry Christmas! Eat, and give the ship a good name!"

Hearing not a sound from the fellows I looked up, and there—looking squarely into my eyes, was the Japanese steward who loved me like poison! I could read my fate without the help of any fortune teller. First, I'd been caught broaching cargo and ship's stores; second, the after gang would ride me after once signing articles. I turned and went aft, a sadder and wiser man.

I never heard a word about it the next day, but the trouble came about later just the same.

In Philadelphia we began loading, watching the after load draught. When it reached the seventeen foot mark the "John Ena" began to look trim. The riggers were busy each day bending sails, sheets, tacks, reeving off buntlines, putting on double and single seizings, mousings, and all the paraphernalia they generally attended to.

Came the day when the U. S. Shipping Commissioner came aboard for the signatures of the crew, witnessed by the captain and his mate. When it came my turn to sign, George Heyward stepped over to me.

"You needn't sign on," he said coldly.

I wouldn't have felt a punch between the eyes as much. I turned away from the rest of the men, wondering what I had done to bring about such a situation. I thought it was the Christmas "treat" for the fellows.

There was nothing to do but pack my bag. I went for'ard to say goodbye to the gang, then went ashore as though in a dream. Beached, and no prospects in view.

I made my way across Delaware Avenue and headed up South Street. I felt sick, and I guess I showed it when I walked into Jimmy Hyland's shop.

Jimmy had cashed my advance note, and I dreaded seeing him, for now I had no way to pay it off.

"Well, Jim," I said heavily as I entered, "I have bad news for you."

"What's wrong, Burnett?" he asked. He acted surprised, but I learned later he'd known all along about what had happened.

"The mate aboard the "John Ena" doesn't want me as part of the crew," I said, "And I don't know why."

"Too bad," said Jimmy, "Did you do something wrong?"

"I don't know, Jim," I said, bewildered, "I did my work like a man, and he didn't give me any explanation."

"Well," said Jimmy consolingly, "Don't get excited, laddie, for if you don't go in that ship we'll get you another. I'm expecting the bark "Dirigo" from New York in about three weeks, so cheer up! You can take your bag upstairs, and turn to your right. There's a little room just as you turn, and you can use it until we get you signed up on another ship."

The bed in the little room was harder than the sidewalks of New

York, and the room itself no more cheery than a morgue, but I was none the less grateful for it was much more than I had expected.

Now came days when I felt hungry. Not because they didn't feed me at Hyland's, but my appetite seemed to crave more fuel because I was broke. From time to time I hocked a few clothes to buy cigarettes and have a few coins to jingle in my pocket. Pride forbade my letting my Dad know.

Shipping was dead as a mackerel, and the ships that rode at anchor needed ninety fathom of chain, while the ice in the river made sheathing a necessity. I went aboard every vessel that looked promising, but in each case the answer was the same. "We don't need anyone now."

Finally I decided to go to the shipping commissioner's office, for I knew that if there were any chances at all, Mr. Quinn, the commissioner, would know of them.

He informed me that the "Dirigo" was expected in that week, and that there might be a chance for me. Finally I told him how I had been discharged from the "John Ena."

"You know why, though, don't you?" Quinn asked.

"No," I admitted, "I don't."

"Why," he said, surprised, "I thought you knew. They said you were the cabin boy who figured so largely in the mutiny of the bark "Manga Reva," commanded by Captain Townsend!" He looked wisely at me over his pipe.

"Why the hell didn't they tell me, then?" I exploded hotly, "I've never even been aboard the "Manga Reva"!"

"What's your name again?" Quinn asked intently, thumbing through some papers on his desk.

"Theodore Burnett," I ground out, still raging within.

"H'mmm," he murmured, finding a paper and scrutinizing it carefully, "That explains it. Your name is very similar to that of the cabin boy of the "Manga Reva." His name is "Burdette"." Thus the whole matter was made clear, and I realized why Captain Olson hadn't wanted me on his vessel.

"My advice to you is to go down to the "Dirigo" when she comes in, and see Captain Mallet personally," Quinn said, puffing on his pipe reflectively. "I'll put in a word for you at this end, and between the two, I'm sure he'll consider you for shipping."

"Thank you, sir," I said gratefully, and home I went to the little room to sweat out the Dirigo's arrival.

She came in one January morning, and as I had breakfast with the Hyland's, Jimmy told me that her mate, Fred Mortimer, had been up to see him the night before. He said he had put in a good word for me and was pretty sure I'd be considered.

Feeling encouraged by all this display of friendship, I buttoned up my coat and headed for the commissioner's office. There, as I had hoped, was the clean-cut, bearded skipper of the "Dirigo," Captain Walter M. Mallet.

I approached him directly. "Captain Mallet, will you give me a chance to ship with you on this next voyage? My name is Burnett, and from what I hear, I've been accused of being the cabin boy who started the mutiny on the "Manga Reva." His name was *Burdette*, and Captain Quinn will bear me out in what I say. I've been deep-water before, and up till now I've always had a good discharge."

The captain was a cool one, and a gentleman.

"What ships have you been in?" he asked mildly.

"I was in the bark "Astral" eleven months with Captain Dunham, and on several coast-wise trips."

"Well," he said, without any hesitation, "Just as soon as we start to load you may come aboard."

"I think he's all right," smiled the commissioner.

"Oh, yes!" agreed the skipper, as though he'd never heard of any trouble at all.

I thanked him heartily, relieved at the thought of going to sea again, and happy to be reinstated. I went back to my room, exuberant and hungry, and began to pack.

My sailor bag had a little bit of everything in it, and as I went through it I found a few sheets of music that were popular at the time. And then I remembered . . .

I had heard a great deal about the amateur tryouts at the Casino Theatre every Friday night, and between finding sheet music and the fact that I always sang when I worked, well—I began to figure ways and means of raising money.

I jammed the pillows from the donkey's breakfast bed against the door. Then, standing as before an audience, I began practicing the song "If I Had You." I sang, hummed, and whistled it until it sounded rotten, then I quit.

By Friday night I was in ship-shape order to enter my name on the amateur list. It was a bitterly cold night, but my knees shook with more than the cold before I was anywhere near the theatre. I was out to make a dollar, though, and I had no intention of backing out.

I reached the Casino, took my seat, and after what seemed an eternity of waiting, my name was called and the band tuned up. I got up, stepped up to the footlights, and sang as though I had canary legs.

The applause sounded wonderful, and when they handed me the dollar prize, I all but burst with pride. In less than two minutes I was out through the stage door, every sail set, bound for Dennet's for coffee, pancackes, and cigarettes.

I walked back to Hyland's, planning like a Philadelphia lawyer all the way. When I arrived, a lovely poker game was going on. The players included Jimmy, Mr. Mortimer, the mate on the "Dirigo," and two or three other deepwater men. They looked up as I entered.

"How did you make out?" asked Jim as I came in.

"Oh, fine!" I answered innocently, "I won the dollar!" And then the fun began!

Every one of those old shell-backs had been to see the show, and they certainly pumped me for a goat.

"I'm sorry," Mr. Mortimer said gravely, "That I didn't provide myself with a few belaying pins. You really showed signs of being a damn fine singer. Good for nothing, that is. . . . I don't like to ask you to give up your budding career. However, I guess you better come aboard tomorrow morning, and bring your clothes."

Flying fishes and sperm whales, if that didn't bring joy to my heart! I forgot all the kidding at once.

"Yes, sir!" I said, "I'll be there for seven o'clock!" And, before he had a chance to change his mind, I said, "Good night," slipped upstairs, and turned in.

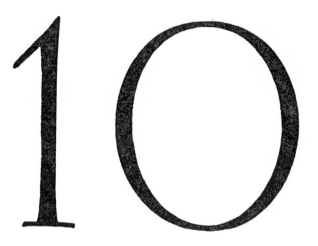

10

The "Dirigo" lay at the dock of the Atlantic Refining Company, Point Breeze, and when I got there early the next morning I stopped at the head of the dock to look her over, as was my habit.

She was a four master, the first steel ship built in the United States, and with those skys'l yards towering away aloft she showed unmistakable signs of strength. I was proud being a member of her crew, and would have been aboard her in an instant if the mate's pet, "Gyp" hadn't kept me from taking one step for'ard until her owner showed up.

Mr. Mortimer called his dog off, and I walked on. The ship was a Bath built vessel, beautifully constructed. The galley was large, and when I reached the foc'sle door I gazed aloft and mused, she's a cuckoo all right, some lofty . . .

I refilled my pipe, then set about the important business of selecting a bunk. Important because it was to be a long voyage. The "Dirigo" had a charter of case oil from Philadelphia to Japan.

The next day, preparations for the "Dirigo's" sea voyage began. It was reassuring to know that the oil which was loaded would stay put when stowed. Mr. Mortimer was always on tap, but we didn't see much of the skipper until about two days before sailing.

When we were about loaded, the mate ordered all hands up to sign articles at the commissioner's office on Front Street. One by one we filed by the commissioner, the line moving steadily along.

The commissioner read off the article like a court clerk opening morning session. "The ship "Dirigo," bound from Philadelphia to a foreign port, namely Japan, or any other port of the world such as the master may direct. Voyage not to exceed twelve calendar months, and back to a final port of discharge in the United States. Now—sign your name in three places. Here, here, and here."

"Yah, yah, vare?" asked the poor fish who was now in front.

"What is your nationality?" asked the commissioner.

"Yah," answered the fellow, nodding his head.

"Your nationality! What country are you from?"

A man came forward from the back of the line. He talked to the poor fish in Scandinavian for about five minutes. And, as he talked, the puzzled features began to clear.

"I'm Svedish!" he announced with an air of discovery, after listening to his friend's explanation. And so it went, on down the line, with about fourteen or fifteen more who hailed from any part of the world but the United States.

The next morning, fourteen A. B.'s and the bo'sun came aboard, all they could carry inside and out. They were singing "It's a Long, Long Way to Tipperary," and at the gangway stood the two mates looking them over.

The foc'sle took on a lovely aroma of twelve different pipe tobaccos and fumes from liquor laden breaths, and a few of the gang huddled together in a corner and sang:

"We're outward bound for a six month's stay
Goodbye—fare thee well
Goodbye—fare thee well."

"Holcheftan!" yelled the Dane at them in deep disgust, meaning shut-up in Danish. But old Joe, the Hollander, opened up his bar room tenor stronger than ever, and sang;

"Good ole fashioned pub
No saloons for me,
I don't want to pay for the pictures on the wall,
I want a decent glass of beer, that's all,

[92]

I don't want to pay for the carpets on the floor,
I don't want a valet or a tub,
It's the good ole time,
Where we used to drink the wine,
In the good ole fashioned pubs!"

Much to the relief of the Dane, as well as the other listeners, the one o'clock whistles piped off and we all went on deck.

After dinner the captain came aboard, and standing with the mate on the poop deck, he gave his departure orders. By four o'clock the "Dirigo" looked ready for her departure on the morrow, and supper over, most of the boys got busy fixing their bunks. Outside, several could be seen pacing the deck, and now and then a hearty laugh let it be known that they were spinning yarns. After awhile, I went outside for a breath of fresh air and to join the gang in the midship house.

We soon broke through the first wall of reserve, and began talking of old cronies. The topic was ships, ships, ships. Tiring of this, I eventually bid them goodnight and went along for'ard.

I stood outside the foc'sle door before entering, feeling the comforting warmth I had felt so often since coming aboard. The security of being where one wanted most to be! That was the answer . . .

It seemed I'd only closed my eyes for a second when a voice at the door bellowed, "All right, you men, turn out for coffee! The tugboat will be here at six o'clock. Rise and shine, all you boys of the Black Ball Line!"

While we drank our coffee, the silence was shattered by the stentorian whistle of an ocean going tugboat. She blew so that she probably woke up the whole city of Philadelphia, Camden included. One by one, we filed out of the foc'sle, each certain it was our towboat. Sure enough, there she came, her sidelights burning clear as crystals.

The bo'sun shouted out his orders to stand by for the towboat, and through a megaphone from the tug's pilot house a deep voice boomed, "Good morning, captain!"

From behind the chart house appeared the man whose answering "Good morning, captain!" was spoken with an unmistakable Yankee twang. It was our skipper, Captain Mallet, well known the seven seas over.

He was a gentlemanly skipper. Tall, clean-cut, with silvering grey hair and a well-trimmed Vandyke. Though he always spoke in an even tone of voice, and never, even in a crisis betrayed any excitement, his orders were always carried out exactly as he issued them. This voyage was not mid-section in his sailing career, and he had rounded the Horn so many times he was never able to remember how many.

Soon we were hearing the welcome "Let 'er all go!" and the orders "All gone for'ard!" "All gone aft!" relayed their glad tune up and down deck.

The tug had been working slowly ahead, but now we heard the three bells to the engine room, followed with a jing-a-ling, and she was hooked up, backing the big bark "Dirigo" out into the stream for a voyage that was to take me nearly twenty-six thousand miles.

Down came the whistle cord, once clear, and three more backing whistles, and all hands waved a last farewell at the spectators on the dock.

The Chinese cook rang the breakfast bell, the mate shouted "All hands to breakfast, bos'un!" Having smelled bacon and eggs, we went on the double, but the bacon and eggs were headed aft. We were treated to oatmeal, a pan of scouse (stew), molasses, and black coffee. Our faces fell, and we ate our breakfast in silence. At times, the distinction between fore and aft made a man's heart bitter within him.

Twelve hours later we bid farewell to our pilot and towboat, and the cry came, "Muster all hands to set watches!"

Mr. Mortimer gave orders to spread out in a line across the deck. With the mates on their respective sides, they started to pick us out, the mate having first choice. I was selected by the mate for port watch, and not sorry a bit, for although hard, he was a good man.

Two other young men chosen by the mate were Harry Manning and Ed White, now both captains. Harry Manning is now captain of the huge liner "United States"—sure proof that he assimilated his lessons at sea. They were both graduates of the New York Nautical school ship "Newport," and they were alert and ambitious in addition to being excellent navigators.

Captain Mallet wanted to get to Japan before the "John Ena" despite the head start the "Ena" had, and conditions would have to favor our ship if we were to beat her. I didn't think the "Dirigo" could outsail the "John Ena," but the race was exciting to think about.

At eight bells we were mustered aft.

"Are all men here?" Captain Mallet asked the mate.

"All hands aft, sir," answered the mate promptly.

Captain Mallet slowly approached the rail of the poop deck. "Now men," he said, "I called you aft to ask your choice in this matter. Do you want me to feed you, or will you have the Act of Congress?"

Congress had passed a bill in 1882 as to what the seafaring man was entitled to in food rations. These rations were issued to the crew on Saturday morning of each week at sea, and in foreign ports. The ration was meager, and there were no luxuries on that list. This was the ration the captain meant. To ask for it meant it was all you got to eat, but asking the captain to feed you sometimes meant that you got more. It all depended on the nature of the skipper.

We talked amongst ourselves, while the captain waited.

"Captain Mallet," I finally said, acting as spokesman, "The men have agreed to have you feed us."

"All right, then," said the skipper, looking pleased, "I'll see to it that you have enough, but I don't want to see any food thrown over the side. That is all."

And right there, something marked me for a sea-lawyer, or leader, for better or worse.

As we got down the coast we got into the spirit of flying fish weather. Off came our heavy clothing, we went barefooted on deck, the nights were balmy and the winds warm. Mouth organs played "Sidewalks of New York" and "Heave For Rio," while all through the dog watches the men made merry. Yarns were spun that fairly made your hands quiver for grasps.

Our food got worse all the time. There was nothing edible that Chinese cook couldn't spoil. The saying "The way to a man's heart is through his stomach," never had a berth aboard a square-rigged ship. Even so, our meals were unusually bad. I stood up at the foc'sle table one day, and offered to fight the man who said it was fit to eat.

"Are you fellows going to let a matter like this continue?" I asked, holding up a pan of half-cooked beef.

"No!" shouted the men, unable to eat the slop.

"Well, let's go aft and see the skipper!"

Aft we went, the whole watch, some with pans of grub, others with the untouched food on their plates.

When we reached the break of the poop, the second mate spoke up. "What's the parade about, men?"

"Sir," I said firmly, "We would like to see the captain."

The skipper made his appearance at once. "Well," he said, with his Yankee twang, "What seems to be the trouble?"

"Captain," I said, "The men and I would like to know if you think this grub is fit to eat?"

Before he had a chance to answer, one of the lads shouted, "Captain, that food isn't fit for a dog to eat!"

"Coptan!" shouted a big Swede who had spent most of his life in Pacific Coast logging camps where food was ample and well-cooked. "I vooden harve dot mon cook for my gang! No—not for my peeg!"

"Be men," said Captain Mallet wearily, "Go for'ard and I'll do all I can to remedy the situation."

We trooped back, feeling hopeful, but in the days that followed the situation improved not one iota.

Our ship sailed into Colon Bay, Panama, on the second of February, 1915. Two of Uncle Sam's Canal Zone towboats came out and took us in tow.

"Has the "John Ena" arrived?" called Captain Mallet.

"Yes, captain," came the answer, "And gone through." The skipper's face fell. He had wanted our vessel to be the first American sailing ship to go through the canal. As it was, we were the second. Roald Amundson's ship "Fram" was one of the first vessels to pass through the great divide, and the convict ship "Success" had gone through just before us.

When we did enter the bay, the government tug put two pilots aboard. I couldn't understand why we needed two, but I soon found out.

At Gatun, the first set of locks, we took aboard six wire cables from locomotives. One each from the bow, one from each quarter, and one from each stern chock, the last two being for backing purposes. The pilots had a finger signal for speeds ahead and astern. Watching them closely, I discovered they would throw the right and left arms forward with one finger showing from the hands, meaning "Throw her in first speed," and so on, up to the showing of three fingers which mean "Full speed ahead."

When we had passed through the Gatun locks, the tug towed us on to Pedro-Miguel, as far as we could go that day. By six in the morning we were in tow across the Isthmus.

As we passed Culebra Cut, folks from the cottages waved, admiring our ship with her towering yards, white painted hull and deck houses.

Everything was fine, except the food. That was so bad that planning a runaway was in the minds of most of the men in the foc'sle.

The end of the day found us tied up to the Miraflores lock. There was a magnificent sunset, the heavy tropical dew settling early, and strange cries of tropical night birds mingled with the mournful croaking of the frogs.

We reminisced until one said, "Vell, I guess ve turn in, because tomorrow dey vill have us yumping like monkeys."

The old Chinese cook was closing the galley door, having done all the damage he could for one day, and whatever he said to his friend the Chinese steward was probably his way of saying "Good night." At any rate, he padded to the midship house, clock in one hand, his Bull Durham in the other.

The gang on the hatch had simmered down to three or four men. Chips was still talking to the bos'un, and we could see Mr. Mortimer coming for'ard along the flying bridge, making his last round before turning in. It seemed peaceful enough.

In the foc'sle house a plot was brewing...

More than half of us before the mast in the "Dirigo" were planning to desert. All of us were angry about the grub. The little card game in the foc'sle went on, but on looking around I noticed that here and there fellows were getting their bags ready in the dark corners of the room.

By going from one to the other, I learned that we had recruited several members for the jungle jump. As I was American born, about the only one in the gang, I took command.

We were a strange mixture. There was Paddy, an Irishman about fifty years of age; two Germans, one a Bavarian, the other a Prussian; a Scotchman, a lad from Glasgow; Wayne Wheeler, a Finn; "Cockney" a London lad; and, lastly, two Russian-Finns. And, of course, myself.

Our venture was a serious one, for I knew the Canal Zone police would comb the jungles for us to arrest us and receive the reward for deserters. My first move was to get Scotty to keep a sharp lookout while I cleaned the galley out. I must have thought I was bound away on a winter campaign through the Alaskan wilds, for I filled a sailor bag with the cabin coffee pot, all the bread, sugar, and milk.

[97]

As I filled the bag, I directed the rest of the gang to get all of Chip's lumber and all the heaving lines they could find. That done, we were ready for the big get-away.

Paddy went over the side, and down the heaving lines, and once down the planks he sang out ever so softly, "Lower away a little more." We did.

"Now make fast." We made fast.

Then, "Hey, fellows!" he called in alarm, "Do you know that the lumber is green, and ready to sink?"

I hesitated only a moment. "Go on ahead," I ordered quietly, "We'll follow."

With all our bags on the fore t'gallant rail, a sentry suddenly appeared not a hundred feet away! We held our breaths, not making a sound, and he didn't notice us. We all heaved a sigh of relief as he walked away.

Paddy dove overboard, and swam away with his shoes lashed to his back. Then the argument broke out.

"Go ahead."

"No, you first."

"What're we going to do with the grub, the bags, and everything else?"

"To 'ell with 'em!"

To cap matters, the Bavarian excitedly whispered that he saw someone coming out of the cabin door aft.

"Are you sure?" I asked, thinking it a stall.

"Sure! I saw him!" the Bavarian gulped and pointed. "There! There he is now!"

"By golly, you're right!" I exclaimed after one quick glance. "Fellows, what do you want to do? Hunter, the third mate, is out on deck and we've got to act quickly!"

It was too late. The third mate had already wheeled, rushing away to call Mr. Mortimer.

Now came action! Every one of us grabbed our bags and made for the foc'sle door, a door only wide enough to admit one at a time. We all reached it at once, and what a bottleneck! Then we heard voices at the break of the poop.

No six men ever jammed through a foc'sle door so fast, sailor bags, rattling coffee pot, and all. Once inside, we threw our bags anywhere they'd be out of sight, and leapt into our bunks, covering up with our blankets and feigning instant sleep. Not a sound to be heard save the deep sigh of an old sailor turning over in his bunk.

Someone entered stealthily from the port side. It was the mate, headed straight for my bunk, flashlight in hand. I didn't budge when the light hit my face.

"Who's this?" he cried, shaking me roughly.

I didn't answer, pretending to be in a heavy sleep.

He shook me again, and I jumped.

"What is it?" I asked, trying to sound frightened. I sat up slowly, rubbing my eyes. "What's the matter?"

Mr. Mortimer was no fool. "You know," he said shortly.

"No, sir, I don't," I said, "I was fast asleep."

"Where's Scotty's bunk?" he asked grimly.

"On the other side, sir, up in the corner."

He turned on his heel and made for poor Scotty's bunk. I laughed inwardly, remembering how we'd all jammed through the door as we came in.

"Scotty, Scotty!" said Mr. Mortimer gruffly.

"Yes, sir?"

"Sir be damned!" Mr. Mortimer was in a fine rage. "Get out of that bunk and get your clothes. Then get aft!"

Scotty reluctantly packed his belongings, and away he went, out on deck and aft with the mate, who saw to it that he got an application of chains and put down in the lazarette.

When they had gone, we didn't dare speak for fear of someone listening outside. Yet we burned to know why Scotty had been singled out. All we could settle on was that Mr. Hunter had recognized him from aft, and told the mate.

We never saw Paddy again, and we all hoped he'd made good his escape. We finally went to sleep, and after that no more escapes were attempted for the mate appointed the third mate to stand watch every night in port thereafter.

After passing through the last set of locks, we were off for Japan, crossing the Pacific at its greatest breadth.

I DON'T BELIEVE OUR COURSE VARIED MORE THAN TWO POINTS NORTH or South of West during the entire run of seventy-two days, until we picked up the Volcano Islands, and not many days later we sighted land. Great, tall mountain ranges with snow covered peaks towering far above the clouds, and we still many miles from shore.

At last we entered the inland sea. Small sampan fishermen dotted the horizon. Once in a while, one would pass not more than a quarter of a mile away, looking strange indeed to sailors who had never sailed this coast before.

Now, in sight of land, our progress was hampered by a dead head wind. The orders for two solid weeks were "Full 'n bye." Every four hours it was "Tack ship." All well and good for a day or so, but after that the swearing was terrific. It seemed we would never reach Shimonoseki.

At last, however, we saw the city lights of Maji. Then the pilot came aboard, and our hearts jumped to every command. Along the shore we could see smoke rising from the fishermen's huts, and sampans making away for their morning catch. Sea and wind united in greeting us as we sailed through the narrow waters, cutting the water like a yacht.

We were now running into steamboat traffic. One, then another, passed us outward bound. They all looked at our beautiful three skys'l bark, craning their necks after we passed, to read the big black letters under her stern, "Dirigo" of Bath, Me.

The sails, all but the six tops'ls and fores'l were clewed up, and it was "You laddies, up'n furl 'em!"

Going aloft to make the last furl is one of the greatest thrills of a trip. At sea, the height above water isn't so noticeable, but coming into port—how grand and noble the old hulk looks when you're standing on the foot ropes of the skys'l yards. The men on the yards are heaving and shouting.

"Come up with 'em, homeward bound furl, boys!" Now they're all snug, and down they come—the young ones never stopping to climb down, but sliding down the backstays shouting, "There's plenty more in the slopchest!"

"Bleckfast allee leddy!" shouted our old renegade Chinese cook, madder'n a hornet because the Jap pilot had insisted on tea instead of coffee.

"Chips, are those anchors all clear?" asked the mate.

"Yes, sir," answered Chips.

"Windlass unlocked?"

"Yes, sir." Both anchors were ready to let go.

In Japan, the women of the working classes as well as the men worked at discharging vessels. And to sailors who had been at sea for four months, the Oriental maidens looked good indeed. They swarmed over the side as soon as we were anchored, and the mates almost went crazy because they couldn't get the men at clearing up the decks.

The foc'sle was full of Japanese, both male and female. They crowded in with tea sets, vases, silks, tobacco, cigarettes, frames and pictures—all done up in silk. They also had kimonos, boots, shoes, sandals, and Saki, the national drink.

I was sitting on the edge of my bunk, trying to read my letters from home. On each side I had Japanese girls trying to sell me postal cards. They seemed to be mother and daughter, and I finally centered my attention on them.

Their post cards didn't interest me. No, it was their glossy black hair done up into a high oval, half-moon fashion, at the back of their heads. Their kimonos were in exquisite floral designs, their tiny feet encased in wooden sandals. Their conversation was limited, consisting of pidgin English sales talks.

Our credit was good, but no cash was given us during our three month stay there. This had been previously arranged by the skipper. The agreement between the captain and the bumboatmen was usually twenty per cent of the sales, and the captain paid the bills. Another good way of bleeding the sailor.

The little Japanese girl who sat on my right was fascinating. Her ways were simple and unaffected, and she was not more than seventeen. Her name was Mitsuko.

A strange affection developed between Mitsuko and myself. I cannot say that I loved her, but she was undeniably attractive. The pert twist of her head bespoke intelligence, and tapering fingers tokened artistry. Her nails, long and perfectly manicured, looked enchanting to a salty seadog with calloused paws.

I was talking with my little Oriental barnacle when the mate stuck his head in the port door.

"Well!" he exclaimed disgustedly, as he took in the smoke, talk, Saki, and souvenirs. "Have you all signed off? Strange—I didn't see the American Consul!" Then he spied the girls. "What the devil. Who the hell is up in the corner?"

"Dot's some Yapanese girls, sir," smirked a Swede.

"Japanese girls!" snorted Mr. Mortimer, "Get out on deck, all of you! You too!" he blasted, looking at the girls, "Don't stand there looking at me! What the hell are we running here? A ship, or some kind of dive?"

"I was reading my letters, sir," I said coldly.

"Yeah!" he jeered, "Now you're in Japan I suppose you're reading characters! Close your hatch!" He turned, "Bo'sun, we'll need all hands to clear the hawse!"

"Aye, aye, sir!" replied the bos'un resignedly. The foc'sle was cleared out, and again all hands were busy.

According to the Articles which hung on the foc'sle wall, we were entitled to fresh fruit after forty-eight hours in a foreign port. We began to talk about it, next day.

"Let's ask the old man before he goes ashore," I said to Smitty.

"Yer bloody well right we will!" he agreed. He had a bit of a limp, and smoked a T. D. pipe broken off short. We were both barefoot as we crossed the "Ship's respect line."

"May we see you a minute, sir?" I called.

"Yes, you can, but be quick."

"Well, captain, according to the Act of Congress, we men are entitled to fresh fruit and we need it badly."

Captain Mallett thought for a moment, then said, magnanimous as a prince, "I'll see to it." He did.

The very next day, while we were eating dinner, the Chinese steward came forward with a basket of peaches.

"Each man, two peachee," he said briskly, passing them amongst us. This was our ration of fresh fruit, according to the skipper's interpretation, and like the old song, "We Never Saw Sweet Annie Anymore."

Once finished unloading, our next port of call was Itosaki to discharge the balance of our cargo. All went well in Itosaki until the last day, when Captain Mallett received orders to proceed to San Carlos, Philippine Islands, to load raw sugar. The charter was good for just so many days, and if the "Dirigo" was late, the owners forfeited the charter.

In the latitudes between Japan and the Philippine Islands at certain times of the year there are winds so light that getting anywhere under sail would take weeks, so arrangements had been made to be towed the fourteen hundred miles. The charter also stated we must carry two hundred and fifty tons of coal for the tug, as it was impossible for her to carry enough bunker for the trip.

Monday morning our tug arrived. One able seaman and two ordinary seamen were ordered in the chain locker, and I was the A.B. to go. The ordinary seamen were Ed White and Harry Manning.

The "Dirigo's" anchor chain weighed about forty pounds to the link, and was tough stowing. We were down in the chain locker, and unable to see what was going on.

We could hear the mate shouting "Aft, anchor away, sir!" Then, all of a sudden, the chain started paying out!

"Stand clear for life!" I shouted to the boys with me. We hung on to the angle iron for all we were worth as bight after bight swung up through the chain pipes, leaving a trail of fiery sparks as it hit the leads. Then we felt the "Dirigo" fetching upon her hawse, and we went to the main deck.

We'd had a collision with a schooner! It was a Jap three-masted schooner which had gotten afoul of the towboat when getting under way. Thanks to the anchor, and the good judgment of the mate, there wasn't much damage done.

Down in the chain locker we went again, the three of us drained of color and a bit wobbly in the knees.

"Heave ho!" This time we were under way.

The tenth in a series of beautiful days found us among the Loo-Choo Islands, now known as the Ryukyus, a group of islands laying south of Japan and north of the Philippine Islands. The tugboat left us on the coast of one of these islands, proceeding toward the trading station, but not before the Japanese captain had told Captain Mallett not to let any man go ashore.

Night came on, and with it a growing ambition to see the half-wild island. The Pacific Ocean in that latitude was murmurously enchanting, it lay as dark blue glass under the full moon, the island appearing in its midst like a velvet silhouette.

Suddenly I noticed a canoe paddling from the island toward our ship. It finally came alongside with its native peddler, a fierce visaged fellow with a shock of straight black hair.

"Tell that fellow we want to go ashore," I said to Saki, a Jap shipmate who was to help discharge coal. We had lost our charter, due to being a day date.

Saki said to the native, making him understand as best he could. "This man will come out later and take you ashore from anchor chain," he finally said.

I was on the foc'sle head, talking with some of my shipmates, when I saw the canoe coming toward our ship again. I went down the iron ladder, looking for Gus, "The man with the joods." He had been christened by one of our poker players, for every time there was a big pot on board Gus would say, "I'm there with the joods."

I finally found him on deck and told him to hurry before our "friend" from shore grew tired of waiting. We dashed into the foc'sle for bartering material. Soap, oilskins, candles—sure to get us a royal welcome! We were ready to slide through the hawse and down the chain into the canoe when something happened. . . .

The second mate was making one of his regular trips for'ard along the flying bridge, when he leaned over the bow and saw the black native holding onto the anchor chains. With all sorts of terrible oaths he made for the galley coal bin, and was back in a minute or two, both hands full of the biggest pieces of coal he could find. He pelted that poor native without a word of warning, and the fellow took off as fast as he could paddle!

The uncivilized tactics of the white man had spoiled our chances of going ashore. We sat on the foc'sle head far into the night, alternately damning the second mate, and—remembering the scene—breaking into guffaws.

We sailed to Kobe, and, the weather being clement, there was nothing amiss at any time. Kobe spelled "homeward bound," because nearly all ships calling there for orders received them with ballast for Seattle or San Francisco.

We experienced a typhoon just two weeks out of Kobe. We had been warned of its approach by some Jap seamen, yet only when the skipper summoned Fred Mortimer to tell him the barometer was dropping sharply, did we know the first real meaning of concern.

The barometer kept dropping sharply. Thirty, then down to twenty-nine point thirty. Then twenty-nine, then—twenty-eight point forty! We were eight hundred miles from the coast of Japan, and the thought of a typhoon, with seven hundred and fifty tons of ballast, and spars towering one hundred seventy-five feet above decks, was not pleasant.

Heavy swells were in evidence, long and high, indicating a serious disturbance not far from our latitude. And then we saw seamanship!

"Mr. Mortimer!" Captain Mallett shouted through his megaphone. He was a poised, indomitable figure on the poop deck. "You can send down on deck the sks'l and royal yards, then lower your t'gallant masts and lash everything!" What an order! Few men today could carry out its equivalent, yet Mr. Mortimer never blenched.

He executed that tremendous piece of seamanship with the ease born of complete knowledge of the problem at hand. Hardboiled, yes. Hard, undoubtedly. But without question, Fred Mortimer deserves to be on the scroll of immortal seamen for that day's performance on a square-rigged ship.

The second indication of the approaching typhoon made its appearance six hours later. The sky became clear and still, blue and ominous, not a speck in the air. Then, that evening, the rigging began to sing its terrible tune, and for three days it continued!

The "Dirigo" behaved beautifully. She was stiff enough to carry her seas in lovely fashion, about four points on her bow. Together, she and Captain Mallett made a combination to inspire any deep-water man.

The typhoon passed, and again we were lulled back into the monotony of ship routine until our fifty-third day at sea, when rumors went for'ard that we would soon pick up Cape Flattery. We had no way of knowing we'd come close to picking it up bodily.

We were under shortened sail, full'n by, with a fresh northerly wind and an evil fog one minute thick enough to cut with an axe, and the next turning into a haze with visibility a mile ahead.

I was in the mate's watch, and our watch was below. We were seated around the foc'sle table having chow, when one of the men happened to gaze up from his mess through the port hole. His eyes bulged as though he were being throttled, yet his face turned white.

"Breakers!" he managed to yell. "Breakers on the port side!"

We rushed on deck, the cry "Breakers!" ringing fore fore'n aft. "All hands on deck!" came from aft. Then, a second later, "Wear ship!"

"Man the weather braces!" Orders poured fast from the poop deck, and we were everywhere, each man working his best, all of us fearing the deadly breakers.

Breakers! The vicious ones, whose every pound and roar thunder death and destruction. There was little hope for the ship, or her crew, that cast its bow on those shores.

With only seconds to spare we managed to wear ship, once again headed off shore on the starboard tack. It had been too close for comfort, and we wondered who was responsible.

The decks cleared up, Mr. Mortimer shouted, "That'll do the watch, but be ready for a call!"

At about eight bells that evening, Captain Mallett sent for Harry Manning, Ted Foresele, and Ed White, our three ordinary seamen. Once they had trooped back to the chart room and returned, Captain Mallett was overheard to say to Mr. Mortimer. "These school ship lads are certainly very clever with their modern day methods of navigation." And, as the remark spread throughout the entire ship, it did little to swell the chests of the three lads.

Yet the best man going can make mistakes, and from all accounts our good skipper found a slight error in his own reckoning that day. The matter of how we had nearly grounded was quickly dropped.

We sailed up Puget Sound two days later, every man on deck standing by to work the ship. We were in high spirits, with Port Townsend just eight hours away and eight months pay coming. It was not our final port of discharge, but the skipper preferred to pay off the men, thereby cutting the expense of wages and food.

At last we anchored, the sails with the prettiest homeward bound furl I had seen for many a day. Five minutes later the doctor's boat arrived, then the towboats, waterboats and launches, bringing ship's tailors, boarding house masters, public house runners, and U. S. Customs officers.

The commissioner finally came along, the skipper with him. We of the foc'sle made ready to go aft to be paid.

"Now," said the commissioner, when we were all before him, "Have you men any complaints to make before we go ahead paying off?"

"Yes, sir!" shouted one, "We have bad food!"

"All right," said the commissioner gravely, "Let us have proof." With that, Captain Mallett's face turned brick red. We were paying off at a Pacific Coast port where the commissioners listened to the complaints of the seamen, and read the official log book of the skipper.

Two members of the crew entered the cabin, carrying with them a five pound can of butter and a plate of biscuits, and looking the commissioner square on.

"Sir, the Act of Congress calls for butter and no substitutes. Am I right, commissioner?"

"Yes, my boy, you are right," nodded the commissioner. "Now let me see this stuff you have in that can."

The seaman who had spoken lay the can on the deck, and cut a semi-circle opening with his sheath knife. "Whew!" he ejaculated as the rancid odor hit him. He handed the can to the commissioner.

"Umm-m, strong," commented the commissioner, averting his face. "Please lay that outside the door before I get sick. Next man. What's your trouble?"

"Well, sir," said the other, a seasoned deepwater man, "We've been getting these biscuits since we left Philadelphia, and in order to eat them we've had to turn the foc'sle lamp down low. Look at these animals, sir." He broke one of the biscuits open, revealing about four soft worms and about a dozen weevils.

[108]

"And you men have been getting this sort of biscuit since you left the port of sign-on?" demanded the commissioner incredulously.

"Yes, sir. And not only that, sir, but you can open any barrel of salt beef on this ship, sir, and I'll warrant you will not stand over it five minutes."

This remark resulted in the commissioner requesting all barrels of salt beef in the for'ard lockers to be opened, while the skipper looked on.

"Captain," the commissioner said, when the barrels were open and the fetid stench was making us all gulp. "This beef must not leave Port Townsend. It's unfit."

Captain Mallett, by the twitchings of the corners of his mouth, was evidently raging within, but outwardly he was submissive enough. We all moved aft, and the commissioner and the skipper went into conference in the cabin.

Fifteen minutes later the commissioner emerged.

"Now, men! The captain and I have arrived at an agreement. If you men accept, we can go ahead and pay off. Captain Mallett is willing to pay each man eight dollars for the bad issue of butter, but, mind you—that is all! And, if you want to take this matter to court it will hold up your paying off."

At this, there was much grumbling and growling, and a few heartfelt oaths. Yet only a few minutes had passed when one of the men shouted, "We all agree to that, commissioner!" The payoff commenced.

Two commodious launches were tied alongside the "Dirigo," their captains bargaining to take what men they could up the Sound to Seattle for a dollar a head. We all went with one launch, for in that way we could stay together until we reached a saloon where the fun started, and often ended, for a homeward bounder.

I often wonder how we ever found Coleman dock in Seattle. I never witnessed a trip like that one! The men were staggering all over the boat, some dancing on the table, others wanting to steer. The parrot's cage in the cabin was knocked over, and the poor bird squawked "Help! Help!" in piercing tones, while bottles were offered to him right and left, to help him recover.

"Heaven help a sailor on a night like this!" I said to the captain of the launch. And, for once, I meant it.

A GAY WEEK OF BEING ASHORE, AND I WAS BROKE. SO, AS I ALWAYS
preferred working to borrowing, I began to haunt the employment
offices.

That morning, the fellow who marked jobs on the blackboard
came out and scrawled "Dishwasher, logging camp." I was on his
heels when he re-entered his office.

"I'll take the pearl diver's job," I announced.

"That'll be one dollar," he said.

"I only have two bits."

"Well, all right," he conceded, after a moment's hesitation, "Pay
the fee on the other side." He told me to meet the boss at the Great
Northern Railway Station in Seattle.

I was there on time, and that afternoon the train pulled out with
an unsavory lot of sailors, cowboys, lumberjacks and beach combers,
all bound for jobs in the woods.

The place we pulled into that night was called Index, Washington.
It wasn't much of an index. All the village contained was a post

office, sheriff's office, general store, a hotel, and a couple of gin mills. There were a lot of Indians to be seen, but I learned later that they only drifted in during the logging season.

The gang boss directed us to the lone hotel and told us we were to stay there. We were walking toward the hotel in a group, when suddenly a violent commotion broke loose in one of the bars we were passing. Guns blazed, tables overturned, and men scrambled for cover.

I stood still for a moment, trying to see what had caused the shooting. A bullet buried itself in the sailor bag slung over my back, the impact startling me well nigh out of my skin. In a cold sweat, I, too, scrambled for cover.

An Indian was killed during the fracas, and the way that bunch of hards took it was something to see. To them, it meant no more than the death of a dog, if as much.

I was a pretty sight next morning, crawling aboard one of the flat cars on the log train, packing my sailor bag with its fancy painting of a full-rigged ship—more attached to the bag since it had saved my life than ever before.

When we arrived in camp after our ten mile ride, we were detailed and conveyed to our various jobs. In order to reach mine I had to cross a cabled bridge over the Snohomish River, a fiercely running rapids. I was ten times as nervous as I'd ever been at sea, but I got across all right.

When we reached the chow hall and entered the warm kitchen I had a fine introduction to the chef. "Here's your pearl diver," said the employment agency man, and that was it.

My wages were one dollar a day, and we fed about sixty white loggers and forty Indians. No china or crockery was used. It was all tin, agate, and iron pottery.

The chef's name was Hans. He was a fine fellow, of Danish extraction. He showed me my bunk in the bunkhouse, but we got there too late, for it had just been taken by a logger. I was put up in an attic, the only place left. The wind howled into my ears at night, inviting me back to sea.

I got into my oldest clothes to report for duty. It was dirty work, and there was plenty of it. I washed dishes, pots and pans, and set dining room tables. I hit the kitchen at five in the morning, and was lucky to leave at nine-thirty at night. All for thirty dollars a month!

About the tenth day I was in camp, I saw a morning paper in the dining room and idly glanced through its pages. On the shipping news page there was a picture of a beautiful square rigger. The underline read, "American three sky'sl yarder about to leave for the Baltic Sea with a cargo of grain from Tacoma, Washington. The American bark "Dirigo" of Bath, Me., Master-Captain Walter M. Mallett."

That night I told the chef I was quitting the next evening and wanted my pay check.

That night Hans gave me a special T-bone steak. When I sat down to it, he said, "Well, Barney, do you prefer sitting down to this meal or a feed of salt beef hash?"

For a moment I wavered, then there appeared before me the new faces in the foc'sle, the new ports, the spread of canvas, and the rolling deck underfoot, and I was lost.

I burned my mattress before I left. So many men were lousy, it was the law for every man who entered camp to buy a mattress for one dollar, and if he quit his job he had to burn his mattress before leaving. Having attended to this little detail, I waved farewell to all and made away for the big pay-off. Fourteen dollars, less cost of mattress, railroad fare, and office fee. I came out with nine dollars.

I made for the railroad tracks where I ran into a Swede whose name I was never to know. He, too, had a bag.

"Which way are you bound?" I asked.

"I vill go to Seattle, but I vait for freight."

"Do you expect one soon?"

"Yah, but ve vill harve to make round up." So, sea bags on our shoulders, we started hiking for round-up curve. Once, my newly acquired friend stooped to pick up a railroad spike. I wondered why, but managed to refrain from asking, though I kept a sharp eye on him.

We heard the signal of an approaching train, and the Swede told me to hurry. The engineer had to slow for the curve, and that was our chance. Suddenly there were a lot of new faces around us. Ten hobos had silently joined us.

We found an open box car, threw in our bags, and in we went after them. Our freight gathered headway, and as I shut the door I saw the Swede bend down with the railroad spike. He was an old hand at the game, for he used it as a chock to keep the door from closing entirely, thereby locking us in for the "bulls." Oh, I learned a lot!

We reached Seattle that evening, and that was the last I saw of my Swedish friend. I made straight for the Carl House, a meeting place for all deepwater mates and masters. I was eager to find out if I could ship on the "Dirigo."

The next morning I went to the shipping office and found out who was shipping the crew for Captain Mallett. It was none other than the famous deepwater shipping office of Max Levy of Coleman dock.

I walked into his office. "Is Max Levy in?"

"No," said the fellow at the desk, "But the runner might be able to help you out."

"Are there any chances left to ship in the "Dirigo"?"

"Sure, my lad. Where are your clothes?"

"Over at Yesler Way."

"Get them quickly," he said, as though there were a fire.

"Okeh," I said, glad enough. I didn't need urging.

I was back at Levy's with my clothes very quickly, and my orders were handed to me.

"Take the ferry to old Tacoma. When you get there, report to Pete McNamara at our boarding house."

"Righto!" Away I sped for the ferry boat.

On the way over I got a broadside view of the "Dirigo," with all sails bent, loaded with grain. An elderly gentleman, noticing my gaze focused on her, came up to me.

"What a picture she makes!" he said fervently, "With those Stars and Stripes painted on her side. Could you tell me why the national emblem is painted on her?"

"Well, sir," I explained, "She is very likely to sail through some parts of the war zone, and being a ship of a neutral country, must carry indentification." And, even as I explained, I knew why there had been a place left for me!

"Oh, I see," he said comprehendingly. "She is very possibly bound for Europe."

"Yes, sir, we are."

"We are?" he echoed, focusing his near-sighted eyes on me with sudden interest. "Are you one of her crew?"

"Yes, sir."

"H'mmm," he said non-committally. I felt he was mentally placing a wreath on my grave.

I met Pete McNamara, and he called me in to sign the articles, and, believe me, they were read off in a jiffy. "The American bark "Dirigo," bound from Seattle, Washington, to Kalmar, Sweden, and any other ports such as the master may designate, and back to a final port of discharge in the United States. Voyage not to exceed twelve calendar months."

"All right, Burnett," he said, "Sign here on number seventeen. Then sign the other two, and your advance note."

After I'd signed all three, and my advance of one month's wages, Pete asked what I needed in the way of slop chest. I suddenly had an uneasy feeling.

"Are we going through the Panama Canal again?"

"No, Burnett," he answered suavely, "I'm sorry to say that the Culebra Cut fell in, and it has to be dredged. Naturally, that means Cape Horn. But then, you have a good vessel under your feet, and I've just shipped a fine cook aboard her." Oh, the lies they told! Anything to get a crew aboard, and a towboat to take you to sea!

We marched off to the waiting launch, stopping long enough at a saloon for us to have one last drink, and all hands went in except the runners, one of whom knocked on the saloon window. When the bartender looked up inquiringly, the runner pointed one finger upwards, meaning "One drink only for each man." They knew they were taking chances letting a crew into a bar where other runners were present.

A short launch ride, and we were approaching the "Dirigo" on the port side. I could hear the familiar bull tones of Mr. Mortimer's voice, shouting to stand by to take the crew on board.

It was then I heard the new second mate's name for the first time. Mr. Jack Malone, and a tough egg he was.

"Mr. Malone!" bellowed Mr. Mortimer, "See to it there aren't any weapons in those bags, and line them up where I can search every man!" The idea of searching for weapons is a sea tradition, but mostly form and sarcasm.

I pushed my head over the side, and the mate grinned. "So you're back again, Burnett!"

"Yes, sir." I said, "I missed the old ship."

"All right," he said, through with his welcome, "Get in line with the rest."

"They're all here, mister!" shouted Jack Malone.

"All right, you may go for'ard now, all of you! Make damned sure you're sober tomorrow morning at five!"

We trooped into the foc'sle, and the fun began. Twenty A. B.'s trying to pick bunks, sailor bags all over the place. It was home again, corn cob pipes, bottles, and all.

I drew the lower bunk way up in the corner, dark as hell itself. Yet, everything went fine until about five that evening, when I heard much scuffling going on. I opened the port door, and looking aft I saw Mr. Mortimer and Jack Malone, fighting like very dogs.

They were throwing right hands, left hooks, shouting hoarsely as they threw their guns in the port scupper.

"We don't need guns!" panted Mr. Mortimer.

"Amen!" agreed Malone savagely. They were both liquored up to a point where there was no stopping them. And, with the skipper still ashore, the ship was theirs.

A little later, Jack Malone came for'ard into the foc'sle with the nerve of a lion.

"All hands on deck, and get under the foc'sle head to see if that turkey is properly tied up," he said.

We looked at each other, doubting our ears. We would have all bet our bottom dollar on Mr. Mortimer.

"Get out of it, now, all hands!" snapped Malone. He was irritated by the way we sat and stared at each other. "Well, do you understand English? Get going, all of you!"

There was nothing else to do. We all marched for'ard under the foc'sle head to carry out his orders.

Then we saw the turkey! No Mr. Mortimer was he, but a real live turkey, sent aboard by the ship chandler for the skipper's Christmas, off Cape Horn.

The turkey well secured, we all returned to the foc'sle, to laugh until our bellies ached! And the more we talked about it, the funnier it got!

The next day, October 14, 1915, we upped anchor, towing nearly all day down Puget Sound, and by five o'clock we were passing Cape Flattery, bound for the open sea.

Soon we had the "Dirigo" under full sail, Cape Flattery astern, a fresh nor'ther with a touch of Alaska chill to it. I was again in the mate's watch, the air was salty and fresh, and it was wonderful to be a young man with fresh sea air in his nostrils, new horizons beyond!

The voyage progressed peacefully, and luck rode with us, the trade winds being both nor'east and sou'east. We passed very close to Pitcairn Island.

Christmas was approaching, and we were getting close to Cape Horn. Off Valparaiso we encountered a severe nor'ther, with such seas that we quailed at looking at them.

The captain's turkey died on December twenty-third, and how the foc'sle gang laughed! Not with malice toward the skipper, but because of the way the old Chinese cook had babied it. He had made up a lot of corn meal balls, and he'd made the poor bird eat by stuffing meal balls down into his gullet. And, as he stuffed, he had sing-songed a constant flow of Chinese at the poor, defenseless bird. No wonder it had given up the ghost!

About three days before we reached Cape Horn, the wind blew in a terrific sou'west gale. Captain Mallett ordered Mr. Mortimer to heave her to under three lower tops'ls, and on one particular day she was really taking punishment. The bell of her foc'sle head was sounding off on every roll. Jack Malone, the second mate, was on watch on deck from noon to four p.m.

At about two that afternoon, I was taking a stroll under the lee of the foc'sle, having a drag on my pipe and enjoying the sight of the Cape pigeons and albatross frolicking about the stern of the ship. Mr. Malone shouted at the bos'un. "Fill the captain's w.c. tank!"

"Yes, sir!" answered the bos'un smartly.

Life lines were strung all about the deck, for our ship rolled her rails under, and the scuppers and ports were not enough to carry off the water about the decks. The bos'un thought to draw the water from the deck rather than rig up all the paraphernalia that went with drawing water over the side, but the second mate thought differently.

"Bos'un!" he shouted curtly, "I want that water drawn from over the side!"

"There's plenty of water on deck, sir."

"I want that water drawn from over the side, I said," Malone snarled. Just then the "Dirigo" gave a terrific roll, and a heavy sea unfurled its crest and filled the decks. The bos'un ran for the mizzen fife rail and held on with all his might.

Once the decks were clear enough to walk on, the bos'un went to the lee scuppers at the break of the poop and issued orders to his men to pass along the wooden buckets from the poop deck. He then filled them from the main deck and passed them along to the man filling the captain's w.c. tank.

There was water on that deck waist high on the lee side, good clear salt water, but again Mr. Malone insisted the water should be drawn from over the side. The bos'un continued to draw water from the deck, not to be insolent, but because he thought the order a dangerous one when the "Dirigo" was continuously rolling her rails under.

Mr. Malone picked up a galvanized iron bucket from the poop deck and walked down the ladder, rage gleaming in his narrowed eyes. The bos'un was bending over, filling his bucket, and—all of a sudden—the second mate lifted the bucket high in the air and smashed it down on the bos'uns head! The bos'un crumpled immediately, rolling over unconscious, his face and neck streaming blood. Mr. Malone stood over him, a peculiar expression of satisfaction on his face.

Dangerous seas were sweeping the deck, and one of the men ran to the bos'un to prevent his being dashed against the lee bulwarks. I wheeled and ran for the foc'sle where the watch below was now turned in. I shouted to get their attention, and they listened carefully. They rose almost in unison, and aft they went, joined by the watch on deck.

Every mother's son of us mustered at the after end of the midship house, where Mr. Malone stood at the mizzen fife rail, a snatch block gripped in his hands, eyed the maddened crew warily.

A big Swedish lumberjack stepped out from the men. "Mister," he said slowly, looking at Malone steadily, "You can pick out any man in this crew to fight you, and he'll fight you squarely just to show you you're not man enough to carry out such a fight without the aid of a snatch block or belaying pin! Are you game?"

"I'll have to get permission from the skipper first," the second mate replied disdainfully as he made for the poop deck as though he were going to make the request. He never came back, though we waited a long, long time.

We finally had to go for'ard about our business, and a couple of men carried the unconscious bos'un aft for medical attention. The affair calmed down, and no entry was made in the official log book. Had the case been the reverse, it would have been quite a different matter.

We rounded Cape Horn on Christmas Day, under three skys'ls, and every stitch of canvas the "Dirigo" had above decks was spread before mild westerly winds. We passed very close to the terrible, gaunt rocks, snow-capped, straight precipiced, with their bottomless waters below.

Cape Horn finally astern, we went on making sennit, now looking forward to chipping rust, painting, then flying fish weather. We were outward bound, and we thought, while keeping watch on the foc'sle had, of the submarine menace and drifting mines. War arguments filled every dog watch.

The second of March we were battling a nor'easter that had blown for nineteen days. We were in the North Sea, somewhere around the Shetland Islands, and how it snowed and blew!

The watch came aft to muster, every man wrapped in oilers and sea boots. They were a tired looking lot, cold, soaked outside and in. We were all irritable and miserable.

"That will do the watch," Mr. Mortimer said, "Relieve the wheel and lookout."

Five minutes later the "Dirigo" was suddenly covered by a powerful battleship searchlight, which flooded her from truck to water line, and stem to stern. What a sight it was!

Our white painted hull, newly painted yards, freshly tarred rigging, white sails, white deck houses, and the men of the crew standing on deck like statues. Then the loud boom of a gun, meaning "Heave to."

The braces were manned with lightning speed. It was then just after midnight, the strong nor'east gale still blowing. The skipper ordered the to'gan's'le and the courses made fast. We were hove to from then until daybreak.

As soon as it grew lighter it was all hands on deck, signalling starting immediately between ships. The battleship proved to be the "H.M.S. Oratava," painted with his majesty's crabfat, or war grey, with a dab of camouflage here and there. More than once I saw her two propellers spinning around in space, for the North Sea runs short and high during storms.

After much signalling, we learned from the poop deck that we had been captured. The blockade was on.

Then came the message, "I will board you with a prize crew." Meaning, men and guns. We watched the "Oratava" trying to put out a boat, and it looked very much as though at any minute both boat and men would be dashed against the cruiser's side, or cut up by her propellers.

In March the days were long. At five a.m. we all had coffee, and about twenty minutes past seven the mate ordered the regular watch below to get breakfast. By this time, the lifeboat from the cruiser was working up slowly under our lee side. It was a tough go, but they were doing it for king and country, and they gave it their best.

They all wore sleeveless guernseys and life belts, and they approached with caution and good judgment. Once within a few yards of our ship they called out for a line. It was snowing heavily, the sea spray freezing wherever it struck, making boarding ship extremely difficult.

The boarding officer was first on deck, followed by the British marines with their guns, good rations, and kit bags. They were ruddy, hardy looking fellows, but they looked almost perished with cold.

I couldn't bear to see them so miserable, so I went to the galley and asked the Chinese cook for the pot of coffee he had on the stove. He was good-hearted for once, and even let me have some pannikins and sugar. It was wonderful to see the grins break out on those stiff, cold faces when I got back with that coffee!

As the day wore on, we heard all sorts of news. It appeared that the Admiralty, wasn't satisfied with matters as they stood, for we were bound for Kalmar, Sweden, with five thousand tons of barley. It seemed suspicious for such a large cargo of grain to be bound for that small place, so they issued orders of capture and directed that we were to proceed to Lerwick, Shetland Islands.

We had been told that the reason the crew was not to be paid a war bonus was because the "Dirigo" would not pass through the war zone or any zone inhabited by "U" boats. Rows and arguments broke out in the foc's'le, then simmered down to nothing. The men crawled into their bunks, and lay there silently brooding.

"If you fellows aren't even going to question the skipper, at least I will," I said. I went aft alone.

I had a talk with the skipper, but came away as dissatisfied with the information I'd received as when I'd gone aft. The next watch on deck I remained in my bunk, refusing duty.

"Sea lawyer, eh?" said the mate, coming into the foc'sle, hard-boiled and impatient, "There are cures for such men. Burnett, what in hell is eating you?"

"Mr. Mortimer, I can easily see how we men were fooled by accepting twenty-five dollars a month. We're in the center of this war blockade, and if "Fritz" finds out it will be just too bad. So, from now on, I'm turning to only for emergencies. Until then, let the prize crew handle her."

"All right, Burnett," he said testily, "Come aft to the skipper and tell him your story." Nothing loath, I went aft, made my demands for war bonus money before the skipper and prize crew officer. The captain made entry in the official log book, then asked me what I had to say.

"Nothing more, sir."

"Go for'ard," he said. "Get your clothes out of the foc'sle, and make yourself at home in the sick bay until you come to your senses."

We battled against wind and sea for fourteen days after our capture, and all that time I refused duty. Then, as we entered Lerwick, the "Dirigo" was blown ashore! The tugboat hadn't enough power to hold her in the wind. To top that, their captains spoke nothing but Gaelic, and what a time the skipper had trying to make them understand!

Finally, after much trouble, we were pulled off the shoal and anchored in a favorable spot. Next, a diver was sent down to see what damage had been done. There was none to report, thanks to the wonderful staunchness of the "Dirigo."

We anchored in Lerwick for three or four days, and were then given orders to proceed to Kirkwall for further examination by the Admiralty.

The first day out of Lerwick, I volunteered to help man the braces. The situation was a desperate one. The Admiralty had sent a large tug to tow us to Kirkwall, and while the captain of the tug figured he had a tough job with such a lofty ship and five thousand tons of barley, he decided to tackle it anyway. All went well until we got outside the harbor, then it was all they could do to hold us.

Our lee shore, with its snow covered cliffs was growing nearer, our crew looking at each other, not daring voice what lay in their minds. Captain Mallett, not wasting a moment, was ordering the mate to make sail as quickly as possible. It was our only chance.

With about sixteen British marines, and our own twenty A. B.'s, things on deck really started humming. But by mistake someone slacked the weather fore brace, and Mr. Mortimer's hair seemed to turn twice as white. He got twenty men on it, and, as I could stand it no longer, I jumped to that weather fore brace with the men and made damned sure the same affair wouldn't happen again.

We got the "Dirigo" off shore after much cracking on, for that's what she was doing. Almost cracking in half, due to the strain of heavy sail spread, big seas, and the fresh blowing gale.

The next day I was called aft to see the captain.

"Sir, did you send for me?" I asked quietly.

"I did," said Captain Mallett. He eyed me quizzically, "Now, Burnett, are you going to turn to? Mr. Mortimer reports you were helping up for'ard yesterday."

"The ship was in danger," I replied.

"Do you know, Burnett, that I can put you in irons?"

"Captain Mallett!" I exploded, "This ship might go to her eternal anchorage any minute. This area is alive with submarines, and you know it, sir. Go ahead, I dare you to put me in irons!"

The British Admiralty officer standing beside the captain looked at me with icy disfavor. "How foolishly you speak!" he murmured disdainfully.

"It may sound foolish to you," I returned grimly, "But you can't deny the facts I've stated!"

"All right," said Captain Mallett resignedly, "Go for'ard."

Four days later we arrived in Kirkwall, Orkney Islands. We anchored there for a week, only to be ordered to Fleetwood, England.

We towed to England through the Pentland Firth, and on the way we passed the S. S. "Mauretania," now a British army transport, on her way to Canada. We admired the beauty of the Scotch countryside while passing through the Firth, deeply inhaling the invigorating air. No wonder we found it invigorating, for it came from the distilleries that turned out good Scotch whiskey!

After two days of towing we came to an anchorage outside of Fleetwood, but, as almost every seaport in England is controlled by dock gate to keep the ships in port afloat, the pilot made apologies for the moon and said we'd have to wait for a spring tide! *That* took two weeks.

Once we lay at anchor in the roads outside of Fleetwood, the examining officers of the British Admiralty came aboard to make investigation for spies. One of our men they took ashore accompanied by an armed guard, bound for a German prison camp.

American Vice-Consul Curtis from Liverpool came aboard, and after matters of importance had been reviewed, the skipper told the mate to muster the crew aft. A cheer from the foc'sle, for we knew it was pay-off!

We assembled, trying not to be impatient until the Vice-Consul made his appearance. He stepped out on deck, and the first name he called was Burnett. I stepped forward.

"Burnett," he said gravely, "I have a bad report about you."

"Bad, sir?" I asked curiously.

"Yes. I understand you refused duty for twenty-one days."

"Sir," I said quietly, "You have heard the captain. Now, won't you hear me?"

"Yes, Burnett, tell me all you know."

"Well, sir, as seamen we are paid twenty-five dollars a month. At the time of sign-on it was agreed there would be no war bonus, because the "Dirigo" was not to pass through any war zone. Instead, the captain took the ship through the lines of blockade where submarines are active, and blow on sight, neutral or enemy. Don't you think, sir, this matter is entitled to a trial?"

"Burnett," he said, "Hold on a minute."

"Yes, sir," I said, wondering, "I will."

He went back in the cabin, and I know not what he said, but he returned after a very short time.

"Burnett?" he said.

"Yes, sir."

"I talked this matter over with Captain Mallett, and he would like to know if you are willing to pay for the food and lodging you used in the twenty-one days you were off duty."

I started to protest, but he motioned me to silence.

"Now, Burnett, I want you to feel you're being given a fair chance. You see, you are alone in this fight. If the rest of the crew had been with you, we could have brought this before a court, and you would undoubtedly win your case. What do you say?" His eyes told me my case was lost.

"I accept, sir," I said resignedly.

I paid off with ninety-seven dollars and ten cents, and sighed with relief to be through with that strange five months at sea. I broke away from the rest of the crew, and spent two pleasant weeks at Blackpool, England, far away from all the turbulence of the times. Then I went to Liverpool, where I booked third class passage home.

We were seven days in crossing, but I was homeward bound. Relaxed, my thoughts turned to romance, and one night while strolling the main deck, I thought I'd found it. I spied a pretty girl sitting alone, gazing at the moonlit sea. I walked slowly up to her.

"The sea is beautiful tonight, isn't it?" I said, by way of opening a conversation.

"Oh yes, monsieur," the girl sighed, "but I am so lonesome!"

"You are lonely?" I said hopefully.

"Yes," she said innocently. "I am Belgian, and I am going to America to be married. My future husband waits for me there. Oh, I wish he were here!"

"Well, I'm sure you do," I said lamely, backing off. "I think you'll like America. We're very—er, friendly."

We saw the Statue of Liberty on the seventh day out of Liverpool, and when I stepped off the gangway at Pier Sixty-one, North River, I had ten cents left from the nine-seven dollars I'd paid off with.

One nickel I used to telephone my sister, the other I used to get to her house to eat. If I was richer in experience it didn't show in my pocketbook.

It was October, 1916, when I arrived in New York, and I was due for all sorts of surprises. We were a neutral nation, and our merchant marine was building. Everything with a bottom in it was dragged into a shipyard to be fixed up, and cargo waited for every available ship.

Although the war was in Europe, the seas themselves were full of raiders. Sailing ships were being used for running blockades. In the hectic living of those war days, the risk only added to the zest of the adventure.

I walked all around the Battery, then over to Water Street and up on Broad Street to see Black Murphy.

"Good morning, *Mister* Murphy," I said, as I entered the rickety old office, dust covered, with its usual pile of seamen's bags in one corner. Oh, I knew him, and he knew me.

"Oh, yes!" he said, crafty as a fox, "I know your name. I shipped you in the —" He knew me, but he dealt with too many men to remember my name.

"Barney is the name, you old blatherskite," I said, grinning. "And how are chances this morning?"

"I've a good berth for a bos'un," he said quickly.

"What is it?" I asked warily. He was too eager.

"A British four-masted bark, loaded with case oil for Freemantle, West Australia."

I thought for a moment, a bit taken a-back because it was a British ship.

"What are the wages?"

"Eight pound for bos'un. Forty bucks a month. You can handle it fine. What d'ye say? Sign on?"

"Okeh," I said slowly, not relishing it too much.

"Just go get your bag then," he said, anxious to have the matter clinched, "And I'll take you down to the British Consulate to sign on."

I went home, told the family, ignoring their dire prophecies that shipping on a British ship would lead to complications. I went on with my packing while they talked.

The British Consulate office was over at the New Seamen's Institute. It was decorated with the flag of Great Britain, and a policeman guarded the door.

"Where yer goin', and what's yer business?" he growled at me.

"I'm to sign on a British four-master for Australia."

"All right, lad," he said, relaxing, "go ahead."

I went up to the long counter and told them what had brought me there. "Oh yes," said the clerk patronizingly. "Do you have your passport?"

"Right here." I handed it to him.

"Oh, you're American!" he exclaimed.

"Yes, sir!" I said proudly, irritated by the trace of patronage that had crept into his manner.

He dragged out three copies with the Crown head of the British Lion, and I signed on for a period of not exceeding three years, to pay off in a final port of discharge in the British Isles. It didn't dawn on me fully what I was doing. That was to come later.

"Cheerio! Have a good passage!" the clerk called as I picked up my sailor bag to depart. I wondered whether he meant a good passage to Australia, or off a jib boom. . . .

That afternoon I boarded the "William T. Lewis" of Greenock, Scotland. Her former, and original name had been the "Robert Duncan" of the same port. She was at one time a hot ship and a fast one, sister ship of the "Howard D. Troop" of Greenock, later called the "Annie M. Reid" of San Francisco.

Mr. Welsh, the mate, met me at the break of the poop.

"Well, what's your trouble?" he growled.

"I'm the bos'un reporting," I said, short and gruff.

"Oh you are!" he said sarcastically. "American?"

"Yes, sir," I said, holding my temper. Being an American seemed to require some sort of apology.

"I'll tell the captain you're here," he said.

I waited. A six-footer leaned from the poop deck railing and called, "Bos'un, I want to talk to you!"

I went up to the poop deck, three steps at a time, and stood erect before Captain Manning of Yarmouth, Nova Scotia.

"What's your name?" he said sharply.

"Barney Burnett of Brooklyn, New York."

"Was Captain Burnett, the Sandy Hook pilot, a relative of yours?" He looked at me appraisingly.

"Yes, sir. He was my grandfather."

"I knew him well." He paused for a moment, then, "Been to sea long?"

"Eight years, sir."

"H'mm. I was captain of a ship when I'd been eight years at sea. Can you handle a job of bos'un?"

"Yes, sir." No use saying I'd more of an eye to adventure than promotion, for his type of man wouldn't understand.

"All right, you may go ahead. But remember! I don't want any barking. I prefer you to bite." The mate made the snowballs in the sailing ships, but it was the bos'un who threw them.

I went for'ard to my quarters in the midship house, and met the sailmaker, a Frenchman from St. Nazaire, and the carpenter, a Russion from St. Petersburg.

The quarters were fair, and supper, damned good food, was on the table. During the meal we talked, and I discovered the sailmaker to be a good fellow, but the Russian spoke of nothing but Nickolof, and the great Russian Empire. I had my fill, and went out on deck to look over the ship.

She was ready for the sea. Loaded, hatches calked, tarpaulined, flying bridge down and sails bent. The tug took us out in the stream where we anchored, waiting for the balance of the crew. As bos'un, I

wasn't expected to be friend of either aft or for'ard gang. My job was
to make myself understood by right or might, from the time the first
sail was sheeted home until it was tied up for the last time.

October fifteenth our crew came over the rail from a ship chandler's boat. It was the usual load for a square-rigger on sailing day.
All hands drunk, some smuggling bottles, some walking, others
reeling and stumbling.

The donkey's breakfast mattresses arrived. Mostly excelsior, they
were seven inches thick when new, sifting down to two inches by the
end of a voyage. When a seaman climbed into a top bunk, enough
dust came through the bunk boards to blind the shipmate under
him.

Mr. Welch, the mate, stood at the rail, his T.D. pipe stuck in the
starboard side of his mouth. "Riff-raff from South Street," he said,
looking at the crew. I was inclined to agree with him.

Captain Manning arrived later, having cleared the ship. He had all
ship's papers with him. "Get your flag up," he told the mate, "and
we'll heave'er short." He turned to me. "Bos'un!"

"Yes, sir!"

"We're getting under way." He looked with displeasure at the
motley crew. "Here you!" he shouted at them. "Have you been deepwater before?"

"Yes!" they chorused. He shrugged resignedly.

I went to the foc'sle door and shouted, "All right, out of there!
We're getting under way!" Out they came, all in good spirits inside
and out.

"Up on the foc'sle head, men!" The thought of getting away from
the cold winter port was exhilarating.

"What, no chanty?" These always helped. "Come on, boys, where
the hell is your spirit?" And away I started,

"Well, we're bound for West Australia
And we're sailing down the bay
We're all signed on with a full month's pay
For that is the sailor way.

The skipper walks the poop deck
While towing down the bay
With a load of case oil
And the tops'ls unfurled
For that is the sailor way.

[128]

With anchors on the catheads
And the cables stowed away
We settle down
We're outward bound
For that is the sailor's way."

The chanty continued, while the mate watched over the bows. The tug stood on ahead, with slack hawser, when the mate shouted "She's up and down!" In short time the port anchor was secure, and a little after that it was "Stand by hawser! Let 'er all go!"

As we passed the tug it was three long blasts, a dip of the British ensign, then down she came to be stowed away until needed for reporting ship to another ship en route.

Captain Manning stood erect at the for'ard end of the poop deck, a calendar in his hands. "Now, you men," he said inflexibly, take a good look at this. It's up to you if Sundays are to remain as Sundays in this ship. Otherwise, there are seven work days in a week."

The passage south to the "roaring forties" went as most trips in square riggers go. Routine work, and new gear rove off for the one-time race track of sailing ships bound for Africa and Australia. Most captains headed their ships far south of the forty-fifth parallel of latitude, weather permitting.

Nearly all the crew were barefoot, and fresh water was plentiful in the barrels at the corners of the for'ard and midship house. The food was good, as food goes in deepwater ships, and our stores were rationed out every Saturday morning along with our lime juice.

Many Americans refer to British ships and British subjects as "lime juicers," but are unaware that American ships were compelled by an Act of Congress to carry and ration out lime juice after ten days out on any deepwater voyage. And, if the ship had no lime juice, to ration out to the man on salt provision diet, there was a fine of one hundred dollars per day for every day there was no lime juice.

Christmas came, and with it an order from the captain to splice the main brace. We were all given a pannikin full of rum, the accordion player of the crew played "Silent Night" and our voices rang out in no less than seven different languages, all saying the same words though in alien tongues.

A few days later we were clear of the Cape and in the Indian Ocean. I overheard a muffled conversation one day when I was working with my watch on the poop deck. A few men of the same watch were working on the other side of the lifeboat, and it was their voices, lowered, that I heard.

"Sometimes I think we ought to throw the bos'un and the mate overboard." The voice I would have known anywhere. It was that of the seaman Leyland of Nova Scotia.

The minutes dragged by until eight bells struck. The mate shouted, "Relieve the wheel!" I went to the midship house, taking a puff on makings as I went. My Irish was up.

"No dinner?" Sails and Chips sensed something was up.

"No," I replied evenly. "Right now I have a date with a guy who would like to throw me overboard." I lit out and went straight to the mainmast, shouting, "Leyland!"

Captain Manning strode for'ard on the flying bridge. It was evident he had heard me. At the same moment, Leyland stepped out of the foc'sle door, bellowing, "You want me?"

"Yes," I said deliberately, "I want to give you a chance to throw me overboard. That's what you want, isn't it?"

"Remember what I told you, bos'un," said the skipper significantly. "Bite like hell, but don't bark!"

Leyland walked aft to meet me abreast of the main mast. Once he was facing me, I squared away for action.

"Come on," I gritted invitingly, "come on, throw me overboard! Throw me to the sharks—if you can!"

I let loose with a left, a right, then more and more as my anger got the better of me. I don't know how many times I connected, for he put up a defense at first although he lacked technique. Such fellows were great for strangleholds, and it was always "May the best fellow win."

We finally tangled, locked, and went tumbling down into the port scupper. I finally broke his hold and got back on my feet, squaring around for round two.

"Come on, here's your chance!" I shouted. He just stood there, his arms dangling at his sides, showing no enthusiasm for resuming the fight.

"Enough, enough!" Captain Manning shouted, smiling in spite of himself, "Let's get back to work."

I went back to the midship house, ate a little, and turned in. It was more apparent than ever that the bos'un had no shipmates, his only course to beat them all at their own game, whether it was seamanship or fighting.

Peace reigned from then on, however. Spirits were high when, after one hundred and fourteen days of sailing, Captain Manning called to the lookout "Keep a sharp lookout for land on the port bow!"

Land was sighted the next morning, and by three that afternoon we were towing up inside the jetty to the long quay of Fremantle. It was a typical sailing ship arrival. Ship tailors, boarding house masters, ship chandlers, and pimps from Madame So and So's favorite anchorage. Bottles were passed around, smuggled aboard by those who could, and I took a smoke until port fever had died down.

The next day we went on with our unloading. The crew was beginning to show signs of unrest. Many of them were frightened by the war. Great Britain was having serious reverses, and now that we had a chance to read the papers, the news was not designed to improve morale. Rumors of clearing out or running away swept the ship, and ideas ran wild.

I belonged to a neutral nation, but, like the rest, I was caught up in the surge of excitement. I had twenty pounds coming the next Saturday night, and a glimmering notion of how I was going to use it. In the meanwhile, I went ashore not knowing what the dissatisfaction was that weighed so heavily on me. I strode into Fremantle's rendezvous for masters, mates and pilots, trying my best to understand the different tongues about me. They were a jolly enough group, but I sat alone, brooding, unable to shake off the feeling that I should get off the "William T. Lewis."

Saturday night found me knocking on the door of a rooming house. I had managed to draw three pounds, and while I was miserable about deserting I knew I would be more so if I didn't.

I sat on the edge of my bed the next morning, wondering what my next move should be. The "William T. Lewis" was not in my thoughts at all, though every other sailing ship sailed through my head. That afternoon I walked all the way to Perth and back, and this I did for a week, never dreaming there was a general alarm out for a deserter from a British ship. One Barney Burnett. Reward, three hundred pounds.

My money soon vanished, and I had left my clothes aboard ship. My shoes were showing signs of heavy wear, yet I drifted, taking in the sights and sounds of Fremantle. I finally started hiking, and got as far as the Northam wheat fields of West Australia.

My peak cap alone told people that I was not only a stranger, but a foreigner. There they wear what is known as the cocky hat.

After a week of sleeping out in the open, asking for food at doors, I wandered down to the railroad station and talked with a track walker there. I asked him if it were easy to beat trains out of there.

"Cobber," he said, using the Australian term for buddy, "You don't 'ave to worry. Just stay under a bloomin' tarpaulin until you get to your destination."

I watched and waited. A train lay on the siding, loaded with grain for Fremantle and Perth, narrow gauge as were all trains there. I made it in between cars, climbing high enough to nose in under a tarpaulin. I squirmed and wiggled, breathing grain dust from the sacks of grain, but I succeeded in working my way all the way in.

The next thing I knew, a man was pulling my feet. I'd fallen asleep, and it was daylight.

"Now look here, cobber," the brakie said, "The next time I catch you, I'll turn you over to the police." He released me, and I got under way.

This was Perth again, and I was hungry. I knew the Salvation Army was supposed to help the needy, and I headed straight there and applied at the window. "Sir," I said, "I'm hungry. Can I get something to eat here?"

"I guess you can have bread and tea," he said grudgingly, "D'you have sixpence?"

"No, sir," I said, wondering how the hell he'd ever come to sign up with a charitable organization. "But if you trust me for it, I'll come back here and pay you."

"Very well," he said coldly, "But be sure you do."

I finished devouring the meager repast very thoughtfully, and when I returned the cup and saucer I told the dour faced lieutenant I'd be back to pay him his sixpence — fast.

I left the place to stroll around town. Signs were posted all over town. "Enlist today for the King's light horse infantry for Egypt," they read, and lower down, "Every man who enlists today receives ten shillings! Fight with the Anzacs!"

The posters opened up a whole new train of thought. It would be a colorful new adventure, and — I could pay that s.b. his sixpence!

Owing for charity rankled sore within. A few more moments of pacing up and down and I walked straight up to the recruiting officer.

"I want to enlist," I said.

"Step right over here, lad, have a seat and be comfortable. Have a cigarette?" Here was welcome for fair!

"Good Lord!" exclaimed the recruiting officer as he read my application. "This man is a Yank!" He came over and grasped my hand strongly, "Yank, let me shake hands!"

They took me to dinner, or tucker, as they called it, then brought me back and I swore on a small Bible faith and allegiance to the King, George Fifth of England. I was given my ten shillings and told to report the next morning at eight. I made for the Salvation Army as soon as I was out.

"Here is your sixpence," I said to the surprised lieutenant who had never expected to see me again. "You know best what you can do with it." I was now in the Anzacs, a soldier of fortune, and all to pay for that miserable tea and bread. Well, so be it.

In the morning I reported to the recruiting officer and along with six other new recruits was put aboard a train for Black Boy Hill, the West Australian training center, and finally we pulled into the most desolate station imaginable and were marched to camp. We were lined up before the lieutenant commander. He looked over the papers, and when he got to mine he said, "Which one of you is the American?"

"I am, sir," I said proudly.

"My compliments for your noble spirit," he said sincerely. I felt like hell, remembering the Salvation Army.

He rang a bell, and an orderly entered. "Have these men billeted for the night, and turn them over to Sergeant-Major O'Donnell in the morning."

The next day we started training. Not even a pair of socks was issued to us new recruits. Those valiant men fought without all the trappings considered necessities by Uncle Sam's army. The British considered them luxuries.

I was shown into a large barracks and told it was for my troop. I wasn't given a mattress, blankets, or clothes.

For two weeks I trained in blue denims, carrying a wooden gun down the hot, sandy roads. Then came the days for final instructions for overseas. All new recruits were summoned to two pyramidal tents, told to be seated and listen for our names.

One by one the men were called. I was thinking of embarkation, riding a spirited steed over the burning sands of Egypt, firing away as I rode. I heard my name called.

"Theodore Burnett!"

"Yes, sir!" I snapped out of the tent and walked the ten feet to where an Australian army officer stood. I stood smartly at attention, and he looked at me. Two bluecoated Fremantle police officers stood beside him.

"Burnett," one of them said, "You are wanted by the law for deserting a British ship."

I was literally dumbfounded, then, "Well, gentlemen," I said, shrugging, "I guess that ends my army career."

The lieutenant commander was very nice. "Lad," he said, "I wish we had about two million Americans like you." He looked at the police, then, "I don't see how I can give this man a discharge, he's been a fine soldier. He's your man, though, no doubt about it." He extended his hand to me, and we shook hands regretfully in farewell.

When we reached the railroad station one officer departed, and I sat and talked with my lone guardian who obviously disliked his task. "I never hated a detail more than I do this one," he said earnestly, "Because you're not the type to go where I think you're going."

When we reached his home in Perth I was served tea, given all the fresh fruit I could eat, and shown into a pleasant guest room. The next morning we left for Fremantle.

Upon arrival we were met at the train by reporters, police, and the "pie wagon." I was put in it, the reporters joining me and my arresting officer, and I was taken before a Fremantle judge, called His Lordship in the British colonies. I was guilty of desertion, and in a British ship in time of war it was a serious offense.

I had no defense, nor did I attempt any. I rested on the mercy of the court.

His Lordship censured me severely, ending with "—and this man shall be confined in prison until his ship, the "William T. Lewis" is ready for sea, and at such time he will be taken aboard on sailing day."

I was being led away, almost before I realized it was over. Back into the pie wagon and out into the desert stretches outside Fremantle. Massive concrete walls loomed up after a short ride, then the main entrance came into view.

I was taken to the finger print room, afterward to a huge shower room, then, still bare-footed, to the clothes issue department and given moleskin clothes which were covered with the "crowfeet" brand of the British penal colony, and a cocky hat. Then I was led to a row of cells, shown into one, and the clanging of the iron bars as they were closed by the turnkey left no doubt that I was truly a prisoner.

At the end of my second week in gaol, I was told I had a visitor. I was escorted to the visitor's cage, and then I got a surprise.

There, big as life, sat Captain Manning.

"Hello, bos'un," he said, gravely.

"Hello, Captain Manning," I said, ashamed as hell.

"Bos'un," he said, looking at me intently, "Had I known they were going to send you up here, I wouldn't have pressed charges. You don't belong in this place." He eyed my straw hat with the ravelled edges, and the number on my coat. "The suit of a convict," he commented. "Would you like to get back to your ship?"

"Yes, sir," I said, very low, "I surely would."

"Knowing the sort of folks you hail from, I almost feel sorry for all this," he said, musingly, "Bos'un, if I get you out of here will you please give me your word of honor that you will go back to the ship and do your work like a man?"

"I give you my word of honor," I assured him gratefully. I wasn't thrilled at the prospect of rejoining the "William T. Lewis," but it was better than being a prisoner.

The warden stood close by the captain, and the skipper turned and said something to him, then turned to me.

"Bos'un," he said reassuringly, "You"ll be out of here today." He left then, and I was returned to my cell. Soon the turnkey came down the block and shoved his pass key in my door. "Burnett," he said, not unkindly.

"Yes, sir?"

"You are released. Follow me." I was taken to the superintendent's office. He looked at me curiously. "You have a great number of friends in West Australia," he observed.

"I have, sir?" I asked, truly surprised.

"When you leave here, read the papers," he said. "Good luck, boy. Go back to your ship. You're serving the empire there just as much as you would have in the army." We shook hands, and I was shown the way out, a trifle dazed.

On the ship I met the cook, the mate, and a few seamen. "Where's the crew?" I asked, baffled by the deserted appearance of the ship.

"They're safe until we sail," the mate said grimly. "From the second mate to the ordinary seamen—they're all in jail."

"No!" I exclaimed, shocked at the thought of fourteen men enduring the rigors of prison life as I had.

"Yes!" he echoed mockingly, "And you'd still be there, my fine lad, if it weren't for the people of Fremantle. Here—read the papers."

I read them avidly. It seemed that the police and the skipper between them had received about five hundred letters demanding my release, protesting the arrest of the Yank who had joined the light horse infantry only to be sent to prison.

I took the rest of the papers to the midship house for perusal. The headlines read "Prejudicing Recruiting," the subhead, "American Withdrawn from Australian Infantry." Excerpts stated that I had been interned in prison without redress, and the commander had stated he would like to have two million men with the same spirit. It didn't stir me one bit, for some obscure reason.

I worked along until Saturday. There was nothing more to do until Monday, and at two p.m. the skipper said, "Bos'un, I'll give you ten shillings."

"I'll be happy with that," I answered dutifully.

After supper I donned the best clothes I owned and went ashore, over the gangway to terra firma, thinking how wonderful it was to have liberty again. I strolled down the quay, and not a thousand feet away saw a great crowd.

As I drew closer I could see a ten thousand ton troopship, and she was loaded. A few more steps, and I could see her name. The "Indarra" of Sydney.

She was laden with troops that had been trained at Black Boy Hill, and were now bound, fully equipped, for Cairo, Egypt. Many were the mothers and sweethearts on that dock, and the tearfully blown kisses were a pitiful sight to see.

I was standing in front of the engine room port door, and the big iron door rolled back. Two of the men started to argue about firemen shortage, and it sounded as though some fireman hadn't shown up.

I looked around to see who knew me in that dense crowd. And, amongst all those faces, I spotted the mate with his inevitable T.D. pipe stuck in his mouth!

The two engineers went on talking. I took another glance to check on the mate, and he was standing pretty well back against the warehouse. The coast was clear, and much cheering was going on. I approached the two engineers and opened up with nice, soft-spoken words.

"I say, chief, won't I do? I'm not a fireman, but I can shovel coal."

"You look like a good man for the job," came the reply, "Come aboard."

"Just one minute," I answered. I glanced around in an apparently unconcerned manner, then I turned to the engineers. "I'm ready," I said, as though I'd just made up my mind.

"Okeh, lad, come aboard."

I took one quick step through the port door, and once aboard I was assigned to the twelve midnight to four a.m. watch. Capacity, coal passer.

I wouldn't show myself on deck, yet I talked freely enough with the other firemen. Every one of them said, "You're an American, aren't you?"

"What makes you think so?"

"Your lingo."

I had cigarettes, and just the clothes on my back. I could never have fired two boilers in those clothes, but the black gang came to my rescue with dungarees and old shoes. We sailed, and after that I dozed a bit, but I was too worried to sleep well. This, I knew, was the worst thing I had done.

At eleven that night I made ready for the watch, and headed for the mess room where the "black pan" was the best food I'd seen since starting to sea. Afterwards I took a stroll on deck.

I'll never know what possessed me to take that pierhead jump. All I knew was that I didn't want any part of the unrest that existed among the crew of the "William T. Lewis."

I finished my first watch in the fire room and it was a tough one, trying to keep up steam on my boiler, watching the experienced men handle theirs. The chief engineer sent for me a few hours later.

"Let's see," he said, as I entered his room, "Your name is Anderson."

"Yes, sir."

"Anderson, the second assistant reports to me that you are a splendid fireman and I've got good news for you. The captain is waiting for you to sign on. We'll go right up to his cabin, and it will only take a few minutes." He looked at me expectantly.

"Oh no, sir!" I exclaimed quickly, "I don't want to sign on. I only want to work my passage to Sydney!"

The captain spoke from behind me in the doorway, "Anderson, unless you want to sign on I will have to put you ashore at our next port of call, Albany. We are due there at nine o'clock this evening."

"No, captain," I said, still determined, "I don't want to sign on."

"All right," he rejoined curtly, "be ready to go ashore at Albany tonight."

When the "Indarra" dropped anchor that night the town looked dark, early as it was. The gangway was lowered, the landing barge approached slowly and was made fast. The purser was busy checking the list of passengers who were disembarking. He eventually reached my name.

"Anderson?" he called.

"Yes, sir," I replied.

"You're ready now?"

"Yes, sir."

"You may go, then," he said.

What little gear I had was in a small bundle, and I started down the gangway. As I did so, the purser called down to the barge.

"Your man is on his way down!" I looked ahead, and there in the barge were the blue-caped police of Australia!

There were two of them, from the mounted division.

"Good evening, sir," one of them said. "Isn't your name Burnett?"

[140]

"No, sir," I said, sounding as Norwegian as could be, "my name is Olaf Anderson. I'm from Horton, Norway, and sorry to be leaving that fine ship. But, you see, I scal not be a fireman. I make a better farmer." On I went, talking about the vast wheat fields around Northam that reminded me of Norway. And how they listened! Waiting for a slip-up!

"You're sure your name isn't Burnett?" asked the other, eyeing me narrowly.

"Vy you keep teenking my name is someting else?" I glared at them.

"We-ell," said the senior officer, "take him to the eggstone for a check-up." From up on deck came the call, "All aboard going ashore!" Our barge pulled away, and for a moment I wished heartily that I had signed on the "Indarra" as a fireman.

I went ashore, accompanied by my two police officers. We arrived at headquarters, and one of the men left while the other asked me to be seated. He went to his desk, sat down, and peered through a book.

"This description fits you perfectly," he said, at last. "All except for the fact you speak such good Scandinavian. Let me see, you want a place to sleep tonight, don't you?"

"Yah," I replied, grinning, "I vil sleep like one little pig!" I then launched into a story about falling into my grandfather's pig sty when I was a little boy, and I really put square edges on the story.

"Well," he said, when he was done laughing, "we have a nice little hotel across the street and we'll go over and find you a room."

The key to my room was at least six inches long and made of wood, and I was given a candlestick to take upstairs as a light. Oh, that was not a new hotel! I bade goodnight to my police escort at the door of my room.

"Sleep well," he said heartily, "and don't worry about the time!"

Yes, I thought to myself, the more time you have to identify me the better. It was about midnight, then.

I lay down on the bed, then noticed there were two windows. I started planning then, for I had no intention of being caught again. I rested for about an hour, then decided that was rest enough for the wicked — who should have no rest at all!

I gathered up my few belongings and turned toward the windows. They weren't fastened, and moved up easily. I looked outside, and what a desolate scene met my eyes! This was one of the last parts of Australia to be settled, and it looked it. There was a low fence between the hotel and the road, and then and there I decided on my course.

One leg out, then the other, a short drop, over the fence and I was headed up the long, dark road. The hike was on.

I hiked all night, and by morning was fourteen miles away. I came upon a small ranch house and knocked on the door.

The woman and her husband who lived there were Irish settlers, and I told them a part of my story. The main gist of it was that I was hungry. They gave me a fine breakfast, talking meanwhile of Ireland, the Sinn Feiners, and the raid in Cork. When I told them I was of Irish parentage they were delighted, and even more so when I said I was an American.

"You look worried," said Mrs. White.

"I am," I said truthfully.

"Don't worry," she said kindly. "We know your whole story." I looked at her, startled, but saw no cause for alarm.

"Have no fear, lad," how motherly she sounded! "You get some rest. I'll kill a chicken, and this evening after dark when you've eaten your fill you take the road. The next place you come to belongs to Mr. Cronin, and although you have to pass through jarra forest you'll make it by dawn."

I slept soundly until about five, when Mr. White wakened me for tea. Again I was plied with excellent food, and afterwards was offered the use of Mr. White's razor.

"Don't be afraid of kangaroos," they chorused as I left them that night. "But, if you're bothered by dingos, just light a black boy." A black boy was a stunted tree of the pine family, growing only about six feet high, its top bristling into a needle shape filled with pitch. I really didn't care to advertise my whereabouts with a blazing fire.

A mile or so away from their place I heard what sounded like the braying of mules. I was startled, but I walked on, telling myself there were probably farms close by.

Then I heard new sounds. They sent a cold chill up my back. Thud, thud, thud! Never in my life had I heard anything like it. In the brush, all about me, I could hear heavy creatures hopping—and it came to me at once. Kangaroos!

"Don't be afraid of kangaroos," the Whites had said. "They're inquisitive, but they won't bother you." I pushed on, hoping they were right.

The break of dawn was a welcome sight. Strange birds fluttered here and there, and ahead was a great clearing. I was tired, and I must have missed Cronin's place, for I hiked all day without seeing a dwelling. That night I saw a beam of light. I came to a split rail gate, and could discern the dim outline of a barn. I didn't stop to wonder if the settler had kangaroo dogs or not. I groped my way toward the barn, found a buckboard wagon in the wagon shed adjoining, and crawled into it. There was a tarpaulin in it, and this I pulled over me. Then I slept, or died. I couldn't have gone another hundred yards.

At sunrise someone shook my feet violently. I woke, and backed out of my makeshift bed to be confronted by a man, obviously the owner. "Well, who are you?" he sounded hostile.

"I'm just on my way to the next sheep station and I crawled in here because I was tired," I said.

"You've quite a way to go," he commented sourly. No offer of tea or food was made, so I drank all the water I could, thanked him for the rest I'd had in his wagon, and was on my way.

By sundown I reached the next sheep station. Witcomb was the name on the mailbox, and the people were nice.

"Know anything about farming?" the man asked.

"Not much," I admitted truthfully, "but I could learn."

"Yankee?" he asked.

"Yes, sir."

"And you want work." It was a statement, not a question.

"Yes, sir." He seemed satisfied, for he asked me no more questions.

I was shown into a stall next to the one occupied by Tilly the horse, and the people gave me two blankets, lots of hay, and a clean feed bag to fill with hay for a pillow. If I hadn't been so tired, I would have whinnied.

Eight pounds a month wages, no place to spend it, and no place to go! A bit of this and I'd be able to get back to the good old U.S.A., and never again would I sell out my birthright!

One evening I spotted a mountie coming down the road on a sleek black horse. His blue cape was very visible.

"Hey you!" he called. "Young fellow! I want to speak to you! How long have you been here?"

"About a month, maybe more," I lied coolly.

"Sure you're telling the truth?"

"Why should I tell anything else?" I parried.

We both stood by the pig sty, he having dismounted, and the ten little suckling pigs clamored loudly for their food. The mountie reached down to scratch one of the pigs.

"I'm looking for a fellow by the name of Burnett," he said, carefully not looking at me, "Are you sure that's not your name?"

"My name is Thomas Kelly, sor," I announced with a rich brogue, "and proud I am of the name!"

"All right," he said, "don't get mad."

"Sure and the Irish never took a prize for the length of their tempers," I said touchily.

"Well," he said, straightening, "I'll stop at the house anyway, and have a talk with your boss."

"Go ahead, if you've a mind to," I said, reaching down for my pails, "they'll be telling you everything."

I waited a bit, petting the little pigs after dumping them their food, my eyes focused on the mountie who was now entering the driveway about five hundred yards down the road. Once he had started talking to Mrs. Witcomb, I made a mad dash for the fields of maize.

How I ran! I panted with fright as I finally crouched low among the cornstalks, not daring to move a muscle. From five that afternoon until dark, when the kangaroos started hopping, I stayed motionless, close to the ground. When I thought it was dark enough I crept slowly to the cow barns and saw Witcomb standing close by the light of an oil lantern. I whistled softly and he heard me.

"He's gone," he called, and I stepped cautiously toward him, wary as a hunted animal. "He's gone, but he'll be back, and if you don't want to get caught you better clear out. Here, take this money." He handed me two pound notes.

I said goodbye, waved my hand, and stepped out into the road, and hiked until two the next afternoon without rest. I came to a bridge over a brook, washed my face and hands and drank thirstily. Then I sat down on the makeshift bridge and fell asleep sitting up.

"Hello," said a girl's voice. "Hello!"

I rubbed my eyes and looked up. There, on horseback, sat a little girl about twelve years old.

"Are you sick?" she asked sweetly.

"No, just tired and hungry."

"Wait here," she said quickly, "I'll be back."

She was back in a very short time. She had a kettle of rich cow's milk, a can of beef drippings and a loaf of bread, and she put them down before me neatly.

"Eat all you want," she said in her clear child's voice, "then mama wants you to come home with me."

I ate my fill, then we went at least a mile and came suddenly into a clearing in which stood a three-sided barn and a small house. A mother and eight children sat outside watching us approach.

Her name, she said, after greeting me kindly, was Mrs. Quimlan. I looked at the eight children, some toddlers.

"Madame," I asked, "where is your husband?"

"He is a colonel in the Australian army," she said, her eyes filling with tears. "Would you stay and work here?" she asked hopefully. "I need help desperately." Her sad gaze encompassed her brood.

"I have to be on my way," I said regretfully. "I don't know enough about farming to help you, and I'd only be another mouth to feed."

"There's a returned soldier about five miles from here," she said, once she made certain she couldn't prevail upon me to stay. "His leg is shot off, and he needs help, but I'm sure he can't afford to pay any wages."

"I don't care about the wages," I said. "All I want is a place to sleep and three square meals a day. I better look up this pegleg soldier."

She fixed me up with a fine pack lunch, gave me the directions to the soldier's place, and I looked at all those kiddies and wondered if any war could be important enough to take their daddy away from them.

Once I reached the edge of the road I hadn't gone two miles when I saw a horse and wagon coming. "Hello, there!" shouted the driver, spotting me. It was the one-legged soldier.

I stepped out into the road then, told him of seeing Mrs. Quimlan, and introduced myself. His name was Clayton Smith, and he wasn't more than my age.

We talked, and I agreed to help him, with no pay for my services. He wanted me to ride back with him, but I refused. No telling where that mountie might be.

Late that evening he came back for me on the wagon trail. I hopped aboard, and we talked the rest of the way in. The two acres he and his wife lived on was a grant given to all returned wounded soldiers, and it had taken them six months to clear it of brush. Their home was a covered wagon.

They had a small shack they called their kitchen, and my room was a tent and two blankets. The whole place was enclosed by a six-foot fence.

"Why the tall fence?" I asked curiously.

"Even that doesn't always keep the kangaroos out," he said ruefully. "And they eat every crop you raise if they're not kept out."

There were no lamps or candles. When it got dark there was nothing to do but turn in, sleepy or not. That first night I awoke to the now familiar thudding and jumping. It sounded as though six kangaroos were doing a war dance around my tent.

For two weeks I stayed with the Smiths, roughing it in the heart of the jarra forest. Then one day I told them I was ready to make the break back to Fremantle, where I knew there would be a ship waiting for me. How I would get aboard without being apprehended I didn't know. I only knew the time had come to try.

Smithy generously rigged me up in clothes, gave me food, a blanket, two cans of Capstan tobacco and paper, and drove me out to the lone sand road leading to civilization. We gripped hands in a silent handclasp. The brief friendship had been a rewarding one.

"Away with ye, lad!" he called as I trudged away into the darkness. "And good luck!"

IT TOOK ONE LONG WEEK TO REACH ALBANY, AND ONCE THERE I WENT straight to the recruiting office and pleaded with the sergeant-major to sign me up.

"Yank," he said kindly, "I'll sign you up, and if you don't make it to camp, just forget it They're after you hot and heavy, lad. I know you, and all about you!"

With all my papers in order I boarded the train. Leaving was delayed, and passengers around me started murmuring uneasily. "I understand they're looking for someone," said one, and I felt cold clear through.

Three police officers reached our compartment, looked at us carefully, and one said, "These laddies are bound to Black Boy Hill. 'Ave yer all yer army papers?"

"Yes, sir," said one of the recruits.

"All right, lads," and they smiled and withdrew.

"Funny," I heard one of them mutter as they made their departure, "I would have sworn he got on this train."

The station master gave the whistle signal to start the train, the gates closed, and the cars began to roll, gradually gathering speed. The click of the wheels sounded like music, but I still had to face the conductor. He came along presently, sharp-eyed, scrutinizing everybody and every bit of luggage. My ticket was for Black Boy Hill, but at Fremantle I left the train to get a cup of tea. I did not come back.

I slipped out of the Fremantle station, headed for the water front, the same dock where the "William T. Lewis" loaded grain. She was gone, praise be, and in her berth lay the "Carrabin" of London, a beautiful four-masted bark.

I went aboard and asked the mate if he needed any men. "I need a bos'un," he said shortly.

"I can take that job, sir. I was bos'un of the "William T. Lewis." I was staking my all.

"Oh, yes!" he said, aroused. "She sailed just two days ago. So you were the bos'un?"

"Yes, sir," I said, quaking inwardly.

"What is your name?" he asked.

"I'll be honest with you, sir," I said. "I'll have to give you a fictitious name, and lay low until sailing."

"Well," he said, "I'll give you one man to help. Now come along and meet the skipper, Captain Richards."

The skipper was about twenty-eight, and hailed from London. He introduced me to the second mate, Mr. Moody. The mate's name was Mr. Black.

"What's your name?" asked the skipper.

"Thomas Kelley of Boston," I replied.

"That's odd!" he exclaimed. "We now have two Kellys on the articles. I'll call you bos'un. Your wages will be twelve pounds a month, and, as near as we know, our sailing orders are for London, England. You will pay off there."

We all shook hands, the skipper opened a bottle, and the third mate came in, a Mr. Taylor, and was introduced. I had never encountered a finer crew aboard any ship.

Early next morning the tug took us in tow for Bunbury, and it was a hundred miles from Fremantle. I relaxed a bit when we got under way.

Once tied up at Bunbury I was given orders to put the full crew on painting the ship a battleship grey from truck to waterline.

We were loading railroad ties for France where trench warfare was going full blast. Supplies had to be brought to the front, and to do this they needed railroad ties. This said in effect that we were to run the U-boat blockade. . . .

My crew worked well. We even got the ship tarred down. She was two thousand, five hundred and ninety-seven tons net, English tonnage, and was a captured German ship, previously the "Susanne Vinnen" of Bremen.

A couple of days before we were to set sail, Mr. Black called to me from aft. "Bos'un!" he yelled, "square up the decks and muster all the crew on the port side of the mainmast."

"Yes, sir!" Inside of forty-five minutes our decks resembled those of a battleship. Then I shouted, "Muster all hands abreast the main fife rail, port side!"

All hands responded on the double, and along came Mr. Black, the second mate, the third mate with him. Mr. Black was spokesman.

"Men," he said, "you are all acquainted with the facts of war. This is a cargo bound to aid England and her allies, yet one of you men has done some talking uptown. I know who it was, and I could point him out. But, instead, all of you will be deprived because of this one man. To make this clear, one of you said in the Blue Goose Tavern that you would clear out one night before sailing. So, now your shore leave has been stopped. Is that plain?"

I looked at the mates, then at the crew.

"What's the matter?" I shouted. "Can't you speak?" There was never a word.

"Well, then," I said, "I'll speak for you! Mr. Mate, this isn't fair to a good crew like this. Furthermore, if we do have a yellow streak in this crew, point him out and we'll give him the fastest trip down that gangway that he or any other man could wish for. Won't you reconsider, sir?"

"The order stands, bos'un," Mr. Black said firmly.

"All right, sir." I turned to the men, "You men have heard that order."

It developed that the order did not apply to bos'un, and the second and third mates were trying to tell me so with eloquent glances.

"I'm not taking this kind of treatment!" I announced hotly, "And after tucker I'm going ashore, and any man who wants to go ashore, just follow me!"

"Bos'un," warned the mate, "as chief officer of this ship I'm telling you that if any member of the crew goes ashore, the police will greet you at the head of the pier. Is that understood?"

"Yes, sir."

"All right, that'll do, men. Supper."

After supper, when the men were ready, they came to my room. "Are you ready, bos'un?" I turned, and there stood twelve men.

"All right! There are thirteen of us, right?"

"Right!"

"Let's go, then."

Over the gangway we went, every one of us singing, while the three mates lined the poop deck railing watching for events to come.

Their coup was well planned. The dock in Bunbury was about six or seven hundred feet long with railroad tracks the length of it, the docks being built out and parallel with the shore. We hopped from tie to tie, singing lustily. That is, until we reached the end of the dock.

There stood a couple of pie wagons and about six policemen. As we arrived, the iron doors opened, we were told to get in, so we all piled into the two wagons and off to jail we went, where we were all thrust into one large cell and snugly locked up.

We all sang, laughed, and raised hell in general, and the echoing wall of the prison added to the noise. We were given blankets, and when we finally stretched out on the floor to sleep we weren't more than two inches apart, all thirteen of us sleeping in a straight line so that the blankets would cover all of us.

Sunday passed quietly, and Monday morning a squad of police, each equipped with a pair of handcuffs, arrived. The gates opened, and we were all shackled together and into the pie wagon we went.

Big Pat Kelly looked at the handcuffs, then at us.

"Bos'un," he said disgustedly, "when we get aboard will you join me in wishing Captain Richards a passage of one hundred and fifty days and then a torpedo? Are you with me?"

"With you!" I exclaimed fervently. "I'd like to convey the same wish!"

The pie wagons eventually came to a stop, and the doors were opened. "All right, men, get out!"

We trudged down the dock to where the "Carrabin" lay, all singled up with a tow boat made fast to her, ready to go. Our handcuffs were removed one at a time as each man stepped over the gangway.

I was bitter to the extreme at this treatment, and big Pat Kelly's face showed he could have torn a man in half. The skipper stood at the poop deck, leaning on the rail.

We drew up at the break of the poop, and I looked at Kelly.

"Bos'un," he said, in his broad Irish, "ye can give him the first broadside. I'll take it from there."

"Captain Richards," I said clearly, "Kelly and I thought it only proper to come back here and pay our respects, for we love this ship and will act aboard her like men, but you and your mates take a good look at that dock now with its people waiting for you to let go all. Believe me, captain, this is the last time the "Carrabin" will leave any dock." I turned to Kelly, "All right, Kelly, now I'm through."

"Now it's me speakin', captain! I only want to wish you a five-month passage, then a fine, well-polished German torpedo. Thank you, sir."

The skipper offered no reply, but ordered to "Let 'er all go!"

Twenty miles into the Indian Ocean and our tug blew to stand by, and shortly afterwards a long and two shorts. By this time every sail was set, and the "Carrabin" looked like the proud ship she was. A farewell salute and we were on our way.

The men mustered aft, and a silence fell over ship and crew as Captain Richards descended from the poop deck and stationed himself between his men and the mates. He was not the sort you could go on disliking, for he was a gentleman.

"Men," he said quietly, "we are now under way, bound for the continent. This can be a happy ship if you want it that way. Now, are there any grudges?"

Five or six of us replied in kind, "No, sir!"

"That's what I wanted to hear," said the skipper, smiling at us. "And lastly, I ask you men not to waste food. There will be full and plenty, but what you have left, take back to the galley. The slopchest will be opened every Saturday night at six. Stores and rum will be issued to the watches every Saturday morning. That's all, men."

I lost my rating of bos'un, and went into the foc'sle, pausing first to admire the way every sail fitted like a "Ratsey." I walked in, and the gang shouted, "Hello, bos'un!"

"Hey, you gang!" I returned, "I'm just as happy sleeping in this foc'sle with you as I was working with you." A big cheer went up, and we all grinned at each other.

I picked a bunk and went to work fixing up shelves and cans for my whack. As the saying goes on British ships—

> "Lime juice and cracker hash
> According to the Act
> So what's the use of growling
> If you know you get your whack—"

Our whack was sugar, jam, milk in condensed form, and lime juice. These we put in containers we could find around the galley, keeping our individual stores over our bunks.

Our ship routine went on day after day with nothing to break the monotony until one night when I was on lookout.

We were somewhere off Madagascar, and about four points off the starboard I could see small white clouds along the western horizon. I walked to and fro on the foc'sle head, sniffing the change in the air. It was a beautiful moonlight night, and the clarity of the air to the westward was plainly apparent. It worried me, for we were flying along on port tack with all sail set.

The little clouds kept coming up over the horizon, gaining in altitude. I looked aft on the poop deck, and there was Mr. Moody, smoking his pipe peacefully and looking over the rail. I wished that he or our watch officer would think of looking at the barometer, for I had the uneasy feeling it would show a distinct rise. I knew, too, that it was not my place as an A.B. to say anything.

Already my right cheek was picking up the change in temperature, and if I'd been up on that poop deck I would have had everything secure. What was coming was a "southerly buster" a storm of gale force that comes off the east coast of Africa, and when it hits it means business!"

At five bells our wind seemed to die down though there was still enough to keep her full, yet the orders I hoped for from the poop deck still weren't given. A few minutes later the buster struck without warning, stopping us dead in our tracks, caught full a-back with all sail set, and the strain so great I looked for anything to happen.

All hands were out on deck within a few seconds, the skipper, mates, both watches—all on the double. One sail after another came in, but it was touch and go by the time we got to the upper tops'ls.

"Kelley!" Mr. Black called, meaning me.

"Yes, sir!"

"I know you're no longer bos'un," he said, biting his lip, "but I'm depending on you for everything up aloft. Make sure it's all secure, will you?"

"Yes, sir," I said, alert to the danger at hand, "I'll do just that."

There was a lot of hard work before the "Carrabin" paid off, and for the next seventy-two hours we were hove to in a gale with squalls that bore the big ship down to port and held her there.

Four days later our gale freshened, though the sun shone brightly and the sky was blue. The "Carrabin" was first one rail under then the other—a metronome keeping time to the furious tempo set by wind and sea.

At ten-thirty that morning we observed Mr. Black peering intently through his binoculars at something off the port quarter. About five miles away we could descry smoke. It meant but one thing. A raider.

Captain Richards brought out a powerful telescope, and we waited in silence while he focused his glass. Our visitor was now on our port beam, bearing directly ahead.

"Mr. Black," said the skipper imperatively, "call all hands."

The captain again focused his telescope on the steamer. She was now two points off the starboard bow. He turned to us, looking grave.

"Men," he said quietly, "The orders I'm about to give you are war orders. I want you men to get everything you value in the way of papers, and strap yourselves into life preservers. I'll give you five minutes. Now, get started!" He turned away, putting the telescope up again.

We all wondered as we went for'ard if our unknown visitor could be the "Emden" or the "Wolf," for both German raiders were on the loose. The thought speeded up in getting our things together and mustering back aft.

"Bos'un," said the skipper, "Did you tell the cook?"

"No, sir," said the bos'un.

"What the hell do you intend doing?" asked Captain Richards tensely, "Leave him behind?" The cry went up for the cook, while the captain chafed at the delay. Then, "Bos'un, clear away both life boats!"

Mr. Smyth, the steward, stood on the flying bridge between the two life boats like a man in a trance. He seemed bemused.

"Steward," said the skipper sternly, startling him from his reverie, "Have the boats food and water?"

"I—I really don't know, sir," Smyth said vaguely.

"Well, you damned idiot," said Captain Richards explosively, "See to it that we're equipped!"

The strange ship was looming closer, the gale force unabated. The skipper watched closely, a calculating expression growing in his tense face. "Mr. Black," he said suddenly, "I suspect this fellow to windward is jockeying into position for gunfire. We have just one other chance aside from the life boats, and that is to run for it. Can she take it?"

"She can," said Mr. Black proudly.

"Then here's the layout," said the skipper rapidly, "Divide your men. Get the fores'l, and the mains'l on first—then your upper tops'ls, then the lower to'gallants, and there can't be one hitch or delay. It's a matter of life and death."

Each of us was given a job, and a strong man to the wheel. Then came feverish activity.

"Mr. Black, four men loosen the fores'l, the rest of you square the cro'j'k yard."

"Be quick, men!" said Mr. Black urgently, "When your sail is loose, shout out 'Sheet 'er Home!' and jump to your next sail. We men on deck will square the yards and set the sails."

"Let 'er go off easy!" cautioned the skipper. The seas were full thirty feet high, and the men at the wheel had to cling hard to the spokes.

Boom!! The first shot came at us. It was high and wide. The "Carrabin" was now picking up speed, the taffrail log now showing nine knots.

We could only see the raider when the giant seas lifted both ships at the same time. Another shot rocketed at us, and it was much too close for comfort.

"Sheet home fore upper tops'l, sheet home main upper tops'l!" Now the fleet-winged "Carrabin" was doing a full twelve knots. So much sail on her could mean suicide in that gale, yet, risk or no, we were running away from the raider.

"Mr. Black!" shouted Captain Richards from the poop deck. He looked arrogant, fighting mad.

"Loosen the main lower t'gallant!"

"Blow me down, sir!" ejaculated Mr. Black, aghast, "D'you think it wise, sir?"

"We're in this together," the skipper said, "Let's stay friends. Loosen the main lower t'gallant!" Again he looked challengingly in the direction of the raider.

"Yes, sir," said Mr. Black, a note of admiration in his rough voice. This was the way clipper ships had sailed, and our fighting skipper would have held his own with any of them.

"Jump aloft, a couple of hands," called Mr. Black, "Loosen main to'gallant! The rest of you stand by to sheet 'er home!" The faces of the men were something to see.

"Sheet home to'gallant!" came the cry, and now the "Carrabin" cut water at fourteen knots, straining like a thoroughbred horse for the finish line. This was driving, reckless driving, and our lives were forfeit if she couldn't take it. "Loosen the royals—sheet home royals!" What a sight it was! All sails set in a gale of tempest force!

For twenty-four hours we ran that way, and for twenty-four hours we never saw our bunks. It was a wild, desperate ride we had, but in the end it was worth it, for we lost our raider.

When we hit the last of the southeast trades in the South Atlantic we sighted a three masted bark. We hoisted our British ensign, and up went the Danish ensign on the bark.

"Let's visit her," said Captain Richards.

The port boat was made ready, and I made sure I was in the boarding party. About nine of us went along, and as the sea was like glass we pulled up under the stern of what was the "Falkatina" of Copenhagen, Denmark, in half an hour.

We were given a rousing welcome. Up the Jacob's ladder we went, shaking hands as we came aboard, and every one of us treated like visiting royalty. We were served hot coffee, cigarettes, and a couple of well-wrapped bottles of liquor were presented to our captain. We were given books, newspapers, and magazines. It was very nice, also puzzling.

I listened as the captain of the "Falkatina" spoke to Mr. Moody, our second mate. "You can tell your captain he can proceed safely right to the mouth of the Thames," he said earnestly, "The submarines have been cleared away." Mr. Moody listened attentively, but made little comment. A little later we said farewell and headed back to our ship.

Our visit over, the "Carrabin" went on her way, all going well until about twenty degrees north of the equator when we sighted a large steamer. We were full'n by, and we ran our colors up promptly as did the steamer, the "Lord Strathcona" of London. She came alongside smoothly, and the two skippers talked to each other through their megaphones.

"Greetings, captain of the bark 'Carrabin', came from the bridge of the steamer. "Where are you bound?"

"Greetings to you," replied Captain Richards, "We're bound for London."

"Have you run across a Danish ship?"

"Yes, sir, we spoke her down in the doldrums."

"Was her name the 'Falkatina'?"

"Yes, sir," said the skipper, "Her skipper told us the English Channel is now clear."

"Captain!" came booming from the megaphone, "I have sealed orders from the British Admiralty for use in the conveyance of orders to British ships only. Will you take these orders?"

"Yes, sir," said Captain Richards.

"Proceed to parallel sixty degrees north latitude and follow in to point of interception with British patrol. The English Channel is impregnable. Keep away!" The "Lord Strathcona" dipped her flag and was off.

"Shocking!" muttered Captain Richards. No wonder the alleged Danish ship had treated us so royally!

Now the days went by quickly, and about twenty-five degrees north latitude it was all hands on deck to change a full set of sails from tropic to heavy weather. Every chance he had, the skipper had all sail on her, and how the "Carrabin" responded! She sailed as though she knew her life depended on her speed, and that any moment a submarine could spell her doom.

The morning of August eighth the cry "Land ho!" came from the lookouts. They had sighted the Irish coast, and an hour later we picked up the patrol ship. As it came closer we learned that it was the "Anthony Aslette" of Grimsby, England.

"Where are you bound, skipper?" they megaphoned.

"Admiralty orders, sixty degrees north latitude, orders received from the 'Lord Strathcona'."

"Very well, sir. The land you see ahead is the Old Head of Kinsale,

Queenstown, Ireland. I am your convoy, Captain Richards, and will stand by you right into Queenstown."

Land was just ten miles away, right through Admiral von Tirpitz' favorite burial ground for Allied ships and their much needed cargoes.

Shortly after we had spoken our escort, the cook complained that he needed coal. "I've got to have coal. Your men were supposed to give me coal yesterday. Now, do I get it or not?" His nerves were as frayed as ours. "I don't give a damn, but if you want to eat, rustle up that coal!"

"All right, cook," said the bos'un good-naturedly, "Don't get your pressure up." Just then our escort called.

"Ahoy! Captain Richards! Get your life boats ready and have your men stand by! There's a submarine lurking nearby, so be quick and ready!"

The wind was light, as is always the case once under land, and there we lay, full'n by, just eight miles from the Old Head of Kinsale. A towboat would have been a mighty welcome sight, but the Navy hadn't sent one.

We'd been wearing lifebelts the past two weeks, but now, in sight of land, we'd taken them off. It seemed unbelievable that anything could happen when we were so close.

The life boats now swung ready for lowering, and we were wondering if we'd have to use them when a quarrel broke out amidships. It was the cook and the bos'un again, going at it hot and heavy.

"I'm trying to tell you, you damn fool," the bos'un shouted ferociously. "Any minute may be our last—and you're worrying your thick head about that damned coal!" The coal was 'tween decks in the fore hold, number one hatch.

The only way I can get coal for that bloomin' stove of yours," the bos'un continued, glaring balefully, "Is by calling for a volunteer. I'm not wilfully sending a man to his doom for you or anybody else!" He turned to us, "Will any of you men volunteer to get coal for the cook's stove?"

"I will!" I shouted, "If another will go with me."

One of the apprentices, named Woolsey, volunteered to go along, and away we went for'ard where we tossed a few hatches off number one hold and slid a ladder down to 'tween decks.

Woolsey got the buckets and a heaving line with clip hooks and down I went. I wasn't there for two minutes when there was a terrific explosion, a roaring boom, and the "Carrabin" shook violently from stem to stern!

I dropped everything and headed for the ladder, thanking God that it hadn't moved during the explosion. Debris was still falling as I reached deck. I ran for the midship house to get my papers, and I had my right foot lifted to step over the twenty-inch threshold when some inner voice warned me not to cross. Instead, I turned and ran for the port lifeboat.

I shot across the deck to the previously appointed boat station, the bow fall on the port lifeboat. I couldn't see the bow, but I could see the stern almost two blocks, the bow down in the water. About eighteen men were clinging to the thwarts and the bow of the "Carrabin" was now under water, the ship listing heavily to starboard.

Eight or nine of us stood on the tilting deck, our feet in the water. I figured quickly that the "Carrabin," when full, would right herself and free the port lifeboat, and I took a strain on the bow fall.

It was a moment that had to be timed. The "Carrabin" lowered, and, the next instant, the "Carrabin" started her final dreadful plunge!

Those last thirty seconds seemed an eternity as we scrambled madly down the boat falls into our one remaining boat. The skipper was the last to leave his beloved ship, and there were tears in his eyes as he took one last look at her.

She was going fast now, and I got into the lifeboat barefoot. There were twenty-nine of us in that boat, and we were barely twenty-feet from the hull of the ship. The cro'j'k yard was under water, and last of all we saw the British ensign fluttering a farewell as the "Carrabin" vanished forever.

It had been just two and a half minutes from the time the torpedo hit us until the final disappearance of the ship.

16

The "anthony aslette" came up alongside, her commander out on the wing of the bridge with his megaphone.

"How many men are missing, captain?" he shouted.

I craned my neck to check the crew. "Kelly is missing, sir!" I shouted.

Captain Richards made a quick survey and found that I was correct.

"One man is missing!" he shouted back, "He was letting go the starboard boat when the torpedo went off!"

"It's all right, captain," came the heartening answer, "We have your man in the engine room."

We all felt relieved that Kelly was safe, but the desire to get out of that lifeboat was stronger even than interest in a shipmate's welfare. Right then we were nothing more than human decoys for the U-boat that had sunk our ship. We were a perfect floating target.

The "Anthony Aslette" had fired two six inch guns and dropped a couple of depth charges as soon as the "Carrabin" had been struck, but the marauder had gotten away and there was no telling whether he was waiting, submerged, to finish the job.

"Captain," boomed the commander of the patrol boat, "When I come around again you'll find life lines hanging over the starboard side. Your men will have to grab them and scramble aboard as best they can, for we are not stopping. Is that plain, captain?"

"Aye," shouted Captain Richards.

Toward us she came, about twenty lines with knots dropped over her side. She was taking a cruel chance to rescue us, but on she came fearlessly, and we were on her in no time, and away. Not however, before the commander of the ship had headed back for the lifeboat and gone through it.

"Why destroy the lifeboat?" Captain Richards asked.

"Well," said the commander grimly, "Just for a short time lifeboats weren't destroyed. Then a Yankee destroyer headed full speed for what appeared to be a lifeboat with unconscious men lying in it. A U-boat had a bead on the lifeboat, using it for a decoy, and as the destroyer crossed the range they fired a torpedo and every man in the crew went down with the ship. Since then we all have orders to sink all empty lifeboats."

Bottles of Scotch and packages of cigarettes were offered us by the rescue crew. To us, those rugged men looked like ministering angels, and we would have fought anyone who found the idea amusing.

We went, a few at a time, to see Kelly down in the engine room. He lay there looking ghastly, in a state of shock. The torpedo had gone off directly under the starboard boat where he had been stationed and it was a miracle that he was alive at all. We tried to act as usual with him, but it was hard with those pain brightened eyes on us.

We made it safely to Queenstown where we piled ashore, almost ready to kiss the soil of Ireland, it looked so good to us.

We thanked the crew of the "Anthony Aslette" again, then were taken to a sailor's boarding house where we were lodged. We looked like a shipwrecked crew, for we had nothing but the clothes on our backs, and many like myself were barefoot. At least twenty of us hadn't managed to save our papers and were without any sort of identification at all.

That night we were fed steak and Irish potatoes, tea and tarts, and God bless the Irish was uppermost in our minds. To be warm, to be fed, to be safe—who said you have to die before reaching heaven?

Captain Richards returned from town later that evening and gave each of us five pounds to buy ourselves necessities such as razors, shoes, tobacco and the like.

We took our money and headed for a pub, thinking we'd have a bit of gaiety after a hundred and fifty-two days of sailing, then being torpedoed to boot. A couple of hours in the pub, though, and we had to admit we were too tired to enjoy it. We reluctantly went back to crawl between clean sheets, and fell asleep almost before we had time to comment on the luxury of putting our weary heads on fresh pillowcases.

After dinner the next day we were called into the foc'sle of the boarding house while Captain Richards held the floor.

"I want you to listen carefully to the following orders," he said tersely, "At ten p.m. we leave here by train for Rosslare, Ireland, and there we embark for Fishguard, Wales. You're not to know the name of the ship nor when she sails. At all times stay together, and I will have no drinking amongst you. At Fishguard you entrain for London's Paddington Station, and until all ship business is finished you will stay at the Aldgate Hotel in Aldgate. The British Admiralty will award the sum of ten pounds to each man for his personal losses at sea. Any questions?" No one spoke, for he had covered his subject with typical thoroughness.

"That's all then, men." He left, accompanied by his mates.

At the appointed time we were taken to the station where we boarded the train. At Cork we had to change trains, and as we waited for our train I had my first view of the troop trains loading soldiers. All about stood Irish maids with shawl-covered heads, weeping as they bid their lads farewell. These lads were bound for France.

We pulled into Rosslare about two in the morning. We walked to the docks in the dark, and I could barely make out the hull of our ship. She was an ocean liner converted into a troopship, her portholes and windows blacked out.

Thousands of boys were boarding the gangway, then we were called. As we came over the top we were each given a life preserver and told to put it on and keep it on.

Cockney and I went to the lounge, and what a sight greeted our eyes! Troops were asleep all over, and also all over the deck, propped up against each other with not an inch to spare. There was no place to sit down, so out we went and paced to the bow of the ship. I peered over and saw she had a mine sweeper on her bow, and I felt sick within. The water slapping against the hull sounded like the mingled tears of the nations at war.

"Come on, Cock," I said, trying to throw off my gloom, "Let's go down to the dining salon and eat."

"Gawd blime," he protested, drawing back in alarm, "I'm not swank enough to eat in that place!"

"Cock, let me tell you something," I said, "You're my guest and I'm inviting you. I've got the money, so come on, shipmate!" It seemed to me that a lack of education shouldn't debar him from accepting a Yank's hospitality. After all, the Yank in question had run away from school.

He accepted then, eager anticipation lighting up his face. We ate and drank, and while we were thus engaged our ship, "The Duke of Connaught," as we discovered by reading the name on our lifebelts, quietly slipped out to cross the Irish sea.

We landed safely the next morning and found our train waiting. Captain Richards went around reminding us we were travelling second class, but Cock, by that time, was feeling so emancipated that he led me to a first class coach.

Sitting opposite were an elderly couple who soon engaged us in conversation. They were so kind and gracious because we were torpedoed seamen I could feel a glow in the regions of my heart. The glow travelled right on up to my face as I looked up and saw the conductor approaching.

"Tickets, may I see your tickets, please?"

Cock never said a word, his bravery having deserted him. The elderly couple produced their tickets, then, as the conductor still waited, the silence grew embarrassing.

"We're riding with our captain," I told the waiting conductor finally, "He has our tickets."

"It seems to me that you lads are in the wrong coach," the conductor said, not unkindly, "And if you stay in it, I'll have to charge you for it."

"We won't have any money until we get to London," I said, feeling cheap as could be.

"Well," he said, kindly, "You'll have to change to second class, then."

"Oh, please," spoke up the old couple, having exchanged glances, "Let us pay the extra fare."

"As you wish, madame," the conductor said. "It'll be five pounds, five shillings." They paid, and off he went, shaking his head uncomprehendingly.

That afternoon we reached Paddington Station, and after saying goodbye to the elderly couple, Cock and I joined the crew. In sailor fashion we followed the captain and we had barely reached the street when the air raid sirens started blowing.

People ran in every direction, trams were abandoned and vehicles left standing as their drivers scattered for cover. None of us had ever experienced an air raid before, and we made no attempt to get out of the street until our skipper herded us into a nearby pub. We were shown into the cellar, and all sorts of people were huddled together there. Men, women, and children from all walks of life, all friendly.

The sirens wailed on. Then, drowning them out completely, we heard a barrage of guns. We could hear bombs exploding, bombs dropped by zeppelins, not planes.

Two musicians began to play "Carry Me Back To Dear Old Blighty," and everyone started singing along with them. Beer was passed, jokes were told, and more songs were sung. I had never seen anything like it. Men you expected to have courage, but these women, children and babies were just as gallant as man could ever be. It made going to sea in a windjammer a very mild business indeed.

Recall finally sounded, and everyone made for the street. We might have been leaving a matinee for all the fuss that was made.

We went on up to our hotel, just above Whitechapel. We were a bedraggled, tired looking bunch, but now we didn't care. We could order the best and charge it. Our credit was good.

The next morning Captain Richards took us down to the board of trade office to be paid off. Each man's name was called, and they were paid off. Then they called "Kelley" and I walked up.

"What's your full name?"

"Theodore G. Burnett," I answered, glad at last to tell the truth. The paymaster looked first at me, then at Captain Richards.

"What's this man's name, captain?" he asked.

"Thomas Kelley of Boston, Massachusetts," said the skipper, innocently enough. His words seemed better than mine, and I received my pay of sixty-nine pounds. I then delivered a little speech we men of the crew had pre-arranged.

"Sir," I said to the paymaster, "We of the crew of the British bark 'Carrabin' have not forgotten the crew who saved our lives at peril of their own off Queenstown, and we feel it our duty that each member of the crew donate a pound to be distributed to the crew of the 'Anthony Aslette'."

"Look here, Yank," he said roughly, "The royal navy is out there doing their duty, and you're not giving any rewards to His Majesty's men. Good day, sir." Plainly, he had never been torpedoed, and a great pity, too.

The next three weeks I lived like a king in London. I was Barney Burnett again, and the Australian police were no longer breathing down my neck. My next voyage would be homeward bound.

One day, coming in from a shopping excursion at the house of Mark Cross, I ran into Kelly, now recovering from the effects of the explosion.

"Hello, Kelley me lad," he said affectionately.

"Take the Kelley off your list, son," I replied, "I'm one Barney Burnett of Brooklyn and the good old U.S.A."

"Glad to know you," he responded, bowing low, "I'd like to ship with you some time."

We went out and had ourselves an evening. The English are not all frigid ...

The following day I made application to leave England. From the London police and immigration department I went to the American Consul for a passport, and with that in order I headed for the hotel. I walked up to the desk to ask for my key and was greeted by a benevolent appearing gentleman who had orders to arrest me.

"You're Theodore Burnett?" he asked pleasantly, as I requested my key. He was in civilian attire, and I saw no reason for not answering him.

"That's what they call me," I said.

"Then perhaps you'll step along with me to Scotland Yard," he said, smiling amiably.

"May I at least have time to get my belongings?" I asked, not knowing what to expect. I was dumbfounded.

"Certainly you may," he said, politely. He was as courteous as though we were going to a private club for luncheon.

Taking leave of the departing towboat, officers and passengers of the
four-mast bark EDWARD SEWALL pause at the taffrail.

Boarding seas fill the main deck, as the four-mast bark HAWAIIAN ISLES takes a dusting in boisterous weather.

The watch on deck stretch the enormous wings of the sea albatross, freshly caught for the Second Mate's camera.

Heeling to the freshening wind, the four-mast bark MUSKOKA *romps along the sea-road to Cape Horn.*

Seamen all ... standing their watch on the pitching, wet decks of the Cape Horn sailing ship SONGVAL.

The four-mast bark WM. P. FRYE sailing through the Golden Gate into her arrival port, San Francisco.

Clewing up and furling her sails, the four-mast bark GRANADA awaits
the towboat, ranging up on her quarter to tow her into Seattle.

Courtesy of the San Francisco Maritime Museum

Legendary San Francisco . . . port of ports for the windjammer sailor . . . sailing vessels discharging at the Howard Street wharves.

Courtesy of the San Francisco Maritime Museum

The four-mast bark ASTRAL lying at the Howard Street wharf, September 18, 1910, shortly after her arrival, 154 days from Point Breeze, Pennsylvania. Her topgallant masts, lost over the side on the Cape Horn passage, await replacement.

Dropping her tug . . . topsails full and straining . . . the ship
CAMBUSKENNETH *makes a picture of unforgettable sea beauty.*

Standing in tall and handsome . . . the four-mast bark JOHN ENA *leaves Honolulu . . . bound on the port tack for "Frisco."*

Courtesy of Carleton B. All

Discharged and waiting for cargo, ranks of sailing ships wait their turn
at the coal tipples in Newcastle, New South Wales, Australia.

The Steward . . . chief of all domestic chores . . . except cooking,
stands on the broad, sea-whitened main deck of the
four-mast bark ARTHUR SEWALL.

Lifting to the broad sea-swell, the four-mast bark WM. T. LEWIS sets

With towboats standing by, the sailors of the four-mast bark
WM. T. LEWIS *unshackle her mooring chains at the Nobbies in*
Newcastle Roads . . . to free her for the sea-run back to San Francisco.

The East Coast four-topmast schooner HORATIO G. FOSS at the dock in Boston, Massachusetts.

He accompanied me up to my room, glancing idly through a magazine while I packed, then back down to the desk where I paid my bill and waved goodbye to those of the crew who were in sight. If they watched me out of the hotel, they saw the police car that I stepped into. I sat down in it gingerly, wondering what came next.

As soon as we arrived at Scotland Yard I was whisked to the British Intelligence Department and let into a room wherein was a large round table with eight men seated around it. I made the ninth, and, as it was tea time, I was served with tea and cigarettes. At last the head man spoke.

"You are Theodore Burnett of Brooklyn, New York?" he asked. It was more a statement than a question.

"Yes, sir," I said. For some reason I wasn't even nervous. You can run just so long.

"You came from Australia in the torpedoed British bark 'Carrabin'?"

"Yes, sir."

"Were you a soldier in the Australian army?"

Here it was. I looked him straight in the eye.

"Yes, sir."

He looked neither pleased nor displeased. He settled back in his chair and gazed at me thoughtfully.

"Now, Theodore," he said purposefully, "I want you to back in your memories and tell us everything you can remember from childhood to this very moment." He paused, meaningly, "And I mean everything."

It took me one week . . .

At the end of the week I was called before the same group and told I was free to sail to the United States. I was giddy with relief.

"Then you've discovered that I'm just homesick and not a German spy?" I asked, after thanking them all around. It was unbelievable to realize the chase was over, and the penalty, such as it was, was paid.

They looked at each other and laughed. Then we all laughed together. It was a high moment.

I was off, after that, in a taxi, in pursuit of the first ship home I could find. It developed that it was necessary for me to entrain for Liverpool where I could board the "S.S. Lapland" for New York.

We were convoyed across by three American destroyers, taking a zig-zag course that lasted thirteen long days, but days without incident.

We docked at Chelsea piers, and I made for home. I didn't even care if my stepmother said, "I told you so!"

My stay at home this time was brief for there was work to do. Even the draft boards were encouraging men with sailing ship experience to keep at their jobs, and I was ready to be on an American ship again. I kissed my stepmother's cheek, shook my Dad's hand, and left. This time, I went with their unqualified approval.

I left my bag at the Seaman's Church Institute on South Street and off to William Pitt's office I went. He recognized me right away, in spite of my long absence, the fine new clothes, and the expensive cigar.

"Hullo, Barney," he said, swinging around in his swivel chair, "Where yer been? Off shore?" He looked a lot older than when I'd seen him last. A lot of people did.

"Just deepwater," I said, not wanting to tell the long story. "How are you, Mr. Pitt?"

"Well, what do you think?" he said candidly. "A little age has been added, but that goes for our fleet of sailing ships, too. We're getting old together." He laughed a bit sadly, and I laughed too. We both knew the day of the sailing ship was about over, yet we both held vigil during the death watch.

He told a story or so to make me laugh, then he said, "Barney, I've a fine schooner for you."

"Well," I said reflectively, "I'm looking for one."

"It's the 'Governor Powers'," he said, watching me closely. "You know her?"

Sure I knew her. She was the largest four-masted schooner in the world! Net tonnage 1850 tons, built in 1905 by Cobb-Butler of Bath, Maine. You couldn't be a sailing ship man and not know her.

"Yes," I said, "I know her. I'll take the foc'sle if that's all there is."

"Well, then, Barney," he pointed outside the wire cage of the office, "There are your shipmates."

I looked, and there sat six or eight seamen, waiting for a chance to ship, their sailor bags neatly stacked in the corner. I looked again, hard, because there sat three of my old time buddies. Poppa Dick, Russian-Finn John, and bald-headed Oscar Nelson of Göteborg, Sweden. It was like old home week. I turned to Mr. Pitt.

"You can count on me," I said, "Depend on it."

The door opened, and the skipper of the "Governor Powers" came in. His name was Viggo Anderson, and he was a Dane by birth, although he had become an American citizen. He was young, not over twenty-six, and, though I didn't know it, he was destined to play an important part in my life.

I joined the sailors, and Mr. Pitt and Captain Anderson started talking right away.

"Every man there can shift over a tops'l quicker than you could shoot the sun," said Mr. Pitt, pointing at us.

"Sounds good," the skipper said, "All Scandinavian?"

"No," said Pitt, chuckling, "One of them is an American who has shipped out so many times he gets his Swedish mixed up with his Norwegian." He meant me.

"That too sounds good. Well, Mr. Pitt, bring them in and we'll sign articles."

"Men, you may come in now and sign," said Mr. Pitt briskly, never one to delay when money was in the offing.

The articles read to Port Hampton Roads to load coal, thence to Portland, Maine, for orders. We signed, and Captain Anderson gave us enough money to take us on to Perth Amboy, New Jersey, where the "Governor Powers" was.

When we reached Perth Amboy, and I finally stood on the deck of the schooner, I took in the details of her vast structure. Her main truck was one hundred and sixty feet from the deck. She was something to see, majestic as all hell.

Captain Anderson and his bride of six months came aboard the next day with orders to get under way, and two days later the "Governor Powers" dropped her hook in Hampton Roads.

Hampton Roads was crowded with troop ships, battleships, tankers and sailing hogs. We couldn't help noticing the camouflage jobs on them, something sailing ships didn't have. I was glad our ship wasn't covered with the nondescript "crab-fat grey." The very lack of it made her stand out like a lady of fashion at a Quaker meeting.

Loaded, and under full sail, we headed out past Cape Henry with five thousand tons of coal for Portland, Maine. As we passed up the coast we saw wrecked ships, oil tankers with just a bow showing, splintered lifeboats, empty lifebelts. Each a grim reminder of the German sea raiders.

Six days later we dropped anchor in Portland. We were not long under the coal derricks, and during that time we were paid off, but we all agreed to sign on for the next trip, pleasing the skipper very much. For two weeks we lay in Portland, then we were out to sea again.

I was in the second mate's watch, and it was our watch below from eight to twelve midnight. At eight bells we filed out on deck just in time to give a hand jibing ship. Captain Anderson was on deck, and the second mate took the wheel while I went up on the main crosstrees.

Once up aloft I started to shift the tops'l sheet, but as I glanced down I saw a vessel of war come up from astern and hail our skipper. It was an American destroyer.

"Is everything all right, captain?" their commanding officer bellowed.

"All's well, sir," Captain Anderson replied promptly. The destroyer gathered speed immediately and was soon lost in the night.

I went on with my main tops'l. I had gotten the clip hooks into the sheet and was holding on to the spring-stay, when—bang! crash! A deafening explosion, seemingly right below me.

I looked down, from the eighty feet I was aloft, and there on our port side was a steamer, her bow rammed clear into our main hatch combings! Our stationary boiler had blown up, and the explosion had been a violent one.

Our four master started to list heavily. Looking down from my precarious perch I could see the crew running out of the foc'sle and making their way aft. The steamer that had rammed us was about four thousand tons, and our port shrouds now lay against her starboard side.

I slid down the starboard main rigging, and the steamer was now listing about ten degrees. Our spars had torn away her wireless and all her starboard lifeboats.

The captain and his wife scrambled up inside the port spanker rigging as it leaned against the starboard side of the steamer, and somehow they managed to get aboard the other ship. We all sympathized with him for wanting to rescue his young bride, but it sat ill that he should be the first to leave his ship.

We were under full sail, listing about thirty degrees. The lifeboats were supported under the keel by strongbacks, the crew working frantically to get them loose. There wasn't an axe handy, the ship now tilting forty degrees.

I was on the starboard high side when I got down and was wearing a heavy blue sweater and my sea boots. I threw my boots into the sea, made the sign of the Cross, and dove into the cold black waters after them.

I swam down to the stern, and I could see our boat was out. As I came alongside, the second mate reached down and grabbed me, pulling me into the lifeboat. The lifeboat didn't have any equipment on it, not even an oar, having been out from the purchase falls when the ship was at a forty-five degree angle, everything in it had been dumped into the sea.

A rough sea was running, and in the boat were nearly all the crew who had reached it by swimming to it as I had. Then, from the high side of the "Governor Powers" we heard a cry for help.

"Save me, boys, I can't swim a stroke!" It was the mate.

The second mate turned to us and said, "What man amongst you wants to go overboard again and save the mate?"

"I'll go!" shouted Larsen, one of the strapping A.B.'s. He dove into the icy water and swam towards the wreck through heavy swells that were littered with debris.

"Jump!" he shouted, when he reached the wreck.

"I can't swim!" shouted the mate desperately.

"If you don't jump now, you can stay there!" returned Larsen, growing justifiably annoyed.

The mate jumped, and we could see that he had a suitcase in one hand! Larsen got him with a grip that turned him over on his back, and swam toward our lifeboat with the strength of a horse.

He was pretty well fagged out when he reached our boat with his human burden, but he had enough breath left to pant "Grab this guy!"

The second mate reached down and started to raise him to the gunwale when he noticed that the mate was still holding tight to the suitcase! For a moment the second mate looked as though he were going to have apoplexy.

"What is that thing you're holding onto?" he demanded in a terrible voice.

"My suitcase and sextant," replied the mate weakly.

"Oh, it is! Well, you rotten stinker—if you don't drop that suitcase this instant, I'm sticking you down under personally!" The mate abruptly let go of the bag, and was then pulled into the boat where he sat, looking sulky over his loss.

We hauled the exhausted Larsen in with us, then looked about to discover our position. At a distance we could make out the steamer, listing heavily. She was almost a mile away, but the sound of voices and oars told us that a rescue party was near.

They finally came alongside and we piled into their boat. Their crew was poorly trained at handling sweeps in a sea, so our men took to the oars with the permission of the boatkeeper, and started toward the steamer. Her name, they told us, was the S. S. "San Jose."

We pulled up alongside of the Jacob's ladder, and all hands got aboard as quickly as possible. I came over the rail to be greeted by our skipper and his wife. It seemed all wrong to see a skipper greet his cold, wet crew as they came out of a lifeboat.

The S. S. "San Jose" now moved slowly on. She had a mean starboard list, and after a bit I walked for'ard on the main deck to see what damage had been done. What I saw was not the bow of the steamer but a terrific mass of steel and iron pushed all the way back to the second watertight bulkhead. I looked down, and all there was to see was the sea itself, washing in and out as the ship pushed slowly ahead.

The steamer was loaded with bananas, and was headed for Boston. About eleven in the morning we were met by tugs and taken to Long Wharf. We of the crew and Captain Anderson walked to the offices of the owners of the "Governor Powers," Crowell and Thurlow.

The long faces of the owners showed wordlessly that the loss of their fine ship had been a crushing blow. They gave us all chairs, and we sat down while the officials and their stenographers made ready to take each man's testimony. Silence descended as Mr. Paul K. Thurlow entered.

He paced up and down for a minute, obviously dissatisfied, then opened fire.

"Men of the 'Governor Powers'," he began, "I'm indeed grateful to know there was no loss of life amongst the crews of either vessel, but I regret deeply that one of you did not stay on the vessel. She was a ship of good oak timber, no cargo, and if she were cut in thirds she would still float. The loss to our company is fifty thousand dollars, and any one of you could have claimed it had you used your heads." He gave a sharp glance in Captain Anderson's direction. "Paper will be passed out to you, and I want you to mark down item for item your losses in the schooner 'Governor Powers'. That's all men. Captain Anderson, I will see you in my office."

No offer was made to buy us clothes and shoes, or anything to help our bedraggled, shipwrecked appearance. We all went to the Seaman's Union, where they got us back into some semblance of being decently clad.

The next morning Captain Anderson met us at the Seaman's Home, and we gathered around him to hear the news.

"Men," he said, smiling, "How many of you want to ship with me in another vessel? Her name is the 'Horatio G. Foss' of Boston, and we go from here to Cramps' shipyard in Philadelphia where the ship is being overhauled. From there we proceed to Norfolk to load coal for Santos, Brazil, there to load coffee for orders. I would like to have my second mate as mate, and for second mate I would like to have you, Burnett. Oscar Nelson, I would like to have you as cook, and John Johnson for my engineer. How about it, fellows, can I count on you?" They shook their heads negatively, except those of of us he had mentioned by name.

So it was that Captain Anderson, Olaf Olsen, Oscar Nelson, John Johnson and one Barney Burnett boarded the Federal Express for Philadelphia to join the American schooner "Horatio G. Foss."

I was to wait five years to collect the fifty dollars I claimed for my losses in personal effects aboard the "Governor Powers."

18

THE "HORATIO G. FOSS" WAS TWELVE HUNDRED AND FIFTY TONS, gross tonnage, eight hundred and forty-six net, and her port of registry was Boston. Again I was the only American in the crew and it was plain from the outset that the crew credited me with knowing nothing because of that. It didn't upset me one damn bit. I could fight if I had to.

Mrs. Anderson accompanied us again, and I wondered as she came aboard how a man knew when he was in love. My shipmates, my skippers, the officers, all of them, seemed to have been bitten by the bug and it seemed to agree with them. I could only shrug and admit to myself that so far the sound of canvas sails bellying out to a fair breeze had twice the allure of the rustle of a taffeta petticoat.

Sixty-nine days later we dropped anchor in Santos harbor. We had no sooner arrived than a bumboatman from shore brought us the joyful news that there had been an armistice. Along with the news he had brought everything from fruit to rum, and I bought five dozen oranges from him and put them on top of the after house. I don't know how the rest of the world celebrated, but I sat on the house combing, my feet on the rail, and ate two dozen oranges!

With no anchor watches, all hands turned in for a good night's rest. The world was at peace, and even the stars overhead seemed to twinkle more brightly. The old hull of the "Foss" creaked and groaned as she relaxed, and the gentle waters of the sea caressed her and sang a murmurous lullaby of a voyage untroubled by submarines.

We sailed from Santos to Gibraltar, Spain, with no interruptions in ship routine. A forty-eight stay in Gibraltar and we were given clearance and allowed to proceed to the port of Cette, France. The port had been given to Switzerland as her port of entry for necessary imports.

The next two weeks were a real homeward bound stretch. The scenery along the coast of Spain was enchanting, and tied up along the banks were fishermen and traders from Italy, Greece and Spain.

The Greek sailor in my watch came up to me where I stood leaning on the capstan gazing shorewards.

"Barney, wait until you meet these French girls. I'll bet you fall in love in Cette. I have been there many times, and the women of that port are—" he drew thumb and forefinger into a circle and clicked his glistening white teeth ecstatically.

In Cette we were placed alongside the quay. Many of the townspeople came down to greet the American schooner, and we entertained the officials of the port. The port doctor, the prefecture of marine police, the mayor. They gave us a fine welcome.

The quay was covered with wine casks, bales covered with straw matting. Here and there a Senegalese trooper walked his post, tall, ebony black, well trained. Along the waterfront were many little French cafes where mademoiselles served coffee and cognac night and day to seafaring folk.

After supper that night all hands went aft for money, including myself. I donned my best going-ashore clothes, and over the rail I went for an adventure in la belle France.

I headed along the canal, stopping to admire the vast fleet of Mediterranean traders. It was spring, and I was half intoxicated by the sights and sounds of Cette. There was music in the air from the little cafes, and a nameless perfume was in the air. I couldn't stand being alone any longer. I walked into the Cafe Brazerie Nationale, and was given a seat at a little table.

The place was full of British, American and Scandinavian seamen, mates and captains. There was dancing, and I looked about for a partner. They were all so pretty it was hard to choose.

The orchestra broke into "Till We Meet Again," and I found myself face to face with a piquant young lady who said, "I am Mademoiselle Yvonne. You dance wiz me? You American, oui?"

I couldn't speak any French, but I did want to dance.

"Oh, oui, mademoiselle," I said eagerly, and the dance began.

After the war of 1914 to 1918 France had a surplus of widows and their daughters and it was a problem for an unattached male to avoid hasty friendships. A French girl will sacrifice anything for her man and she is forever catering to him, but woe to any other French girl who tries to cut in. This I didn't know.

The second number the orchestra played was "Oh, Johnny, Oh, Johnny, Oh." A svelt brunette strolled up to me and said, "I like dance wiz American." At the same time my first partner came over and burst into a barrage of French. Yvonne backed away, threw her chic hat to one side, her tunic to another, handed her necklace to me with a "Please hold thees, cherie," while the brunette stripped until she was almost down to just her skirt.

They went at each other like tigers. I stood holding the bead necklace, and the orchestra swung into the song "Mademoiselle From Armentieres." A crowd gathered, then the police arrived, and there was much excited talking, waving of hands, and shrugging of shoulders, but no arrest was made.

I went back to the ship pondering on the excitable ways of the French. It was provocative, but uncomfortable.

On board the "Foss" the crew was celebrating the armistice belatedly. Oscar, the cook, went on a spree that lasted for a week. We never could find the mate, and it was an odd day that found us all accounted for.

Captain Anderson had many worries. As the unloading of the coffee progressed, the surveyors reported the two full bottom layers wet, a case for the insurance agency. The mate showed up and wanted to be paid off. He had had a terrible fight with George, one of the Greek sailors, threatening him with a gun while drunk. George had pulled a knife in self-defense, then gotten a wrestling hold on him and thrown him into the scuppers, the gun going in another direction. The mate didn't feel comfortable aboard after that.

The skipper finally called me in, paid the mate off, and entered the matter in the log book and had me sign it as a witness. The mate departed, looking relieved, then the captain turned to me.

"From today on, Barney, until a final port of discharge in the United States, you are first mate of the 'Foss.'" He extended his hand, and I shook it heartily, pleased to be coming back into my own again. It looked as though my troubles were over.

George, the Greek, came to me a few days later.

"Mr. Mate," he said, his dark eyes flashing with suppressed excitement, "Could you please help me get paid off? I want to buy the Cafe Internationale, you know it?"

"Yes, George," I said, "I know where it is. I'll speak for you, but the decision remains with the captain." I was sure the skipper would do it. Trying to keep a Greek out of the restaurant business would be a losing game.

The captain acceded, then one by one they all quit. Even the cook. Springtime in southern France, the armistice, the mademoiselles, it was enough to turn any sailor's head.

Once unloaded, the towboat swung us head out in the bay and our starboard anchor was dropped. Our stern lines held us to the quay, making room for another ship to unload. With no crew in the foc'sle there wasn't much I could do, although I was doing the cooking from necessity.

Palm Sunday in Cette was a rare day of clear golden sunshine. I cooked a good dinner for the engineer and myself, and we sat out on the hatch afterwards enjoying the warmth and talking over old times. On the quay, many people were taking their Sunday stroll, and a boatman was in attendance for the convenience of the crews whose ships were out in the stream. The actual rowing distance was only about fifty feet, but it was enough to make a boat necessary.

When we had talked ourselves out I decided it was a fine time to do my weekly washing. True, it was Sunday, but cleanliness is next to godliness, and a little sudsy labor seemed less offensive than dirt. And so it came about that at two that afternoon I brought an armload of dirty clothes from the cabin and threw them on the mizzen hatch. Then I went for'ard for my bucket of water.

As I went for'ard I heard a call from over the port side. I dropped my bucket and went to the rail.

It was the boatman, and he had two French girls with him who wanted permission to come aboard and see the ship. One look at the girls and permission was granted.

Once over the rail the girls introduced themselves as Vivian and Marie. Their English, spoken with more than a trace of French accent, was charming. I showed them the entire ship, introduced them to the engineer, and wound up by serving them cake and coffee.

As they sat and chatted with us I noticed every tiny detail of the petite Marie. She was demure with a twinkle, that was the only way I could describe her.

"Would you dance with me this evening, mademoiselle?" I asked her hesitantly.

She looked puzzled, not understanding the word "dance." I performed a little dance step with two fingers, hummed a bit of music, and she started to laugh. "Oui, oui, je comprends, danser!"

"Well, will you?" I persisted doggedly. I racked my brain for a word or so of French. At last it came. "Avec moi!" I jerked out, tapping my chest emphatically. She laughed again, looking up at me through her lashes.

"Certainment, monsieur," she replied demurely.

I remembered my abandoned washing, and tried to leave the girls with the engineer while I got it over with. But no, they were enchanted. A big man doing washing? This they must see! They established themselves on the hatch, talking volubly in a mixture of French and English, their eyes following every move I made. I could feel my face getting red, but I started washing out my socks, wishing I could toss the damn things over the side.

Marie watched me for a few minutes. Then she stood up, removed the jacket of her fitted suit, and gestured to me to sit down.

"You no savez wash," she said, dimpling. "I show you how." I sat down, bewildered, and she lay her jacket in my lap and went to work capably and energetically at washing my clothes!

"Ah, monsieur," murmured Vivian, whose bright eyes were taking it all in. "C'est l'amour!" I knew what she meant, but she was teasing. I wasn't.

I was falling in love over a bucket of suds. . . .

My whole wash was done in half the time it would have taken me. Marie had donned her jacket again, and the girls were leaving the ship. I looked into Marie's eyes and held her hand, saying goodbye, until the boatman grew impatient.

"Tonight," I coaxed urgently. She nodded quickly, and disengaged her hand. Over the side she went, nimble as a sailor, and I went groggily about my work. These French women certainly had something, as George the Greek had said.

I could scarcely wait to get ashore after supper. I went to the Grand Cafe, and had the waiter show me into a booth where I had an unobstructed view of the whole cafe and its occupants. As I sat there, I saw Marie.

She was talking with the chief of marine police. It didn't seem odd, for the town was small and she could easily have known him. What was strange was that when she finished talking with him she flitted out of the place and was instantly lost in the crowds outside. She couldn't have seen me, and I told myself she'd be back.

Six drinks later I went back to my ship. Marie had not come back. I couldn't figure out what had happened, for I would have sworn those brown eyes were sincere. I tossed and turned for a long time before I went to sleep.

THE NEXT DAY THE SKIPPER SENT ME FOUR MEN AND A SECOND MATE.
There was a great deal of activity aboard. The prefecture of police,
accompanied by Lieutenant Farber of the dope squad, came over the
rail and I answered many questions and showed them over the ship.

The lieutenant explained that one of the ships had brought in
contraband, and to me it could have been diamonds or tobacco,
almost anything. I never thought of dope.

About ten a.m. Marie came aboard. She walked up to the chief of
marine police and whispered to him in French. He listened intently,
answered her in French, then smiled. I was eaten with jealousy. At
last she came over to me.

"'Allo, m'sieu," she twinkled, "You are angree?"

I looked into that pair of eyes, and I wasn't angry at all. "Of course
not!" I said stoutly, "I'm just glad to see you."

Lieutenant Farber looked back at me and smiled. I smiled back at
him. The world was a wonderful place again, and if my eyes had had
teeth, Marie would have been devoured in a minute.

"Barney," she said, looking prettily confused, "tonight you come to my house, oui?"

"Sure—I mean, oui," I said, feeling all clumsy and confused again. "What time?"

"Come for aperitif, then we have le diner, cafe and a petit cognac, oui?" She was irresistible.

"I'll be there, Marie." Can a duck swim?

"Can I see the cab-ine?"

I took her in and showed her around. She was interested in everything with a naive curiosity that made me feel fiercely possessive and protective.

"Tres jolie, very beautiful," she said, adding wistfully. "Where is your chamber?"

"Right here," I said, not sorry to have her see the sign over the door that read "Certified for Mate." I took her in and closed the door.

She looked at everything without comment. That is, until she saw the picture of a girl. She picked it up and looked at it closely, then put it back carefully.

"Your sweetheart?"

"No," I said, truthfully enough, "not now."

She picked up the picture again, turned it face down on my desk, tilted her chin at me and smiled.

I took her in my arms, and it was a long time before we found our way out of the room "Certified for Mate."

After that, we were always to be seen together. On shore, at dances, cafes, even house parties. One night as we sipped a demitasse at a sidewalk cafe, she told me she worked as a police department auxiliary with the dope squad.

Cette was so close to Marseilles that the dope peddlers came down often to sell to those who had the habit. Algerian troopers, Spanish and Italian fishermen. The feminine element, too, unfortunately, didn't lag far behind in buying forgetfulness at a price. The things she told me were interesting, but so sordid I didn't want to hear them from her lips. I wanted to take her away.

The following Sunday was Easter, and Marie came to the ship in the morning with a small bouquet of posies for my cabin. The day was perfect, yet nice as it was I had to tell Marie I couldn't leave the ship until after supper. Duty, no less.

Marie left a few minutes later, after promising to meet me that evening. The distance to shore was short, and I stood at the rail to wave to her. Captain Anderson stood on the quay, and even as I watched he greeted her in French, she waved her hand to me, and they walked away together.

The afternoon seemed interminable. I was jealous. The new crew thought their mate a bear, and I couldn't blame them. After supper I went up to the poop deck to haul down the colors, and as I did so I threw Marie's bouquet as far as I could throw it.

I went ashore after supper, and went in every cafe I came to. I danced with anyone. I was miserable.

I finally decided I'd rather be alone, so I walked to the Cafe Internationale and had George give me a booth. I ordered coffee and cognac and sat over it, brooding darkly.

It wasn't long before Marie appeared, telling me how she had been to the ship, then to every cafe, looking for me. What had she done? Why was I so cruel?

I was silent, fingering my glass. I was ashamed of myself for my black Irish temper.

"You come home with me now, yes?" She put her hand on mine, and I got up and followed her like a man in a trance.

Her apartment was on the second floor of a building. The front room had French windows opening on a balcony. All along the quay were moored two-masted trading schooners of all nations bordering the Mediterranean. It was a moonlit night, and through the opened windows came breezes from the sea.

We talked of love and jealousy and hate, and she cried while I stroked her hair and cursed myself for a jealous fool. This was no port romance.

It was late when I left her little apartment and started for the ship. I slept well, having made up my mind, and next morning I was at mess table bright and early. The skipper shot a sharp glance at me. "I think my mate has fallen in love," he ventured, smiling.

"Then you and I are of the same opinion," I shot back. "We're the same age, yet you're the father of a boy."

"You are serious, aren't you?" he said.

"Give me a day or two to answer that question," I returned, levelly enough.

That afternoon I was invited to tea aboard the British ship "Ponjam," and was told I might bring Marie. She was delighted, for it was a new experience for her, and I—well, I was proud to be seen anywhere with her.

The "Ponjam" had all sorts of monkeys aboard, brought from India, and one of them mischievously grabbed my cap and ran to a safe place to inspect it at leisure. Marie laughed at his antics, and I laughed too.

Tea was served by a coolie servant, and with it we had rich Scotch shortbreads, a decanter of fine brandy, and Abdullah's finest cigarettes of Turkish blend.

Chief Officer Harry Babcock offered us the same long-tailed monkey that had grabbed my cap. "I can assure you," he said, his eyes twinkling, "he'll make things very lively aboard your ship."

"I'm very grateful to you for my—I mean, our new shipmate," I replied.

"Do you wish a birth certificate?" he asked solemnly.

"No," I said, "but I would like to know his name."

"His name is McGinty," Babcock laughed.

"Hooray for the Irish!" We all laughed together.

Marie, McGinty and I bid the British crew farewell and went back to the "Foss." I invited Marie to have supper with us, and while she made friends with McGinty I went on deck to check with the second mate on what he'd had the men do during the afternoon. The cook was so ignorant I knew he'd have to go overside. Cooks seemed to be at a premium.

Supper over, I took Marie home. I went back to the ship thinking long thoughts of love. When I took time out to think about the ship I worried about the second mate. He seemed to be a trouble-maker. A fault finder, and always surly.

Each night I saw Marie, and each meeting brought us closer together. At last I spoke of marriage.

"Would you like to stay in France, cherie?" I asked anxiously, wondering if she'd leave her country for me.

"Non," she said firmly, shaking her head. "We can be happy in America, mon cheri. Let me go with you. I weel be cook on the sheep!"

Her French practicality was better than all my daydreams. I began to see where it might be possible. I told her I'd see the American Consul the next day.

True to my word, I paid a visit to the Consulate the following day and told him of my plans to marry.

"You are the mate of the 'Horatio G. Foss?'," he asked coldly.

"Yes, sir."

"Now look here!" he said loftily, "we can't authorize any marriage. I therefore advise you, sir, to forget about this hasty love affair, as the only way you could obtain a marriage license would be through the State Department in Washington, D. C."

"Consul," I said quietly, "I'm here for the purpose of marriage, and you tell me I can't marry. Well, I'm going to marry the woman I love, and I might add that neither you nor the government of the United States will tell me when I can marry or whom I will marry, and I'm marrying her here in France. Good day to you, sir!" I turned on my heel and walked out, leaving him staring thoughtfully after me.

Marie was waiting for me outside.

"Marie!" I exploded hotly, "you get your passports and papers fixed up, comprenez?"

"Oui, mon cheri," she whispered. She knew all had not gone well inside.

I hotfooted it back to the ship. The skipper was waiting for me on the poop deck.

"Well, Mr. Mate, we have orders," he announced, as soon as I came within earshot.

"Good news, captain?" I asked, biding my time.

"As good as could be expected," he said sourly. "We go from here to Torrevieja, load salt for Boston from there." He wanted to get home sooner to see his new baby.

"Well, sir, that's that," I said regretfully, "but I can't go unless my wife ships with me."

The skipper's face lit up like a flare on a dark night. Before he could say anything I went on.

"She is a wonderful cook, and what she doesn't know I will teach her."

The skipper just looked at me.

"Are you serious?" he asked.

"Yes, sir. If Marie can't ship you'll have to find yourself another mate."

"Well," he said, sighing deeply, "I don't want to lose my mate, so I guess I will have to sign your wife on the articles. When are you getting married?"

"Captain," I said, "I want you to marry us outside the three mile limit. The authority in this port, the American Consul said 'No', I said 'Yes', and I told him I'd marry my wife and carry her back to America in the 'Foss'."

Captain Anderson fell silent, pondering awhile. At last he looked at me straight on.

"You're certain you're in love with Marie?" he asked, an odd note in his voice.

"Absolutely," I told him unwaveringly.

"Am I to understand that she'll cook for us?"

"Yes, sir."

"How soon can Marie come aboard?"

"She is packing now."

"Have you notified Commissioner Cussack of the marine police?"

"I'll do that today, sir."

"The stores come aboard tomorrow. We should be able to get under way by Friday."

"Very well, sir," I answered, not moving a muscle in my face. "I'll see to it that everything is stowed away in its proper place."

"That green berry coffee you will have to have the men sweep together, and put the hatches on until we reach Spain. I'm going ashore now and clear the ship. Just remember this—I did not see your wife come aboard. Savvy?"

"Yes, sir!" I said, and touched my cap.

I WAS QUICK ENOUGH IN GIVING THE SECOND MATE HIS ORDERS. THEN
I flew like a homing pigeon to Marie's little apartment.

"Mon mari," she whispered, nestling in my arms, "Mon cheri." A
tear found its way down her cheek.

I kissed the tear away. "Don't be frightened, cherie. I've arranged
everything."

I looked about the tiny apartment. Her hamper trunk was packed,
but I wanted to be sure she had everything she'd need for a long
voyage. I gave her a list, money, and enough kisses to keep her courage up whilst she shopped. I was as edgy as a caged lion.

Straight back to the ship I went. I made sure the decks were
cleared up, and after supper I went back ashore.

Marie and I danced, and it was like a dream. Her friends surrounded us, and gifts were given to us no matter where we went. An
American was taking away a French bride, and they would not let
her go empty-handed. No matter how poor they were, they all managed to give something.

It was after midnight when we returned to her apartment, and there we found a surprise party. Supper, dancing, farewells, champagne! It was beautiful, a real bon voyage party, and through it all I could only see Marie.

When I got back to the ship I glanced into the cook's room, and was glad to see that he was gone. I lay down in my bunk, clothes and all, for I had to be up in two hours.

At five-thirty I went for'ard to the galley, cleaned up the stove and lit a fresh fire. By six-thirty I had made fresh coffee, and stood at the rail sipping a cup. The sun was getting higher now, and it was another shimmering spring day.

At a little after ten a two-wheeled cart pulled up abreast our gangway and out stepped Marie.

I don't think she ever looked more beautiful in her life. Her little chin tilted proudly as she directed the ancient coachman in disposing of everything she owned in the world. The sudden irrelevant thought came to me that it was only fitting my bride should be wed to me at sea. Only it was no longer the sea and a woman. It was *the* woman and the sea.

I brought her to the after cabin and called the crew to bring her trunk, hamper and suitcases aboard. She had brought sheets, pillow cases, napkins, tablecloths, and even a supply of tobacco for me. She had all our gifts, too, and they included many bottles of fine cognac.

We treated all hands to drinks, and while we were gay as could be, we'd glance apprehensively at each other from time to time. We couldn't wait to be out at sea, safe.

After the crew left the cabin, Marie donned a white apron and went for'ard to the galley. Every day she was learning another word or so of English, and I in turn added a bit more French to my vocabulary. A few questions from her, and she turned to making lunch for us. She cooked like a Frenchwoman, which is to say, the lunch was the most appetizing the crew had ever eaten.

At about two that afternoon a large dray stopped abreast of the main rigging. The driver handed me his invoice and, as I looked at the items, it was clear the skipper meant for us to eat. Among other things, I noticed he had included a large order of French bread!

On and on the stores kept coming, and Marie and I worked diligently getting everything put away. The crew, not having any cause for worry, had celebrated more than we had, and they weren't quite as active as they might have been. We didn't care.

Then I noticed large cases of pork shoulders, weighing easily four hundred pounds each. We debated about rigging a purchase, but I was sure we could carry them over the gangway. The driver of the cart agreed with me.

"All right," I said, wanting to show off a bit for Marie, "I'll take one end if you two men will take the other end. Let's go!"

We all lifted together and approached the top of the gangway slowly. I was walking backwards, and suddenly my foot slipped. I fell heavily, and the steel-strapped edges of the case fell directly on my shinbone. I didn't want to frighten Marie, yet I couldn't help groaning, and the crew quickly removed the crushing weight.

The case had cut a full inch into my right leg, and I bled like a stuck pig. The drayman was powerfully built, and he picked me up and carried me to my bunk. Marie bravely went to work staunching the flow of blood, and a doctor was called from shore.

The doctor ordered salt and warm water washes to prevent gangrene, and I lay there and sipped the brandy the ship's chandler had sent down and felt like a bungling fool.

Captain Anderson came aboard, and Marie served an excellent dinner to everyone. I had mine in my bunk of necessity, and he came down to see me afterward.

"Are you going to be able to get about on deck tomorrow?" he asked, looking perturbed.

"I'll lay you money I'll be there," I said, trying to forget the pain in my leg. I'd make one fine bridegroom if I didn't recover.

"All right," he said, restlessly. "How's the new cook?"

"Captain," I said blissfully, "She's tops!"

After supper Marie went ashore to finish her passport affairs. I gave her what money I had left, for she had none of her own. I had overdrawn my pay of $120.00 per month by one full month, and resolutely closed my mind to the dead horse I had to sweat out.

Several hours later she tiptoed aboard and came to my room in the after cabin. She turned the door knob slowly and peeked in. My oil lamp burned low, and she didn't know I was awake. I moved out of my bunk despite the pain in my leg, and such an embrace!

Marie had lost both parents in the bombardment of Lille in 1915. Her brother, aged thirty, had snow white hair from the horrors of the trench warfare he had seen with the 72nd French Infantry. Now she was bound for a new life, and when I told her about life in America she looked like a child hearing about Christmas for the first time.

"Now, Marie, if you stay in the galley until we are away from Cette, everything will be all right," I whispered. "If anyone comes aboard asking for you, hide in the ship's coal locker. Comprenez?"

"Oui," she whispered, looking frightened.

"You get breakfast at five, and I'll keep lookout." Again I put my arms around her. She was happier than she'd ever been in her life, and so was I.

In the morning, breakfast once over, I helped our valiant cook clear the table, carrying the dishes to the galley for her. I planned the dinner, and gave the menu to Marie, telling her to call me if she was puzzled, worried, or just plain lonesome. I didn't say it exactly in French or English, but the language of the heart. She understood.

Captain Anderson called me aft. "Mr. Mate," he said, "As soon as we reach the three mile limit I will perform your marriage. Until then, I don't know anything about Marie being aboard."

"Very well, sir," I said. My leg pained me, but I bit back the hurt. Barney Burnett was getting married, for better or worse. I felt humble as hell, a big, hulking seaman, beside my petite Marie. I didn't have to promise to cherish her forever. It was just a formality to be gone through, for in my heart it was already done.

I left the captain, trying my best not to hobble as I departed. And then, from over the side I heard a few shrill whistles. I looked over, and there was a group of officials from the Department de la Marine Francaise.

There stood Commander Cussack, Lieutenant Farber, and several police of the dope squad. Captain Anderson greeted them as they came over the rail, six in all in their blue caped uniforms.

"Ah, bonjour, capitaine, will you mustaire the crew?"

Captain Anderson called all hands to muster aft. Everyone showed up except Marie, who was hiding in the coal lockers as she had been told.

Captain Cussack looked over the sheet.

"Oh, capitaine!" he exclaimed reprovingly, "There is one person missing!" My heart sank to my boots.

"There's my crew," said the skipper, looking surprised, "That's all there is." He didn't sound too happy.

"Mais non!" clucked Captain Cussack emphatically, "There is one more, and we are here to wish her bon voyage. She is Mademoiselle Marie Dheilly."

"Mr. Mate," said the skipper sternly, "Is Marie aboard?"

"Yes, sir," I said reluctantly.

I ran to the coal bin.

"Marie, Marie!"

"Oui?" her head appeared timidly.

"Come out, please!" I took both her hands to help her, gave her a gentle kiss, and took her aft.

"Marie," said Commander Cussack, once she had joined the line-up, "Today you sail away from your native France. We of Cette love you, and my colleagues and I have come aboard to say goodbye and bon voyage." He turned to me. "My best wishes, mate. May I add, if Marie were not with you, I do not believe I could permit your sailing today!" He smiled, extending his hand. He was a fine man.

The tugboat gave several impatient blasts. The hour of sailing had come.

"All right, men! Take a line! When you're ready, let 'er all go. One man to the wheel!" The "Horatio G. Foss" moved slowly away from the dock, the villagers cheered and waved, and the crews of the nearby ships whistled and flung their caps in the air. It was anything but a secret elopement.

I stood on the foc'sle head, waving to the many friends I had met during my stay in Cette. We had to pass the jetty that projected out from the town, and thus we were at close range. I could see a man standing there, searching the decks of our ship with binoculars. It was the American Consul. I was glad Marie was not in sight. Then I did something wrong, but the impulse was irresistible.

As we slid by, I thumbed my nose at him.

An hour later the "Horatio G. Foss" was headed out into the Mediterranean, the towboat blew to stand by and let go our hawser. The towboat captain saw Marie at the rail, and he blew three long whistle blasts then lifted his megaphone.

"Bon voyage, mademoiselle!" he shouted, "A long life and a happy one!"

"Vive l'Americain!" shouted his two men lustily. Marie lifted her small plump hand in farewell.

It was May twenty-fourth, 1919, and outside the three mile limit

Captain Anderson summoned Marie and myself, with the engineer John Johnson, to his cabin. He was ready to perform our marriage on the high seas . . .

It was a glorious day, and outside, from the jigger truck, flew the Stars and Stripes. Inside the cabin the ceremony was brief, but nonetheless sacred and binding. The marriage was entered in the official logbook, and signed by all present. I kissed my bride.

At coffee time the next morning, the chief got out of his bunk and closed the fire box door, then opened up the draught. A strange noise came from the boiler. He jerked open the door, and out jumped McGinty—frightened, cold and shivering.

The chief called Marie, and she called me. I took McGinty into the galley where it was warm, wrapped him in a flour sack, and put him down to rest. After breakfast I went in to see him again, and he seemed to be growing weaker. I held him in my arms and fed him warm milk from a teaspoon, and this continued for an hour or so while the pitiful little creature looked at me sadly with his mournful eyes.

At four bells he passed away. We all felt badly, for we had grown found of the little prankster. I got a box from the store room, put him in it along with some weights, and wrapped the pathetic little cargo in canvas. We lowered him, cut the rope, and—down went McGinty to the bottom of the sea!

After five days of smooth sailing we reached Alicante, our salt loading port. There were no docks for large vessels and we all anchored in the roads, the harbor wide open to the sea and the storms from the southeast and southwest which played havoc with small harbor craft and fishermen.

Captain Anderson was taken ashore to enter the vessel, hatches were opened and stacked ready for loading our twelve hundred and fifty tons of salt. Some of the stevedores who rigged stages at the main and mizzen rigging for the passing of salt baskets were eyeing Marie in a way I didn't like.

I limped about the deck, the gash in my leg still bothering me, giving orders to the crew and glaring at the stevedores. I was ready to jump the first man who attempted any familiarities with Marie.

When Captain Anderson returned he summoned me to his cabin. "Barney, this is Saturday. After lunch I want to take you and your wife ashore for a wedding supper at the Hotel Almira, and we'll take in a show. I also want you to know I've reported both stowaway and marriage to the American Consul."

"It sounds good to me," I said warmly. "We have just one problem to settle, and it'll be important when we're out to sea again. I've got to find someone who'll teach me how to make good bread." Neither Marie nor I knew how.

"Over here on our port side is the steamer "Panay" from Panay, Philippine Islands," said the skipper, "How about your running over there to see what the cook says?"

"All right, I'll go now," I said, anxious to get it over with.

"You'll make the yeast and bread?" he asked, his eyes twinkling, "What a man won't do for love!"

"I'd do anything for Marie," I said doggedly. I was to prove it before I was done.

Once aboard the "Panay" I introduced myself to the mate. "My name is Burnett," I said, "I'm mate on that four-master anchored over there, and we have a problem on our hands. We have to learn how to bake bread."

He took me down to the cook, a little Filipino, who chuckled merrily when I explained my errand. "Oh, sure!" he said obligingly. "I show you how to make bread and yeast. American army show me. now I happy to show you." He plunged into the details and I wrote down everything he said. Sometimes bridegrooms have to learn how to cook, too.

I thanked the cook and the skipper for my cooking lesson, then dashed back to the "Foss." Captain Anderson, Marie and I then dressed to go ashore for the wedding party.

Over the side we went, into the ship's lifeboat that was equipped with an engine. Marie was growing accustomed to the Jacob's ladder, and a charming sight she made as she swung down, her expressive eyes brimming with anticipation.

Once ashore, the skipper told us to meet him at the Hotel Metropole at seven o'clock. The delayed hour gave us leisure time to stroll through the picturesque old town and see some of its attractions. The market place was situated in a block surrounded by a six foot stone wall, the booths well sheltered from the blazing sun. Marie and I eyed the exhibits, and wound up by buying many fine foods for the "Foss." These, including about two dozen rabbits, we sent to the ship before continuing our tour.

The Spanish love to promenade, and Marie and I walked arm in arm along the broad avenida, stopping here and there for an aperitif. Mantillas were plentiful, and I stared in fascination at the sloe-eyed beauties who wore them until Marie jabbed me indignantly in the ribs.

"I do not like these flirts!" she said hotly, and after that I kept my eyes where they belonged.

We met Captain Anderson at the appointed time, and the patron of the hotel showed us to a table for eight. The skipper had invited guests to make the dinner more festive.

Dinner was superb, the wines excellent. Champagne, the finest Spanish sherry, coffee and cognac were served, then after dinner the table was cleared and a spirited Spanish senorita came to dance on its broad surface.

She had to be lifted up, and I gallantly took her and set her on the table, mantilla, castanets, heady perfume and all. Between the champagne, sherry and cognac, I was beginning to feel quite gay. I turned around to smile at Marie as I sat down. Her dark eyes were snapping fire.

"You're a married man, now," said the skipper, laughing, "Isn't he, Marie?"

"Ah, oui! Oui, capitaine," she said vehemently. She was jealous, and the stare she levelled at me was something to see.

The ensemble played, and the vivacious dancer whirled with graceful abandon on our table, clicking her castanets, and stamping her high heeled shoes. I was careful to give most of my attention to Marie. I was beginning to learn what it took to be a model husband.

Our guests had arranged for seats at the Teatre Valencia, the town's best theatre. When we got there we were directed to seats in the front row. The show was something like American vaudeville, and included one act that nearly started a revolution.

A Spanish senorita, dressed as a British sailor, came out on the stage, and her act called for opening a bottle of beer as part of her song and dance routine. We were all enjoying it when the entertainer suddenly looked out into the audience.

"I would like the American guest to share my cirvaza with me," she said, beckoning at our row.

I looked at the captain, and he looked at me.

"She means you," he said.

"No, you," I didn't want to get in more trouble.

"You!" said the singer, pointing directly at me.

I didn't want to seem rude, so I started for the stage. Then Marie went into her act! She grabbed my arm and pulled me back, holding me firmly.

"Non, non, non!" she exploded in shrill protest. "You are my husban'!"

The delighted audience applauded. "Bravo! Bravo!" they shouted approvingly.

I sat down quickly. The act on stage proceeded without me.

After the show we returned to the hotel for more champagne. We invited all the entertainers for dinner on board ship the next day. It was daylight when we left.

After much difficulty we got the engine started on the lifeboat and headed for the "Foss." The anchor watch was on the job, and he helped us aboard.

"Bon soir, capitaine, and merci beaucoup," came from Marie, sleepily.

We'd had a fine time.

THE WIND WAS OUT OF THE WEST, AND FRESH. THE "HORATIO G. FOSS" sailed better now than she had in the past eight months. We averaged nine knots per hour, with a list of ten degrees and a home wind.

Marie would come out on deck to look wonderingly at the vast spread of canvas. She liked it all, the clean tang of the salt air, the hoarse cries of the gulls, the rhythmical rise and fall of the ship. She hummed snatches of French songs as she worked in the galley, and the crew smiled sympathetically at her happiness.

I tried making the first bread, and although my yeast had fermented well, the first batch of bread raised only three inches. It was edible, but that was about all, and many were the remarks passed among the crew about going home to their mothers if I didn't do better.

The wind finally hauled to the north, giving us our chance. We eased the sheets, and were soon travelling at a ten knot clip. Marie came to me as I stood my watch on deck, the eight to midnight. Astern were the shore lights of Spain and Portugal.

"It is goodbye to my native France!" She looked up at me pleadingly, "Barney, please always be good to me, because I love you so much!" I stroked her hair, and murmured terms of endearment to her, while the man at the wheel obligingly looked the other way.

"Now, Marie," I said, when her tears had subsided, "You go down and turn in. Get some sleep, because I'll have to wake you about four-thirty. You're cook on a windjammer, remember?" The commonplace words restored her, and she became practical again, her moment of farewell behind her.

"Goodnight, my Barney, and do not worry. The bread she is set, and the fire is what you call it—?"

"Banked," I said, grinning.

"Oui." She slipped away.

For two weeks every member of the crew was happy. I noticed the skipper was taking a northern route, and this I didn't like because of the prevailing westerlies. Most ships leaving Europe take a southern route. The slap-bang of the sails is mighty rough on running rigging, and the "Foss" had only two sets of sails. One was rotten and rat-eaten, and the other was old.

Leaving Gibraltar in our wake we made a run of about a thousand miles on a parallel of thirty-nine degrees north latitude. Our sails were taking a beating, and every watch both night and day something had to be lowered for sewing up the seams. There came nights when we lowered everything, put the wheel in beckets, and forgot it stoically until the next morning.

Our potatoes were going bad, and many of them had to be thrown overboard. We had no icebox, our supply of fresh meat was gone, and we started in on salt provision and lime juice.

On Sundays, as a special treat, Marie would kill and skin four rabbits for dinner. She was fast becoming a fine sea cook, and she turned out succulent dishes from the fish the men caught from the side of the "Foss." Albacore, bonito and dolphin lunged at our white rag bait, and it was great sport bringing them in from the jib boom.

One man would hold the burlap bag, another would pull the wildly thrashing fish up and throw him in head first. The bonito was the hardest one to hold. We had nine big fish strung up under the main boom, a sure sign we'd eat for awhile.

The winds continued light, yet every night we encountered heavy squalls. We were now thirty days out and the second mate was agitating the crew, stirring up trouble with his reckless talk. Marie could hear the talk in the foc'sle by listening at the food slide door, and what she heard alarmed her.

"Capitaine," she said gravely to the skipper one day, "Watch second mate. He say you no capitaine."

"Thank you, Marie," said the captain, "I'll keep an eye on him."

Two weeks later, when I had the four to eight a.m. below, Marie ran aft, shaking me out of a sound sleep.

"Barney! Barney! Be queek! The second mate, he make much trouble." She began to cry.

I was in my shorts, but I shot out of my bunk and up on deck. As I reached it, I made one jump from the poop deck to the main deck and dashed for'ard where McDonald was having a round with the engineer.

I grabbed McDonald without warning, swung him around, and led with a vicious right. With quick short jabs I worked him down to the lee scupper, and he fought back savagely every inch of the way. Suddenly he stopped.

"What the hell are you fighting about?" he asked.

"I don't know yet," I answered. "What the hell are you fighting about?"

"I wanted water on deck," he said.

"You'll get water when the engineer has enough steam to give it to you! Now listen here, don't let me hear any more of this sort of trouble." I turned to the engineer, a fine, quiet fellow. "Are you all right, chief?"

"All right, sir," he said stoically.

I went aft in my shorts, back to bed. "Marie," I said, as I pulled the covers over me again, "if that fellow opens his mouth to you, at any time, just let me know."

"Oui, Barney," she said. She giggled appreciatively, "You fight like the boxaire!"

"At least I was dressed like one," I agreed wryly.

It wasn't another week before I noticed a strange uneasiness in the crew. It was something I couldn't define, yet it was there nevertheless.

Came the morning when the skipper gave the second mate some orders.

"Yeah?" said the second mate. "You don't know where you're bound, or how to get there!"

I came up from the cabin. Captain Anderson was standing on the for'ard side of the poop deck, the second mate on the deck. The argument waxed hotter.

"You're nothing but a white-washed Yankee, you son of a bitch!" snarled the second mate. The skipper tensed.

"Mr. McDonald, I have a witness to that last statement. I'm disrating you to A.B. Barney, I'm entering this in the log book. Will you sign it?"

"Yes, sir!" I said fervently.

The captain went to his room, and a few minutes later he had me call the second mate. McDonald came down into the cabin, his hat on his head.

"Take that hat off, McDonald," I said warningly. "These are the captain's quarters."

He started to object, thought the better of it, and unwillingly removed the hat.

"Manley McDonald, I will read to you the charges made against you as entered in the log book," said the captain. He read the statement clear through. "Now, have you anything to say?"

"No, sir," said McDonald stonily.

"Then sign your name on this line." The skipper watched him scrawl his signature. "Good! Now, take your clothes and go for'ard into the foc'sle. Mr. Mate, have Arne Lindholm come aft to take the berth of second mate."

About five hundred miles north of Bermuda, a pea soup fog settled down and all hands were busy taking in the four tops'ls and flying jib. A strong gust of wind, then a stronger one, and the "Foss" listed heavily.

Captain Anderson remained cool and resourceful, standing in the weather mizzen rigging, watching and listening.

"Take in the spanker!" he suddenly shouted, but he was a fraction too late. Everything zipped and cracked. The mains'l went to ribbons before we even had the spanker down. Then the mizzen, ripped from head to foot; the outer jib sheet carried away, while the chain pennants gave out fireworks. And it all happened in a matter of moments. . . .

In the after cabin, everything was thrown to leeward or port side.

What made it all so strange was the wind of gale force coming out of the thick fog. Now it was increasing to a violent nor'easter.

I worried about Marie, and one hove to I went to her rescue, securing everything in her galley. On deck, I watched for her whenever her fears drove her outside. I didn't like the gale and fog. They were a bad combination when we were in the steamer lane.

The next three days we encountered the same peculiar combination of weather. I wouldn't let Marie go for'ard, for our ship was taking a beating. One sea swept our deck, splintering the 8" x 8" strongbacks on our main hatch. We were hove to, and rolling our guts out.

Once, and only once, she rolled until her starboard cathead came within inches of the sea. I thought of the salt cargo and prayed it wouldn't shift. I worried about having brought Marie along. I could have sent her by steamer, she would have been safer. Then I thought of her unwavering confidence in me and grew ashamed.

For four days all our frightened cook could serve us was soup and stews. Our table in the cabin wouldn't hold food, and the skipper, Marie, the engineer, second mate and myself ate on the cabin floor with our feet braced against anything that was solid, making as light conversation as possible to allay Marie's fears.

Sixty days out and we were again in a dead calm, still about five hundred miles north of Bermuda. We had long since exhausted our supply of tobacco, except the skipper, who smoked cigars. All hands were kept busy patching and repairing, and we were by the wind, under full sail, making little headway.

Our provisions in general were very low. Every morning Marie fed us cornmeal flapjacks with Brazilian honey, and though her eyes were now dark-ringed her tremulous smile was still a fine thing to behold.

Two feet of water sloshed in the hold, and the engineer pumped out three times a day. We were half hungry, discouraged, longing for a sight of land.

Came the red letter day when Captain Anderson sighted a steamer through his binoculars. Closer and closer she came, until she was within a mile of us.

"Run up the ensign and our numbers," cried the skipper, "she'll report us!"

"Yes, sir." I started away, then turned back. "Captain, we don't have many stores. Do you want me to semaphore him for provisions?"

"Mr. Mate!" he snapped irately, "Haven't we had enough bad luck? Do you want me to have a salvage claim against this vessel after we've already pumped out two hundred tons of our cargo?"

"No, sir," I said resignedly, "But what would you say if I were to ask him for some tobacco?"

"If he'll give it to you, go ahead," said the skipper, softening a bit.

I ran for my flags, and jumped to the top of the cabin with the spanker for background. I waved my signal flags, glad that the ship flew the British flag as British ships all carry men who are adept at semaphore.

"We are sixty days out of Spain, and out of smokes and tobacco," I signalled. "Can you spare any?"

"Stand by," he flagged back. The steamer's deck was thick with passengers, all staring at our battered ship.

Minutes later the reply was signalled. "Look for can buoy now being dropped overboard. Contains tobacco. Good luck, cheerio!"

"We all thank you," I flagged in return, "Cheerio!"

Through the binoculars I could see the can buoy in the glassy sea, bobbing a good three hundred yards from the ship.

The crew looked longingly at the drifting buoy which might have been in China as far as they were concerned. Suddenly the second mate tied the log line around his waist, dove over the side and swam to the buoy. He brought it back, the hearty cheers of the crew spurring him on.

We helped him over the side, and he stood there dripping and triumphant, holding the tubular buoy.

"With sharks around, you must have wanted that tobacco pretty badly to swim for it," I said. It had been a daring, almost a foolhardy stunt in those waters.

"Me?" he laughed heartily, "Not me! I don't use the stuff!" Strange are the ways of a sailor.

We gathered round, and the buoy disgorged nine plugs of tobacco. We all shook hands with Arne, but he just grinned, brushing away our gratitude good-naturedly. "It was nothing," was all he would say.

We could spare no bread for breakfast as the flour was running low and what there was, was damaged. Marie went on serving us our cornmeal flapjacks.

She was crying one morning when I invaded the galley. The ship had resumed its rolling, and each time she poured batter it ran first to starboard, then to port.

"Le petit gateeaux, c'est terrible!" she sobbed.

"Don't worry, darling," I said, trying not to smile. "Two weeks more and we're home." She managed a smile for me.

We were crossing Georges Bank when we sighted a swordfisherman out of Gloucester. Their skipper talked with ours.

"Out very long, captain?"

"Sixty-eight days out of Spain," said our skipper.

"Long time, captain."

"You wouldn't have a piece of fish to spare, would you?" asked Captain Anderson hopefully.

"Why, yes, captain, I'm sure we have. By the way, you wouldn't have a bottle of good cognac, would you?"

"I certainly have," replied our skipper. "I'll bend it on a heaving line, so stand by."

I heaved the line from the poop deck, the bottle of cognac in the middle. They, in turn, bent on a big piece of swordfish. A "Thank you, and good luck" and the fisherman was off, for he had both power and sail.

Seventy-one days out, and a cry from the lookout.

"Land off the port bow, sir!"

I was in the galley, checking my bread in the oven while Marie made fresh coffee. I put my arm around her and we both grew a bit misty-eyed. We'd made it in spite of everything.

Captain Anderson ordered all sails trimmed to full-n by. "Mr. Mate," he said, "we will signal Cape Cod light station for a towboat."

I handled those flags like a U. S. signalman. I couldn't wait to go ashore with my bride. I pictured how her eyes would widen in wonder at the tall buildings, the traffic, the smartly dressed women—in short, everything that spelled the good old U.S.A.

Early the next morning we saw a towboat headed for us. He came alongside promptly.

"Captain!" he called, "have your men take our hawser."

"All hands on deck!" came the cry. Marie brought coffee and we drank it dreamily, hardly able to wait until we were in port.

After an hour or so our tug slowed down for the pilot boat. "Get a ladder over the starboard side! Stand by for pilot boat!"

The pilot came aboard, a big six footer.

"Erickson is the name, sir," he said to me.

"Glad to know you, pilot. Marie, will you please see that the pilot has hot coffee?"

"Oui, oui, mon chere."

As we were towing, we had all sails drawing, and Captain Anderson treated the pilot to a couple of cognacs.

"Oh, Mr. Mate! Would you do me a favor?" the pilot called presently.

"Yes, sir."

"Will you stay close by? I'm not used to stretching my neck at tops'ls and I'm afraid I'll get dizzy."

"How about some more coffee, pilot?" I asked, straight-faced.

"I'll go for that!" he said eagerly. Marie brought coffee, and I noticed she was smiling demurely.

Marie couldn't stay in the galley. She was at the rail, holding her little dog Kiki and talking to him. "Regardez, mon fils, c'est America!" she said to him excitedly, rumpling his ears. She could hardly stand still. Her excitement was contagious.

"Your wife, captain?" the pilot asked lazily, his eyes fastened admiringly on Marie.

"No," the skipper replied, shaking his head, "my mate's wife. I married them in the Mediterranean."

"Remarkable!" exclaimed the pilot, taking another look at Marie. "A real French bride!" He made it sound as though I had brought home a Zulu.

At eleven a.m. our tug slowed down off Gallups Island for U.S. Quarantine. The doctor boarded us, mustered all hands, and issued a certificate for a clean bill of health.

We reached Boston Harbor, and out came the customs and immigration boats. We moved slowly ahead now, at least eight U.S. Government officials aboard, plus press representatives from the Boston Post, Boston Globe, and Boston Evening Transcript.

Cameras clicked all over the ship. The excitement, it seemed, all centered about the mate and his French stowaway bride. We posed for many pictures, and they were anything but flattering. We looked hungry, ill-clothed, tired.

The reporters were very pleasant. They made much over us, and I kept wondering why they'd come aboard. In all my sailing passages I'd never seen one on board before.

We were called to the captain's cabin to answer to U.S. Immigration officers. They spoke French, as did many of the reporters who were veterans of the war. Marie looked worried, yet it could have been fatigue. It seemed to my anxious eyes that she drooped a little under the questioning. In her lap sat Kiki, barking warningly at anyone who approached his mistress. In her plain little housedress my bride looked as much like a typical French peasant of the soil as it was possible to look.

Captain Anderson was told to drop anchor on East Boston Flats until the next day when we would proceed to the National docks. Anchor down, all officials left, the skipper with them. He sent provisions back to the ship, including fresh grapefruit.

"Quelle beeg o-range!" said Marie, her eyes widening at the sight of the golden globules. She had never seen a grapefruit.

The skipper had sent steaks, too, and what a dinner Marie cooked for us that night! After all those days without good food, or even enough bad food, we ate steak until it hurt.

The next morning, after Marie had made us all a fine breakfast, we dressed in our best—which wasn't very much. Outwardly we were a pretty shabby-looking pair, though obviously much in love.

We had been told to report to the Immigration officer at Long Wharf at ten a.m., and off we went, Marie holding Kiki under her arm so he could see the sights, too.

"I weel be back to make for you the fine dinnaire!" she called to Johnson, the engineer, as we left.

We took the East Boston ferry, but on the ferry everyone looked at us curiously. I couldn't understand it. As soon as we got off the ferry I bought a newspaper. The explanation was in the headlines.

"French Girl Stows Away in American Sailing Ship" read one. "Captain Marries Couple On High Seas" read another.

I began to study the articles. "The mate, a typical Jack London character, and his bride showed no strain after the hazardous trip of seventy-two days crossing the Atlantic," and so on, column after column. Pictures, headlines, articles, in every paper!

Undismayed, Marie, Kiki and I made our way down Long Wharf to the immigration offices. We were confident that from that time on life would be just one long smile.

We were escorted into the office of Mr. Sullivan, the commissioner, and he introduced us to Mr. Clark and a Mr. Hagberg. They asked me to be seated in the guest room while Marie was told to follow Mr. Clark and Mr. Hagberg, the inspectors. I thought nothing of it for I was too accustomed to government regulations to give it a second thought.

I waited for about an hour. Suddenly Marie came out, escorted by a matron who took out a pass key and admitted them to what is commonly called the "big cage." I started up, and someone put a hand on my arm. It was Mr. Hagberg. He led me into his office.

"Sit down, Mr. Burnett," he said, seating himself. "Now, you are Theodore G. Burnett, first mate of the American schooner 'Horatio G. Foss'?"

"Yes, sir," I said, promptly and proudly. I was expecting trouble, because of the American Consul in Cette. I remembered how I'd thumbed my nose at him. A fine thing to do!

"Where were you born?"

"New York City, New York."

"Now tell me," he said, his voice laden with all sorts of unpleasant insinuations, "Where did you first meet Marie Alfreda Dheilly?"

"You mean my wife?" I shot back swiftly.

His face reddened, and his eyes grew hard. "No," he said deliberately, "I mean just what I said. The United States Immigration does not recognize your marriage."

I looked at him full on. "I met my wife in the port of Cette, France," I said. "She, like many other French people, visited the waterfront to see the different ships of all nationalities. We fell in love, and the rest is in the official log book."

"I see." Silence fell between us. "How long did you know Miss Dheilly before you brought her on board your ship?" he asked finally.

"I knew Mrs. Burnett just two weeks when I decided that I wanted her to become my wife," I said, trying to keep firm rein on my temper.

"Did you know what your wife was doing for a living before you met her?" he asked sarcastically.

"Yes," I said hotly, "She was aiding the French Maritime Police in rounding up smugglers of dope from Alexandria and Algeria!"

His expression never altered.

"And did you know that you claim as your wife a woman whose record shows she was a prostitute in France?"

I stood up, the room spinning giddily around me, and I saw everything through a red haze. I had only one thought in mind, and that was to kill the bastard . . .

Mr. Clark, who had entered the room quietly, grabbed me and threw me down in a chair, and he was plenty rough in doing it.

"Sit down!" he thundered.

22

"Perhaps six months on deer island would quiet this fellow down a bit," Mr. Hagberg said to Clark.

"Mr. Hagberg," I said, shaking with rage, "For what offense could you send me to a penal institution for six months?"

"See here, that's enough out of you!" he said roughly. "We want answers from you and nothing else! You know your wife was a prostitute when you married her!" He paused, eyeing me contemptuously, "Didn't you?"

There was something so deadly sure in his attitude that the truth suddenly dawned on me.

"No! No! No!" I cried desperately. Then I broke down, and cried openly. Even men can cry.

They didn't say a word. Something in the quality of their silence led me to believe they were as shocked as I at the moment. They had thought I had known ...

"That's all," said Mr. Hagberg, sounding as though all the sap had run out of him.

Mr. Clark led me over to a wash basin and gave me a towel.

"Better fix yourself up," he said, not unkindly.

I was shaking uncontrollably. I felt as though I were going to vomit. I turned to Mr. Clark.

"What do I do now? Where's my wife?"

"She will be all right," he said, looking at me in an odd manner. "She's in the next room."

"Can I see her?" I asked pleadingly. The first shock of revelation was wearing off, leaving me to face some unalterable facts. I had loved Marie, not knowing. Knowing, I still loved her. What had forced her into such a life I had no way of knowing. But I had been her husband long enough to know that she was essentially good and sweet and true. If anything had changed, I loved her more. No wonder she had looked so frightened!

"I guess you can see her," he conceded, sounding puzzled that I should want to. He led me into the big cage.

There were about a hundred women in the cage, all cases for the immigration authorities. I went to the matron at the desk and asked to see my wife. They sent for Marie.

She appeared, completely beaten. She ran to me, put her arms around me and sobbed until she was almost in convulsions.

"Mr. Burnett," said the matron, a Mrs. Grace, "You will do better by letting her rest—especially after what she has been through."

I thought of what I had been through, and wondered what they had done to my pauvre petite. Her sobs would have pierced anyone's soul.

"Come back tomorrow, won't you please?" asked the matron. She was trying to loosen Marie's frantic hold of me but she was doing it gently and she looked kind.

"Thank you, madame," I said, swallowing hard, "I will."

I kissed Marie, but she was so hysterical I doubt she felt it. I went to the visitor's check-out gate, an iron-barred gate which always had a turnkey and watchman on duty. He opened up for me, and I left.

As I walked alone up the long wharf there were cameras clicking. Reporters tried to bombard me with questions. I shook them off. It was hell.

I made my way to the U.S. Shipping Commissioner's office for pay-off and the whole gang was there waiting for the skipper. Kiki nestled in my arms, seemingly understanding the trouble we were in. I talked to no one. Life had caught up with me in spades.

A Union delegate was present to defend Manley McDonald, but I barely heard the proceedings. All hands were paid off, discharges were given out, and I was free to go. My pay, after eleven months, came to two hundred and fifty-six dollars.

I returned to the ship, forgetting to say goodbye to my shipmates. I was trying to straighten out my whirling thoughts. In short, I was the fellow whose ideals and philosophies had still been in knee pants.

I trudged back to the ferry, and every step of the way I saw Marie. I knew that I loved her for herself. Whatever her profession had been, for whatever reason, had nothing to do with it. She had been clean, sweet, fastidious, ever since I had known her. She was human. So, God knew, was I. I was damned if I was going to let her go because she had made some mistakes. I'd made quite a few myself. I lifted my chin.

On board ship I was greeted by Johnson. I tried to explain why Marie was not with me. The cabin phonograph was playing "Till We Meet Again," and I directed such a glance in its direction that he turned it off.

I found a room in an old frame house on Maverick Street, not far from Maverick Square. The price was three dollars a week. It was an attic room with a bed which looked as though some of the boys from Bunker Hill had slept there. In the roof there was a glass skylight, plentifully endowed with chinks and holes to ensure ventilation.

I moved everything from the ship, including Marie's hamper trunk, our wedding gifts, and Kiki. I tried to keep busy, for every moment I wasn't occupied I thought of Marie.

My appetite dwindled to nothing and I slept scarcely at all. I missed my wife. My wife who couldn't speak our language, and who wasn't apt to get a square deal from a port that had won no medals for its treatment of immigrants.

I bought an inexpensive little suitcase and loaded it with the things I thought Marie would need. I came to the cage door.

"Who do you want to see?"

"My wife, Mrs. Burnett."

"No Mrs. Burnett here," the surly fellow said, looking through the registry.

"What?" I demanded incredulously.

"No one here by that name," he intoned slyly, "But there is a

French girl here, a Mademoiselle Alfreda Dheilly. Do you know her?"

"All right," I said, between clenched teeth, "May I see her?"

"I'll have to check that suitcase," he said, opening the gates.

"This is just like a jail, isn't it?" I said sarcastically.

"Don't know," he grunted, pawing through the things I'd so carefully packed for Marie. "I've never been in one."

I was so full of repressed anger that I shook. This turnkey held a government position, and by virtue of it he could be as boorish as he chose and I could do nothing about it.

He returned the bag to me, the things I'd folded so carefully all mussed and tossed, and showed me into the women's ward. I asked to see my wife.

They brought Marie out, and I was frightened by her appearance. She was completely broken by our separation, and she had been none too well nourished during our long voyage to undergo the physical and mental stress she was being subjected to. She leaned against me and cried so desperately that the matron led us to her private room to keep the other immigrants from being upset.

Marie tried brokenly to tell me about losing her mother and father, and how she had turned to prostitution to keep body and soul together during those dark days in France. I told her how much I loved her, and of my confidence that we would be vindicated. Things I didn't believe, but I kept my bitterness within.

She told me the doctors had put her through a rigid physical examination. She laughed and cried alternately. "I was all right, mon mari, you know? But these men! They looked at me as though I were the leper! I would not have married you if I had not been all right." She grew so hysterical I had to call the matron. Our home-coming. It was fine.

I had been told many things, but of these I said nothing to Marie. Some said my only chance was a lawyer who would obtain a writ of habeas corpus. One woman, a Miss Catherine Eaves, asked me if I had the money to engage legal counsel. I had two hundred and thirty dollars left, and that was all I had in the world.

"You better get a lawyer," Miss Eaves said decisively, "And be sure you get one who is familiar with immigration cases."

I inquired about a lawyer at the immigration station. They told me that a Mr. Keating and a Mr. Harbridge had most of the cases there. I went looking for Mr. Keating, and—to my ultimate sorrow— found him.

He promptly requested a deposit of fifty dollars as a retainer, and after a week I discovered that amount could be charged off as a gift. For, after that, I was never able to find him again.

More people were becoming interested in the French girl each day. Ministers and priests visited her in the cage, asking for more information concerning her plight. School teachers, housewives, business people, the rich and the poor, wrote letters. They came to hearten her with their visits, and they proved by their actions that the underlying human quality which had made America great was not dead, just buried alive in the welter of everyday living in a post-war world.

Every time I saw Marie I tried to give her a few dollars from my dwindling funds. It was to no avail.

"Non, non—mon chere, you need it more. 'Ere, wat can I do weeth it?"

I became almost miserly, begrudging every penny that would not advance our case. Yet, after two weeks ashore and less the fifty dollars I had given the attorney, I knew I'd soon have to go to sea in order to keep money coming in.

I found a berth on the S.S. "Lake Worth," as A.B. at eighty-seven fifty a month, and bade Marie goodbye. She understood why I was leaving and we clung to each other for only a moment in farewell. We were learning to avoid embraces, for they only led to tears on Marie's part and such agitation on mine that I felt I'd go mad if I couldn't effect her immediate release.

Kiki and I went to the Seaman's Union Hall in Boston where the crew was being assembled. This time I felt no thrill at the prospect of going to sea. I was shipping out because I knew no other way to make a living.

Our round trip from Boston to Norfolk took three endless weeks, then I was back to visit Long Wharf.

I found Marie vastly improved both in spirits and appearance. During my absence she had made many friends in Boston. They had brought her gifts of fruit, flowers, candy, and clothing. French people had brought her books in her own language, and a sewing kit with things to crochet.

She was in her fifth week of internment.

Deputy Commissioner Sullivan and the inspectors were not committing themselves publicly these days, for the ball had roll all the way to Washington, D.C., where a Mr. Skeffington was in conference with the French Ambassador Jusserand. The stowaway bride was no longer merely local news.

I found a new job to be near Marie. This time it was for Uncle Sam at the munificent salary of one hundred and twenty dollars a month. The job was at Gallups Island, and Captain Bryant of the U.S. Public Health Service was in charge.

My job included three meals a day and a nice room, but my duties consisted of taking care of five hundred white rats and feeding them and driving a two-wheel dump cart about the island behind a horse named Jerry. Jerry had served twenty years with the Boston Fire Department and was allergic to bells. It was a far cry from the sea, but it didn't matter.

I eventually grew tired of dealing with four legged rats, as that was one matter in which I had some choice, and even Jerry's eccentricities failed to charm me after awhile. I went looking for another ship.

Winter was coming on and the fight continued to keep my wife from deportation. Each time I came to the immigration station the insults and humiliation I had to undergo were almost more than I could bear. I clenched my fists in my pockets and bit back the words I longed to say. I was in trouble enough.

On December tenth I was notified that Marie had pneumonia. Half beside myself I rushed to Kearney Hospital where she had been sent.

I found her feverish, vague, unhappy. She was scorned by patients and nurses alike because of the slanderous reports circulated by the commission. Her shallow breathing and racking cough did little to allay my fears. And what I had done was to take her away from those who loved her, and knew her background, to set her down in a strange country—a defenseless target for malicious tongues.

I left the hospital and walked aimlessly for a long time. Christmas was approaching, but the joyous Yule season was a mockery. I only knew I had to go to sea again. I went to Union Hall, and a job came up on the S.S. "Agria," clearing for Hampton Roads. I took it. I had no choice.

A full crew signed articles and we all worked the first day. The dog

Kiki made friends with all hands aboard and kept a good watch over my bunk. He needn't have. I wasn't sleeping anyway.

The next day orders were received from Washington to lay up the S.S. "Agria," and, as we'd signed articles, there was nothing the skipper could do but pay us one month's wages. To me, it was an unbelievable bit of good luck.

I collected my eighty-seven fifty, and with it I made Marie's Christmas the best I could. She was recovering slowly from her bout with pneumonia, but she was very weak. I grew to dread her questions every time I saw her.

"W'en do they let me out?" she would ask, trying to smile. Then she would cry.

Christmas Day I arrived at Long Wharf with a basket heaped with presents. Kiki's harness was festive with a huge bow of red ribbon. Outside there was a heavy snowstorm, and the soft fall of the velvety flakes made it seem like a true Noel.

The big cage was thronged with visitors. I sat with Marie, watching her covertly for signs of fatigue. We enjoyed looking at the strange assortment of presents being opened by people around us. All languages could be heard, yet the spirit was the same. Even in the big cage the tidings of the gentle Savior could be heard.

Commissioner Sullivan appeared to make his Christmas visit to the inmates of the big cage. He finally made his way over to where Marie and I sat.

"Merry Christmas," I said, trying to mean it.

"What have you got in that basket?" he demanded curtly, ignoring my greeting, "Whiskey?"

"No, sir," I said, clenching my jaw to bite back words that might have gone hard for Marie. If I hadn't thought first of her I would have let him have a Coke bottle right between the eyes. Oh! his arrogance and righteousness were something to see, for he was on the right side of the law.

After Christmas I went on the pilot boat "Liberty" for two weeks of bitter cold experience putting pilots aboard incoming ships of Grave's Light, Boston Bay. I came back tired, despondent, expecting to be greeted by more trouble.

To my surprise the public was actively aggravated. They were demanding a fair trial for the stowaway bride. Mrs. Eaves, Mrs. Walsh, Mrs. Goodwin, and Father Pacquette all came to me. "Ask William

Lewis to take your case," they urged. "He is a brilliant colored lawyer, and was star quarterback at Harvard."

Mrs. Eaves agreed to go with me for an appointment. We both sat facing Mr. Lewis, and my hands were clammy cold. I'd heard that he never took a case unless he knew he could win.

"Now, Mr. Burnett," he said courteously, once the introductions were made, "tell me all the facts in this case."

I told him everything. I didn't omit the slightest detail for I felt it was my last chance. He listened attentively, making notes from time to time without comment.

"Was this marriage of yours entered in the ship's official logbook?" he asked, and added keenly, "And witnessed?"

"Yes, sir," I said. "I will notify Mr. Grant of the U.S. Shipping Commissioner's office any time you wish to see that book, sir."

"Mr. Burnett," he said quietly, "do you know how much this will cost you?"

"No, I don't sir," I said, "but I'm listening."

"It will cost you two hundred and fifty dollars," he said. My heart sank within me.

Mrs. Eaves looked at me, then at Mr. Lewis.

"I happen to know that Mr. Burnett has no funds," she announced gently. "But that needn't stand in the way. I'll be more than happy to pay the amount necessary for this unfortunate couple."

"You're a fine woman, Mrs. Eaves," said the attorney, smiling approvingly at her. "Our first move will be to get a writ of habeas corpus." He turned to me, "And you, Mr. Burnett, don't go far away."

"Can I make a short sea trip?" I asked. We needed money again.

"Not more than three weeks, then be back here to report to me. Keep your business to yourself and say nothing to anyone. Mrs. Eaves, I'll attend to this matter, and it may take a trip to Washington after I have spoken to my client. Good day, sir and madame, and I thank you."

Mrs. Eaves and I left his offices together, and for the first time I began to feel the stirring of hope within me.

I WENT DOWN TO THE SEAMAN'S UNION AND FOUND A BERTH IN A CON-
crete steamer, the S.S. "Polias" of Boston. Then I dashed back to say
goodbye to Marie.

She was overjoyed with the good news I had for her. Her eyes lit up
with the old sparkle and she talked more animatedly than she had
since her internment. She was beaming when I left her.

With my sailor bag over my shoulder, and Kiki's leash in one hand
I was off for the "Polias." Kiki pranced ahead of me as though good
times were just around the corner, and I stepped along more briskly.

Once aboard the vessel I learned that our sailing orders directed us
to proceed to Hampton Roads for coal, then back to Searsport,
Maine. The skipper's name was Captain Tom Cotter of Newfound-
land, and the bos'un was a German named Haufman. The others I
didn't know.

A northeast snowstorm set in as we headed out Boston Bay, and
both wind and sea mounted as we passed Nantucket Island. I had
the twelve midnight to two a.m. lookout, and as I walked the foc'sle
head I noticed how stiff the concrete ship was. She never rose to the

sea, just plowed through it rigidly. She was a war emergency vessel, and I wasn't long in making up my mind about her. She was dangerous.

We loaded our coal and headed out of Hampton Roads for the trip down east. It was supper time and I was standing my trick at the wheel. The captain paced to and fro on the bridge, apparently wrapped in thought.

The second mate came up, and I noticed he was holding a plateful of food. He shoved it almost under the skipper's nose.

"Tell me, captain," he said sneeringly, "is this food fit for a ship's officer?"

I cast a side glance at the twenty-two-year-old punk who called himself an officer. One look was enough. I wondered that the skipper didn't spit in his ear and give him a new set of brains.

As I looked, he deliberately took the plate, food and all, and threw it with all his might over the port wing of the bridge and into the sea.

"Is it necessary to throw ship's property into the sea?" asked Captain Cotter with ominous quiet.

"Aw, to hell with it!" retorted the second mate. He left the bridge, swaggering.

"He's a bad actor, captain," I said.

"Yes," agreed the skipper, looking after him reflecting, "but he's not through with me."

We headed up the Gulf of Maine after five days, and a strong nor'-wester that blew with every sea that hit us made much ice on deck. As we headed for Searsport the next morning a heavy vapor rose from the sea in the zero weather and the "Polias" groped her way, fog signals blowing at regular intervals.

I was on the foc'sle head, bundled up like an Eskimo, talking to Haufman the bos'un.

"Well, and what do you think of her?" he asked, meaning the ship.

"She's a Jonah, and I'm going to pay off," I said.

"I think I will, too," he said slowly. "I don't like the feel of her. We can take a train out of here for Bangor and change trains for Boston."

"That sounds good to me." I was glad someone else shared my opinion of the ship. "You know, bos'un, I don't know how to explain it, but it's just as though a voice were warning me to get the hell off this ship. I never felt that way before. Some I haven't liked, but this one is different."

We went together to the skipper to ask him if he would pay us off.

"What seems to be the trouble, men?"

"There isn't any trouble, Captain Cotter," I said hesitantly, at a loss to express my feelings clearly. "It's the ship herself. I have no faith in her. Call it superstition, or getting soft if you like—I still want to leave her."

"All right, men," he said, knowing it useless to try to keep us, "I'll pay you off."

Haufman and I struggled through two feet of newly-fallen snow to the Bangor and Aroostock Railroad Station. There we boarded a combination passenger and log train for Bangor, a half-day trip. The passenger coaches were old-fashioned, each equipped with a pot-bellied wood stove, and we talked with trappers, loggers and farmers as we travelled along at a snail's pace.

At Bangor we changed for Boston, a twelve-hour run in a more comfortable train. We alighted from the train at North Station and stopped to buy a morning paper. The headline caused us to look at each other in shocked surprise. "S.S. Polias Runs On Siley Ledge In Snowstorm. 12 Perish."

"My God, Barney!" said the bos'un feelingly, "you were right!" He glanced through the article and handed it to me. "Read this," he said significantly.

"Second mate leaves wreck with eleven crew members against master's orders," the account read. "All twelve frozen to death in the ship's lifeboat. The balance of the crew rescued by coast guard."

The second mate had been defiant once too often.

I left Haufman and hurried to the offices of Mr. Lewis, congratulating myself as I sped along that I had obeyed my hunch.

"Well, Mr. Burnett," Mr. Lewis said, once I greeted him, "I'm glad you're not amongst the missing! Sit down and make yourself comfortable. I've arranged the habeas corpus proceedings and tomorrow you will appear in Federal Court with your wife. She, of course, will be escorted by a matron. Be at Long Wharf by ten a.m. and tight lips in the meanwhile. That's all for now."

I deposited my sailor bag, picked up my mail, and started out for Long Wharf to see my wife. The guard who let me in acted almost human.

"Your wife is certainly going to be glad to see you," he commented as he unlocked the iron doors.

"You mean she saw the papers?" I asked, horrified, for the names of the dead had not been published.

"They read the news to her," he said, "and she broke all up, wondering if you were among the missing."

I burst into the big cage, and immediately several of the internees called, "Marie! Marie! Your husband, Marie!"

I caught sight of her and held out my arms. She ran into them, laughing and crying all at once.Her nerves were about at the breaking point, and no wonder! We clung to each other until she calmed down, then I told her the news I'd had from Mr. Lewis.

"You theenk thees time they let me out?" she asked hopefully.

"I think they better," I said stonily. I was afraid to promise anything. She was smiling when I left her, holding the fruit I'd brought to her. She didn't drink or smoke.

At ten, the next morning, I was in the big cage.

Marie was all ready and waiting, her matron escort close at her side. We made an odd looking couple. I was wearing a well-worn mackinaw, old trousers, and my sea cap. Marie was attired in a cheap housedress, a black coat that came within six inches of the ground, and a hat that dated back five years.

We left the Long Wharf Immigration station and walked up State Street toward the Federal Court. Cameras clicked at us from all directions when we reached the courthouse. Marie looked straight ahead, holding tightly to my arm.

The court room was packed, and the crowds were still lingering outside the building. Marie, the matron and I sat down in our appointed places and court was called to order.

The first of the trial went by like a dream. The U.S. attorney, Mrs. Lewis, Federal Judge Morton, and officials of the U.S. Immigration Department exchanged words regarding technicalities which neither Marie nor I could understand.

Mr. Grant of the U.S. Shipping Commissioner's office was on tap with the official log book of the "Horatio G. Foss," and his gruff presence reassured me greatly.

After a full hour of legal pros and cons the Judge requested time to review the case, and the case of the United States versus Marie Dheilly was adjourned.

"Be patient," Mr. Lewis advised us kindly as the court room was cleared, "it's all in your favor."

With our matron escort, Marie and I started back for the big cage at Long Wharf. It was a silent walk.

As we entered Long Wharf's iron gate, the very snapping of the lock caused Marie to break down.

"W'at 'ave I done?" she cried hysterically, "W'at 'ave I done?"

The matron took her from me.

"Please go," she said firmly, yet not unpleasantly. "I'll give her a sedative for her nerves, and see to it that she rests."

I left, Marie's piteous weeping sounding in my ears as I walked away.

The case had been adjourned until further notice, and once again I was faced with getting a job. Seafaring was all I knew, yet I couldn't ship out.

As I walked along the waterfront of East Boston a five mast barkentine, the "Falkatina" of Copenhagen, Denmark, caught my eye. Discouraged, I went aboard and asked the skipper for a job. He gave me the job of bos'un.

Every day I scanned the papers for news of our case, and reporters tracked me down even to the "Falkatina."

The commissioner circulated a rumor that Marie was to be deported, and after that my bag was kept packed and my passport in order. I was ready to go.

The rumor turned out to be nothing more but a scare, and Mr. Lewis advised me not to let such malicious tales worry me. I knew he was right, yet it was difficult advice to follow.

On February 18, 1920, Mr. Lewis advised Mrs. Eaves, Marie and myself that the decision would be given in Federal Court by Federal Judge Morton on February twenty-eighth. The end was near.

The "Falkatina" was to be ready to sail about the sixth of March, but I told the captain I was not going to sign on. He complimented me on the assistance I had been able to give him in preparing the ship for sea, and wished me the best of luck.

On February twenty-eighth I was again at Long Wharf at ten a.m. Marie and I both looked much the same as we had previously, with the difference that we were looking forward to hearing a definite verdict one way or the other. We both hoped for good news, but were steeled for the worst.

Outside the Federal Court building it looked like a holiday. Hundreds of people had turned out for what the newspapers called the "greatest human interest story of the day." Cameras clicked again. This time Marie and I both smiled.

We took our seats in the crowded court room. There was no jury, and a preview of the case was given. Then the Judge rapped his gavel for quiet. The U.S. Attorney was about to speak his piece for the U.S. Immigration Department.

He referred to Marie as a woman of the world. A bad woman. A wicked woman. There were other terms, too. All to describe a girl who, I had since learned, had followed the suggestion of her own grandmother to keep body and soul together in starving France.

When he was finished he sat down, looking highly pleased with himself and his summation of the case.

Mr. Lewis stood up. He was calm, unhurried, dignified. He began his plea, and the spectators bent forward to catch every word.

William Lewis was a born orator. He didn't shout, he didn't exaggerate, he just told facts with a simple, moving eloquence that brought tears to many eyes.

He spoke of our laws, the flag, the authority of a ship's captain on the high seas. Then he spoke of the accusations regarding Marie's past life. He lingered, letting the shameful words sink in. Then he added deliberately, "I would have to hear these accusations against this French girl directly from the mouths of the French authorities themselves before I would believe one word."

He paused to take a drink of water, and there was utter silence in the court room. He turned then, and faced the people.

"There is, it seems, an objection to the marriage of this couple. Who is there so powerful on this earth that they shall tell us whom we will marry? Is this objection because she has sinned?" His voice rose, and he looked accusingly, not at Marie and myself, but at the spectators.

"Let he or she in this court who is without sin to cast the first stone!" He looked challengingly around, and his glance included the government officials. "That is all."

A terrific ovation broke out from the spectators, but the Judge quieted them by rapping loudly with his gavel.

"Quiet please!" he thundered. He settled back in his chair, once it was silent. "Attorney for the United States, Mr. Lewis, attorney for the defense; ladies and gentlemen present at this court session—I have reviewed this case, and I have read the entry of this marriage in the official log book of the 'Horatio G. Foss.' The conduct of these two persons involved has been excellent all through this long internment. Under our laws I cannot see why I should not recognize this marriage. It has been according to law, it is legal. I hereby place Mrs. Burnett on a two-year probation period." He looked over his glasses at Marie. "Should you break any of our laws, or become involved with the law, you would have to report to us."

"You don't look like people who get into trouble," the Judge continued, "therefore I say this; the court recognizes the marriage of Theodore G. Burnett and his bride Marie Dheilly and considers them man and wife, married on the high seas on board the American schooner 'Horatio G. Foss.' "

He smiled at us paternally before he rapped his gavel smartly.

"Court is now adjourned!"

Pandemonium reigned in that packed courtroom! There were handclasps, hugs, kisses. Utter strangers kissed Marie, and threw their arms around her while photographers clustered round for pictures.

Marie smiled at everyone shyly, clinging tightly to my arm as though I might vanish. From time to time she surreptitiously touched her eyes with her handkerchief, trying to wipe away the welling tears of happiness.

Reporters surrounded us, firing questions at us as fast as they could.

"What are your plans?"

"Where will you go?'"

"How do you feel about this?"

"Mr. Lewis, our lawyer, deserves the credit for the verdict," I told them repeatedly. "He, and Mrs. Catherine Eaves, who made it possible for us to engage him. You ask what we're going to do? We intend to be like any other young American couple. To work, to get ahead, to be happy. All we wanted was the opportunity to pursue our happiness, and Judge Morton has given it to us."

The press drew away from us finally, and the crowd separated to let us pass. They smiled at us as we smiled at each other.

"W'at we do now, mon mari?" Marie asked timidly. We were at last outside the courthouse, and she reached up and touched my cheek with her fingertips.

"Do?" I echoed, smiling down at her. "The thing to do is to stay as happy with each other as we are now. Do you think that's too large an order?'"

It wasn't. For twenty-five years, until the death of my stowaway bride, we were.

THIS BOOK WAS DESIGNED BY WARD RITCHIE.
THE DRAWINGS ON THE TITLE PAGE AND COVER
WERE MADE BY ROBERT WEINSTEIN, WHO
ALSO COLLECTED FROM MANY SOURCES
THE PHOTOGRAPHS USED AS ILLUSTRATIONS.